Reading History in Children's Books

Also by Catherine Butler

FEMALE REPLIES TO SWETNAM THE WOMAN HATER (*ed.*)

FOUR BRITISH FANTASISTS: Place and Culture in the Children's Fantasies of Penelope Lively, Alan Garner, Diana Wynne Jones, and Susan Cooper

ROALD DAHL (*ed. with Ann Alston*)

TEACHING CHILDREN'S FICTION (*ed.*)

Reading History in Children's Books

Catherine Butler and Hallie O'Donovan

palgrave
macmillan

First published 2012 by
PALGRAVE MACMILLAN

Palgrave Macmillan in the UK is an imprint of Macmillan Publishers Limited, registered in England, company number 785998, of Houndmills, Basingstoke, Hampshire RG21 6XS.

Palgrave Macmillan in the US is a division of St Martin's Press LLC, 175 Fifth Avenue, New York, NY 10010.

Palgrave Macmillan is the global academic imprint of the above companies and has companies and representatives throughout the world.

Palgrave® and Macmillan® are registered trademarks in the United States, the United Kingdom, Europe and other countries.

ISBN 978–0–230–27808–0

This book is printed on paper suitable for recycling and made from fully managed and sustained forest sources. Logging, pulping and manufacturing processes are expected to conform to the environmental regulations of the country of origin.

A catalogue record for this book is available from the British Library.

A catalog record for this book is available from the Library of Congress.

10 9 8 7 6 5 4 3 2 1
21 20 19 18 17 16 15 14 13 12

Printed and bound in the United States of America
by Edwards Brothers Malloy, Inc.

For Charlotte and Nathaniel, with all my love, past, present and future.

C. B.

To the memory of Rosemary Sutcliff, who not only taught me almost everything I know about British history but also created some of the most memorable characters in children's literature.

H. O'D.

Contents

Acknowledgements

Many people have had a share in this book's making, directly or indirectly, knowingly or otherwise. While we cannot acknowledge every individual by name here, all deserve – and have – our gratitude. Some specific debts must, however, be acknowledged. The Faculty of Arts, Creative Industries and Education at the University of the West of England, Bristol, UK, awarded Catherine Butler a semester's research leave in order to write the book, a period of concentrated time that was crucial in allowing its timely completion. We are grateful too to Ronald Hutton and Isobel Butler, who read and commented on parts of the manuscript, and particularly to Edward James and Farah Mendlesohn, who found time in their busy schedules to read the final draft at very short notice. Their insightful comments proved invaluable.

We would like to thank N. M. Browne, Victor Watson and Dennis Hamley, three of the authors mentioned in these pages, for corresponding with us about aspects of their work. Dennis Hamley was also amongst those who generously gave us access to books, articles and other information, as were Mark Bradford, Kate Chedgzoy, Peter Bolger of ICT Gateshead, Peter Hepplewhite of the Tyne and Wear Archives Service, Penelope Harnett, Edward James, Tony Keen, Farah Mendlesohn, Katherine Roberts, Frances Thomas and Shana Worthen.

We have been informed and inspired by innumerable conversations with friends, colleagues and chance acquaintances. In particular, we have found in our polymath friends on *LiveJournal* and *Dreamwidth* an unfailing source of information and suggestions. Amongst those who answered our specific queries or suggested texts to us are David Bratman, *LJ* user Breathingbooks, Teresa Claudino, Emma Comerford, William Flesch, Francesca Forrest, Debbie Gascoyne, Dorian E. Gray, Helen Hall, Rosie Hopkins, *LJ* user Houseboatonstyx, Deborah Kaplan, Kit Kapphahn, Valerie Keefe, Harriet Monkhouse, Alison Page, Brandy Painter, Sarah Prineas, Sheenagh Pugh, Dana Skirrow, Sherwood Smith (sartorias), Gillian

Spraggs, G. M. W. Wemyss, Shana Worthen and the LiveJournal Rosemary Sutcliff community, sutcliff_talk.

Hallie O'Donovan would also like to thank her daughters Becca and Cara for their shared love of so many of her favourite historical novels, and for their huge patience and minimal eye-rolling when she just *had* to talk (again) about this book.

1
Introduction: That Was Then?

This book is about the representation of history in children's literature.[1] Its subjects are the ways in which children's books shape their readers' understanding of, and relationship with, the past, and the manifold issues and paradoxes generated by the activity of writing about a different age. Certain themes will thread their way through this volume, appearing in diverse forms in the contexts of individual chapters. Many of these concern the authorial dilemmas faced by those who write about the past for a juvenile audience, and the interpretative choices made by their readers. For example, historical novels for children must negotiate the fact that many attitudes now generally considered bigoted or otherwise unacceptable (such as a belief in the legitimacy of slavery or the subordination of women) were almost universal at various points in the past. In a world riven by the effects of cultural mistrust and incomprehension, writers seem to face a difficult choice: that of presenting a sanitized past, with at least the sympathetic characters displaying an ahistorically liberal sensibility; or appearing to normalize and perpetuate those attitudes through fiction.

We will consider some of the approaches that have been taken to this problem, but will also recognize it as one manifestation of a more general ideological and philosophical conundrum. As has long been recognized,[2] historical books for children typically accommodate both a confidence in the essential continuity of human experience over time and an historicist insistence on the radical difference, and even inscrutability, of the past. The first of these underpins the belief (implied in the very practice of writing and reading historical works) that learning about the past is both possible and worthwhile, and that past human lives are sufficiently like our own to enable us to empathize with and understand them to a significant extent. The second justifies the idea that the past's differences from the present are important, that change is real and profound and that this should be acknowledged in any representation of the past. The coexistence within individual texts of these apparently contradictory positions will be a recurrent subject in what follows, whether applied to social *mores*, to historical language or to the general proposition that literature (especially for children) should exhibit some form of 'relevance' to contemporary readers.

Another of our concerns is with the relationship between the aesthetic and the informative aspects of children's historical texts. Much critical discussion of children's literature has treated its pedagogic or didactic potential with a degree of disdain, as something that children's literature has moved beyond in its historic progression from instruction to delight. This tendency has been particularly pronounced with regard to explicit instruction in personal morality, even if other forms of moral teaching (for example, about the duty of humankind to the environment) have arguably filled its place. However, even factual pedagogy has sometimes been seen as a dubiously valuable (because utilitarian) form of literary experience. Although reviews of historical books frequently make a point of assessing the meticulousness of the author's research, children who 'read for informational, not emotional, satisfaction' have received relatively little critical attention (Mendlesohn 52).[3] We will consider the value placed on accuracy in historical texts, and the ways in which this may be set against other considerations, such as ease of comprehension, entertainment, ideological norms and the perceived desirability of creating characters with whom modern child readers are able to identify.

The possibilities of viewing people in the past either as fellow members of a trans-historical community or as inscrutably alien already suggests a degree of instability about the basis on which depictions of the past are founded. That difficulty is only compounded by the problem of deciding whether to prioritize those depictions' aesthetic qualities or their informational function. Indeed, instability is evident in the very phrase 'historical fiction', which combines an implicit claim to factuality (i.e., to being an accurate representation of the past) and membership of a class of writing defined by its departure from fact. When Cynthia Harnett writes in the Postscript to *The Load of Unicorn* (1959) that her historical research has given her 'solid foundations [on which] I have built up a story which is *only* a story, but I hope may not be too much "fiction"' (223), she betrays something of the uneasiness of the relationship between fact and fiction, and this too will be a recurring topic.

The scope of this book

The remainder of this chapter will largely be devoted to defining the scope and structure of this book in more detail. In terms of scope, we will outline the parameters of our study along three different axes: geographical, temporal and generic. That is, we will explain our decision to confine discussion to texts dealing with British history and to use a series of chronological, period-based chapters rather than a more obviously thematic approach; and we will justify both our practice of examining texts from a broad range of genres rather than a select set, and of considering genres together rather than discretely. Since we will be commenting on the current contexts of this literature's production and reception, and (where pertinent) on its relationship with contemporary education and culture, we will pay particular attention to material likely to be available to children in the UK today. In effect, this means that many of the books considered in this volume will be of recent date, although we will also address older works, such as the books of Rosemary Sutcliff and Joan Aiken, that continue to have a child readership.

Much of what we have to say about historical books for children applies to texts set in any part of the world. Nevertheless, *Reading History in Children's Books* is centred on British, and particularly English, history.[4] Largely this is for reasons of practicality: the field of historical writing is too large to be discussed in a volume of this size in anything approaching a comprehensive fashion, and for our purposes a geographical limitation is preferable to one based on genre. Restricting ourselves in this way also enables us to consider the part that nationality has to play in historiography and historical writing, and to investigate what it means to have a 'national story'.

In addition, British history happens to be conveniently diverse. At different times Britain has been conquered from abroad and has colonized countries in five continents; it has been seen as peripheral to world events and as central to them; it has been well documented and tantalizingly unknown; and it has seen periods of great ethnic and linguistic change, yet incorporated these into narratives that speak eloquently of a distinct and continuous national identity. These numerous incarnations mean that different historical periods pose distinct challenges for anyone wishing to represent Britain in children's fiction or non-fiction. The main body of this book comprises a chronological series of chapters, each of which focuses directly on issues of pertinence to the representation of a different period. This allows us to consider specific historical circumstances and general theoretical and critical issues at the same time. Rather than see these as uniquely applicable to a particular period, however, the understanding gained in one chapter will frequently be applicable to others. What emerges will thus be a cumulative or palimpsest portrait of a literary and ideological territory as much as a linear, developmental argument.

Criticism is often conducted within generic boundaries; that is, a book or article will devote itself to realist historical fiction, to time-slip fiction, to non-fiction and so on. There are good reasons for this approach. Genres are defined in terms of shared conventions – conventions that are assimilated by readers who, on picking up a book, are often primed (by the title, the author's name, the jacket copy, the imprint, the book's position within the bookshop or library, or other prior knowledge) to expect certain generic features. These expectations may be confirmed (the status of Michelle Magorian's *Goodnight, Mr Tom* [1981] as realist fiction is not qualified by any forays into the supernatural or time travel) or they may be overturned (Penelope Lively's *A Stitch in Time* [1976], which seems to present itself as a time-slip story, turns out to be – more or less – a psychological novel set in the present day). Either way, the reading takes place within a framework of expectations that is governed by existing conventions and is understood by both writer and reader. Genre thus defines the 'rules of the game' – and to discuss different genres together might seem to invite confusion.

Nevertheless, we have decided to take just such a cross-generic approach, in the belief that it will offer two useful perspectives that more generically focused discussions tend by their nature to ignore. The first of these stems from the observation that, while criticism is typically carried on in terms of specific genres, children are not asked to engage with history in quite that way but inhabit a world characterized by generic intersection and hybridity. For example, a primary-school topic on the Tudors for Key Stage 2 under the English National Curriculum might involve studying the sixteenth century not only in history lessons but also in art, English and other subjects. In the course of this cross-curricular study, children may be asked to read books in a number of different genres, including fiction, non-fiction and hybrid texts such as those in Scholastic's 'My Story' series, which take the form of fictional diaries supposedly written by children living through significant historical events and include factual appendices providing historical context.[5] Outside school the same children may encounter history through another Scholastic product, Terry Deary's popular 'Horrible Histories' series, which combines historical facts with slapstick humour, fictional vignettes and cartoons, and has proliferated beyond books into audio-books, songs, a TV series, a stage show and a popular web site. 'Horrible Histories' trades on its claim to leave out 'the boring bits' of history in favour of an emphasis on blood, dung and the bizarre, and as such it might appear to be a 'dumbed down' or simplified version of the subject, but from the point of view of genre it sets a complex interpretative challenge. At what point do selectivity, exaggeration and surreally anachronistic references take the books out of the category of non-fiction altogether? How does this 'transmedia phenomenon' (in Kate Chedgzoy's phrase [116]) address the commonly perceived tension between entertainment and education? It behoves anyone considering the ways in which children are presented with historical literature not to be dogmatic with regard to which genres are in play and how they are being deployed in any individual act of reading. Relevant too is the consideration of whether different genres are held more or less strictly to account in terms of their historical accuracy. We may suspect that treatments of historical material within comic, fantasy and science fiction texts are judged with less rigour than those in realist historical fiction: a multi-genre study enables the comparison to be made.

The second advantage that our cross-genre approach will offer involves the recognition that generic borders may be undermined in a different way – not as a side-effect of the cross-curricular and multimedia strategies employed by teachers and publishers, nor as part of a literary strategy that partners writer and reader in a postmodern game, but in a more contingent and perhaps more radical manner. This is a point best made by way of example, and to this end we will here consider Jill Paton Walsh's time-slip fantasy, *A Chance Child* (1978), and Geoffrey Trease's historical novel, *Bows Against the Barons* (1934). These books' generic labels appear to offer a firm classification and an assurance of distinctiveness, with time-slip books being a sub-species of fantasy and historical novels of realism – but what does this mean for the practice of reading?

A Chance Child is Jill Paton Walsh's only fantasy for children. A writer more associated with realism, she has on occasion exhibited a somewhat partisan preference for that mode, protesting against any suggestion that 'a book in the realistic mode can explore only outer reality' ('Art of Realism' 35). Perhaps then it is not surprising that in *A Chance Child* she seems in places almost reluctant to admit to its fantasy elements – or, at any rate, anxious to show how firmly its fantasy is tied to historical reality. The novel concerns Creep, a child from modern times who runs away from his abusive mother. He finds himself near the canal, in a wasteland of rubbish, broken machinery and old cars. Coming upon a workman, Jack, who is sorting out different lengths of chain, Creep asks where he can go. Jack helps Creep set off down the canal on an iron boat with a little hut built onto it.

> 'The cut goes on, or back, from here,' said Jack.
> 'I'll go back,' said Creep.
> 'Just as you say, gaffer,' said Jack.
>
> (14)

When Creep disembarks farther down the canal, he finds himself at the time of the Industrial Revolution. While his brother Christopher seeks him in twentieth-century England, in the early nineteenth century Creep witnesses children being abused as he himself has been abused: in mills, on the canals, in the potteries, in the forge. The children can see him but he is invisible to adults and, like a ghost, he feels no hunger. It is only towards the end of the book, when he witnesses a mother standing up to a mill foreman who has been abusing her son, that he is freed from this state of suspense and becomes properly part of that earlier history. Unlike most time-travelling protagonists, Creep does not return to his own time: he stays and grows up, eventually writing an account of his life, which will in time be discovered and read by his brother in the town archives.

The reader is, of course, free to speculate about the metaphysics of all this. The wasteland where Creep first finds himself seems to be a liminal space, and the canal representative of Time itself, stretching back into the past and forward into the future. Perhaps the workman who sends Creep on his way is a kind of industrial-age Fate, measuring out different lengths of chain like a cross between Lachesis and Jacob Marley. Perhaps he is simply a workman, met by chance. It is easier to establish that Paton Walsh has gone to extraordinary lengths to tie the narrative of *A Chance Child* to historical sources and to the discourse of the historical method. She includes no fewer than three paratextual notes aimed at showing how little of her fantasy is actually invented. The first is the book's dedication, to nine named individuals and 'innumerable others like them' – historical victims of the Industrial Revolution whom Paton Walsh has presumably read about during her research for the book. These include 'William Kershaw, aged 8, a "piecener" whose mother beat his master over the head with a billy-roller' (5). (Thus even the climactic incident of Creep's story is shown to have been drawn from historical record.) Then there is the admonition on the next page that 'The landscape of this book is fantasy, and yet for every place described in it, some such place exists somewhere' (6). Finally, at the end of the book stands an 'Author's Note', in which Paton Walsh describes the research she undertook.

As well as this external apparatus, there is much internal bolstering. The author models the process of research. Creep's twentieth-century brother, Christopher, suspecting with remarkable acuity that Creep may have gone back in time, determines to discover what has become of him. Accosting a history teacher, he asks how he can set about researching an ordinary person from the past. The teacher gives him (and the reader) an impromptu lesson in social history research, sending him off to the main town library with instructions to look up the Parliamentary Papers. Many of the cases Christopher researches there resemble the ones in Creep's own encounters, so that when we eventually come to the 'Author's Note', the implication seems to be that those encounters are not to be regarded as fiction but rather as dramatizations of the historical record – a record that readers are encouraged to consult for themselves. By contrast with this assiduous historical research, the mysteries of time travel remain notably unexplained and, indeed, unconsidered, even by Creep himself.

Although *A Chance Child* is a fantasy, few realist historical novels are more tightly coupled to history. It is worth asking then why Paton Walsh did not simply write an historical novel, or even a work of non-fiction, about the conditions of child-workers in the nineteenth century. One answer is that the time-slip genre allows for a direct examination of the *relationship* between the past and the present. That relationship turns out to be a complex one. Part of the narrative's effect is to show that the past and present are not that different from each other. The industrial landscape Creep moves in is still recognizable in the twentieth century: his brother Christopher is able to find a message from Creep scratched onto a canal bridge. Nor is oppression alien to the modern world. Creep's story gives us no opportunity to congratulate ourselves with the thought that things like that 'don't happen nowadays'. They do, and in fact Creep is more easily able to make a home and life for himself in the nineteenth century than in his own. Unlike most time-travelling protagonists, Creep does not feel out of place in his new surroundings, and spends little or no time either marvelling at how different things are or trying to get back to the twentieth century. Even in his own time Creep seems like a throwback, with one visitor to the house exclaiming, on catching sight of him: 'It's terrible! It's like the bad old days!' (41).

All the same, Paton Walsh does not hold up the conditions of the nineteenth-century industrial working classes as in any sense a desirable alternative to twentieth-century life: indeed, the book depicts them as appalling. Even if Creep finds a place there, and eventually manages to escape from utter poverty, his is not an easy life, nor one free of danger. As an adult he is crippled while working on the canals; and even though, by the time he writes his autobiographical account, he considers himself 'well set up' as a printer's assistant, it is plain that this is a comparative term.

A Chance Child is a book full of anger against the child cruelty and exploitation that was a feature of the English Industrial Revolution. Paton Walsh provides a graphic and detailed portrait of that cruelty in its various forms. The time-slip genre facilitates this: being both invisible and impervious to hunger, Creep is at greater liberty than a child of the nineteenth century could plausibly be to move from place to place, and hence to witness different scenes of maltreatment. Nevertheless, Paton Walsh also resists the potential of time-slip fictions to view the past as something alien, where strange and terrible things happen and which can be judged from the safety and comfort of an enlightened present. Hers is a unique adaptation of time-slip conventions to the purposes of what is, in some respects, a disguised realist novel.

By way of contrast, Geoffrey Trease's 1934 book *Bows Against the Barons* presents itself as a 'straight' historical novel. Set in twelfth-century England, it contains no time travel and no supernatural elements. The hero, Dickon, is a peasant boy who runs into trouble with his liege lord and is forced to take refuge in the greenwood, where he falls in with Robin Hood and his men. For Dickon, the move to the forest is also a move to a world of new ideas. As a peasant, he had been resentful of the tithes he had to pay the priest and the service he owed the lord of the manor, but had not thought that there was any way to change the situation. Once he joins Robin he realizes that there are other possibilities. 'Don't call me "sir" ', Robin chides him early in their acquaintance. 'We're all equal in Sherwood – comrades. What's the sense of getting rid of one master and taking a new one?' (22).

Even this short speech indicates some of the ways in which *Bows Against the Barons* is as much a book of the 1930s as of the 1190s. The word 'comrades' is especially pointed, given Trease's socialism, and this is just the first of a series of passages evidently written to speak directly to his own time rather than to King Richard I's. A little later, when a smith addresses the crowd at a kind of medieval rally, he begins: 'Fellow workers, whoever you are, Normans or Saxons—COMRADES' (34), and later the battle cry in the decisive encounter with the powers of oppressive aristocracy is: 'ALL POWER TO THE WORKERS!' (136). In a chapter tellingly titled 'Hammers and Sickles', Robin draws on the famous Bolshevik symbol to make the point that he and his men owe their strength to the common people:

> 'Thank these people,' grinned the outlaw. 'It was the hammers and sickles did it, to-day, not the bows and bills of Sherwood.'
>
> 'Ay, the people,' broke in the blacksmith. 'And if every man who used hammer or sickle used it as we've done, there'd soon be an end of masters.'
>
> (61)

Communist sentiments (unlike Soviet-era symbolism) were not unknown in the later Middle Ages, and were perhaps most famously voiced in the preaching of John Ball during the Peasants' Revolt of 1381, but we may wonder how meaningful they were likely to have been either to Dickon or to Robin, and whether a twelfth-century outlaw could plausibly have developed a class-based social theory of the type that Dickon goes on to learn about:

> Soon he realized that it was true what these men were saying, that the King and the Barons were equally useless to people. If they could be got rid of, with their wars and taxes and selfish sport, everyone would be far better off.
>
> (31)

Robin in effect aims to overthrow the feudal order and install what would to all intents and purposes be a workers' republic. Only death prevents him, and the book ends with Dickon and Little John agreeing that Robin's ideas will have their day, even if (as Little John prophetically puts it) 'things will come about slower than we thought. Perhaps not in our time at all' (152).

Bows Against the Barons was Trease's first novel. In the 'Author's Note' for the 1948 edition, 14 years after its first publication, he wrote that he had intended his story to be more historically accurate than those that had preceded it in the Victorian era, in which Robin Hood (implausibly in Trease's view) was represented as a man willing to fight against the tyranny of Prince John and the Sheriff of Nottingham, yet also to kneel at the feet of the returning King Richard (7). Trease thought it more likely that he was a rebel hero in the tradition of Wat Tyler or Jack Cade, who wanted to see the whole rotten feudal system overthrown. Despite this profession of allegiance to historicity, today it is hard not to read *Bows Against the Barons* as a book drenched in the politics of interwar socialism, and indeed the textual revisions that Trease himself made for the later edition suggest that he recognized that it was in some ways too closely tied to the language of its decade. The workers' battle cry disappeared, the blacksmith now addressed the crowd as 'neighbours' rather than 'fellow workers' or 'comrades', the reference to hammers and sickles was replaced with the more general 'tools', and the chapter of that name was retitled 'Friends in Need' (69, 41). Similar changes were made throughout, although Robin remained a class warrior in terms of his political vision and ambitions.

For Trease in 1934, Robin Hood was a foreshadowing of the rise of socialism in his own time, and for a reader today the book occupies a strange generic borderland in consequence. It is an historical novel (Robin's men wear medieval clothes and their enemies live in fairly realistic castles), but it also has elements of prophecy, allegory and topical propaganda: Trease's sympathies are certainly directed towards all those suffering under the yoke of parasitic 'masters', and not just the Norman variety. *Bows Against the Barons* is also in some respects a product of the existing literary heritage of Robin Hood: Trease follows Sir Walter Scott rather than history, for example, in making the division between Normans and Saxons a live political issue at this date, and he alludes ironically to the literary image of the Middle Ages in calling his first chapter 'Merrie England'.

None of these considerations makes Trease's novel a fantasy, but they tend to dislodge its moorings from the there-and-then of late twelfth-century England where Trease apparently wished to fix his story, and to send it floating up towards the present day – or to Trease's 1934 present, at least. In some respects, indeed, the experience of reading it resembles that of reading a time-slip fiction. Robin and his followers are essentially modern in terms of their beliefs and attitudes, mediating the past through a sensibility contemporary with that of Trease himself. To read *Bows Against the Barons* today is thus to view the Middle Ages through the double lens of today's world and that of 1934. In fact, we might note (as Kim Stanley Robinson once put it)[6] that many realist historical texts feature at least one 'time-travelling character in disguise', often the protagonist, who exhibits a modern set of attitudes hard to account for from their supposed upbringing and surroundings. Such characters may then act as a bridge between the reader's world and that of the book, although this advantage is gained at the price of anachronism.

Generic hybridity in books such as Trease's is thus far from exceptional, even if *Bows Against the Barons* offers a particularly clear example. One of the subjects of this volume will be the ways in which tensions inherent in the concept of 'historical fiction' can be productive of new forms of meaning and expression, which are difficult to articulate using the critical discourses based more firmly within one or other genre tradition. The critical reorientation we propose is designed in large part to offer a framework for such discussion. Could it be, for example, that the juggling of contemporary and historical perspectives we have identified actually offers advantages to the historical novelist? Hester Burton, author of the 1962 novel about Horatio Nelson, *Castors Away!*, offers a useful perspective on Trease's method in *Bows Against the Barons*:

> I am quite conscious that I choose an event or theme in history because it echoes something I have experienced in my own life. For example, when I described the autumn of Trafalgar in *Castors Away!*, I consciously relived the summer of 1940. Both seasons were a time of danger, stress, and joy; in both we were threatened by invasion and were fighting for our lives. In the courage of Nelson, I felt again the inspiration of Winston Churchill [...].
>
> (162)

This idea that contemporary events may illuminate the past, and even be a way of 'reliving' it, is significant and suggests another sense in which historical novels, like time-slips, can address the relationship between past and present. Bearing Burton's words in mind we might cite *Cue for Treason* (1940), a later novel by Geoffrey Trease, set in the London of William Shakespeare. This story, which tells of a treacherous plot linked to a production of *Henry V*, appeared at a time when England was again under threat from continental Europe, and fear of fifth columnists was rife – a fact likely to have affected its reception as a patriotic book. The same echoing of historical events was taken up as a deliberate strategy by Laurence Olivier four years later when he dedicated his 1944 film of *Henry V* to the British forces on the eve of D-Day. Indeed, Shakespeare himself used the technique in the same play, comparing Henry's expedition to France with the contemporary expedition of the Earl of Essex into Ireland (V.Pro. 30–5). It is an established tradition of historical writing, in other words, to make use of the parallels between the time depicted and that of composition. There are no postmodern tripwires here, no forcing of readers into a self-conscious awareness of the artificiality and convention-bound nature of the act of reading. Rather, it is an attempt to use the knowledge already present in writer and reader as a booster station, to intensify the immediacy of the past.

In all this, the differences between genres do not disappear, but they do tend to become more marginal. Paton Walsh, while producing a time-slip novel that implicitly compares the late twentieth and early nineteenth centuries, virtually ignores her fantasy structure, and the question of *how* it is that a modern child comes to find himself in past. Trease, writing a realist historical novel, does so in unabashed consciousness that readers will find echoes of their own present in his fictional past, and includes a 'time-travelling' character in the person of a socialist Robin Hood. We suggest that too great a respect for generic boundaries may blinker critics from attending to what actually happens in children's books, and thus lead them to underestimate the degree of flexibility with which both writers and readers approach the formal properties of genre. Instead, it is more useful to consider these generic boundaries with an understanding of their inherent permeability.

The shape of chapters to come

The main body of this book takes the form of a chronological series of case studies, starting with the Roman invasion of Britain and ending with stories set in the near future. This span of history contains wide variation in terms of its familiarity to modern readers; the richness and reliability of the historical record; the ways in which history mingles with legendary or mythical material; the extent to which children may feel personally involved with the events being represented; and the range of children's texts that deal with the period in question. Although the issues addressed in this book apply to a greater or lesser extent across the historical range, a chronological approach will allow for a more nuanced picture of the ways in which different periods of history are presented and read in children's literature, and the functions they fulfil in contributing to an awareness of, and relationship with, the past.

We begin with the Roman invasion in 'The Eagle Has Landed' (Chapter 2). Here our focus will be on the ways in which authors in the decades of the 1950s and the 2000s position their texts with regard to the invasion itself and the cultures involved – those of Rome and of the Britons. The possibilities for writing about this period of British history are clearly influenced by the nature of the historical record, in which all the written sources are Roman, the Britons being illiterate at the time of the invasion. This imbalance naturally introduces questions of bias within the source material. More important, however, is the extent to which the point of view of the implied reader in children's texts is made into an ideological battleground for concepts such as 'progress', 'ecology' and 'civilization', which are in turn projected onto the Romans and the Britons.

At the centre of 'Once, Future, Sometime, Never' (Chapter 3) is Arthur, a figure who stands at the very end of the story of Roman Britain. Along with Robin Hood and a small group of others, Arthur occupies a fault-line between history and legend. At different times and by different writers (including archaeologists and historians) his existence has been treated as a matter of fact and of fancy, and he has in any case undergone a series of radical reimaginings. Post-Roman soldier, Celtic chieftain, paragon of chivalry, resistance fighter, imperialist, Christian prince, pagan consorter with wizards, cuckolded corner of a tragic love triangle – Arthur has been all of these. A symbol of British resistance against the English, he went on to be co-opted as a symbol of Englishness itself, as well as an enduring national hero of the Welsh. Writers who choose to address the Arthurian story have to negotiate these protean qualities, either narrowing Arthur's range or else finding a way to accommodate his contradictions, and also to come to terms with a thousand years of storytelling about him from Celtic, French and English sources, which stand between us and whatever historical reality he may possess. As the most famous person from a period of history about which little is known and from which almost no written records survive, Arthur has been a perennial challenge to historians, whether or not they consider him to be historical, but he is no less so to writers interested in presenting the past to child readers.

From the individual figure of Arthur we move to a chapter that deals with a long span of history, stretching 600 years from the Norman Conquest to the Restoration. The primary subject of 'She Be Faking It' (Chapter 4) is authenticity: cultural, linguistic and material. Here we investigate the concept of anachronism, considering the competing demands on historical texts, on the one hand to represent the material and cultural world of the past accurately, and on the other to offer modern readers a means of understanding that past and of establishing an affective connection with it – for example, in the form of characters to whom those readers might be expected to 'relate'. Although these can be seen as opposing aims that must be reconciled as far as possible through compromise, some authors have used them to create new ways of presenting the past to children today.

In 'Dreams of Things That Never Were' (Chapter 5), we extend the discussion of authenticity to include a more detailed consideration of genre, concentrating on texts set in the eighteenth and nineteenth centuries, and especially on those that eschew any attempt at the mimetic representation of history in favour of stylized, satirized or otherwise altered versions of the past. Some texts, for example, make use of alternative history to view historical events in the mirror of the might-have-been. Others use historical settings for orientalist or touristic purposes, treating history as a landscape for costume adventure, and prioritizing the pleasure of the reader over any obligation (or pretence) to historical accuracy. Some are ambiguous as to the nature of the liberties being taken, a feature particularly common in intertextual works that use older texts as a basis for pastiche, sequels or other forms of reworking. And there are texts that take famous historical figures whose lives are frequently well documented, and give them parts to play in uncanonical histories. All these kinds of text represent history, but do so in ways that are unabashedly *not* offering to be faithful representations of the past. They may, however, offer a second-order discourse about the construction of historical accounts, about the contingency of events and about the illusory nature of history's seeming solidity. There is always another story to be told, and another version of the stories that already exist.

As we move into the twentieth century, the nature of history undergoes a qualitative shift. With the advent of film, sound recording and photography, and (for more recent events) family stories and personal reminiscences, evidence of the past is no longer preserved merely in physical remains and written records: it has a face and a voice, and this affects the ways in which we imagine such seminal events as the Second World War. The history learned in school and from books may overlap with the personal memories of relatives and friends, and indeed authors. Personal testimony and autobiography are central elements of many books about the Second World War in particular, which was, for the generation of writers born in the 1920s and 1930s, the time of their childhood. In 'Ancestral Voices, Prophesying War' (Chapter 6) we will be considering the issues involved in combining personal experience (especially child's-eye experience) with the larger events and structures that go to make up public accounts of 'history'. We will then extend the discussion to include books that move beyond the past of living memory into the near future. Books set in the future may seem to have little to do with the representation of history. However, they are likely to draw on the images and events of history in order to refigure them as speculation, prophecy, dystopia, fable and allegory. A consideration of future books, in other words, can tell us a good deal about the cultural position of the past in the authors' present.

Most of the books discussed in *Reading History in Children's Books* cover a relatively small period of history, typically bounded by the protagonist's childhood or adolescence. In 'Patterns of History' (Chapter 7), we will consider the ways in which texts convey the larger-scale aspects of history. Texts carry implications about the shape, direction and, in some cases, purpose of historical change, which may, for example, be represented as an ascent into moral and technological progress, or else as an inexorable decline. Such features may be at their most obvious in genres involving time-travel, which allow direct comparisons to be drawn between different periods, but they are implicit in any representation of the past. Recent reports by the Office for Standards in Education, Children's Services and Skills (Ofsted), the UK Government's school inspection service for England, have highlighted the extent to which children lack an understanding of chronology, and hence of more general concepts related to the nature of historical change that rely on chronology as a foundation. In this final chapter we consider the ways in which historical fiction in particular promotes certain models of history, albeit often in an implicit and unexamined way. Given the strong ideological tenor of many such models, we believe that their open discussion is a vital component not only of historical education but also of critical analysis.

2

The Eagle Has Landed: Representing the Roman Invasion of Britain in Texts for Children

The events around the Roman invasion of Britain can be framed as narrative in a number of different ways. At one extreme, they may constitute a story of the bringing of civilization to a savage land; at the other, of a brave defence by patriotic islanders against an unprovoked imperialist attack. The question is not merely one of 'taking sides': for modern British children, this is also a question of identity. Do historical narratives encourage them to see themselves as having more in common with Rome, or with the conquered Britons? What alternative positions are available? If this period of history is part of 'our island story', to invoke H. E. Marshall's classic book of 1905, who exactly are 'we'? Children's authors have used a variety of strategies for addressing these questions. They may, for example, adopt either Roman or British narrative perspectives, or they may attempt a more complex imaginative reconstruction of the ways in which these two cultures interacted, one that leaves arguments about the rights and wrongs of invasion somewhat to one side. They may create a multivocal text that (by any of a variety of means) presents us with opposing points of view, perhaps in quite stark form, without necessarily attempting to reconcile or arbitrate them. Or they may move the scene into a fantasy alternative to history, in which the terms of the debate can be recast. All these are amongst the strategies we shall consider in this chapter.

In comparing the Romans and the Britons, one asymmetry that immediately presents itself is the fact that, in comparison with those who immediately preceded and succeeded them, the Romans appear easier to 'know'. They left many still-visible traces on the landscape and in place names, kept written records and had an historical sensibility easy to recognize as 'modern'. Moreover, the only accounts we have of their British campaigns are Roman ones, by Julius Caesar, Tacitus and others. In many ways we have a continuing investment in Roman culture, which has had a formative influence on contemporary British society. The same cannot be claimed for ancient British culture. Children in English primary schools, to take one relevant example, are taught the classical myths as part of the National Curriculum, but very little of the Celtic myths of their own island, or even of the Teutonic mythology that was the historic heritage of the Anglo-Saxons. One reason for this, no doubt, is that Greco-Roman myth permeates mainstream European literature, music and art in a way that, with relatively few exceptions, Celtic and Teutonic myth do not.

For the purpose of this chapter we will consider these matters by examining a selection of fiction and non-fiction published over the last century, concentrating on the two decades of the 1950s, which saw a particular flourishing of children's books set in this period, and the 2000s. This involves some deviation from our normal practice of primarily considering books easily available to modern child readers, but will allow us to observe some of the changes in the presentation of this period over the last 60 years, and the relationship of these changes to more general developments in education and society.

The historical background to the Roman invasion

In order to provide a context for our reading of books about this period, it will be useful to say something about its history and the sources available to the authors we will be discussing. For classical Greek and Roman commentators Britain had always been a fairly peripheral point on the map, about which relatively little was known. The tribes of the channel coast had been involved in trade with the continent for some time, but when Julius Caesar described Britain in his account of the Gallic wars, he was doing so as an explorer into savage regions. The story of the Roman conquest of Britain begins in 55–54 BC with Caesar's two forays into British territory, and resumes almost a hundred years later with Claudius's invasion in AD 43. The subjugation of modern England and Wales took another generation, including the defeat and capture of Caratacus (in the 50s AD), the destruction of the Druidic stronghold on Anglesey (AD 60), the rising and subsequent defeat of Boudicca (AD 60) and the entrenchment of Roman rule through the late 70s and 80s AD by a succession of Roman governors, the most famous of whom was Gnaeus Julius Agricola. The building of Hadrian's Wall in the 120s AD marked the eventual limit of Roman imperial expansion into Britain, and for the purposes of this chapter we shall consider the phrase 'the Roman invasion' to cover the whole period from 55 BC to AD 120.

The major sources for this period of British history are Caesar's own account of his campaigns in his *Gallic Wars* (a text long familiar to schoolchildren studying Latin), and Tacitus's *Agricola* (AD 98) and later *Annals* (AD 109). The work of Caesar and Tacitus has the advantage of being written by people either closely involved in the events described or personally acquainted with those who were, but for the same reason neither author is remotely disinterested. The *Gallic Wars* is a masterpiece of style, but it is also a piece of self-justification and aggrandizement, written with an eye to immediate political advantage rather than historical accuracy, and what it has to say about the Britons – both praise and dispraise – must be read in that light. For example, Caesar goes out of his way to praise the Britons' courage and their skill with horses and chariots; but while his admiration may well be genuine, it also serves to make them seem more formidable opponents, and his victories over them that much more impressive. Equally, his description of the Druidic practice of sacrificing criminals (and, if necessary, the innocent) in giant wicker figures, tends to demonize the enemy and thus to justify the Roman invasion. As Ronald Hutton puts it, Caesar 'had the strongest possible motive for misrepresenting native customs in order to portray the Gauls as peoples deserving of conquest' (*Druids* 96) – and what applies here to the Gauls applies to the Britons by extension. None of this invalidates Caesar's claims, but it must certainly limit the weight we are prepared to put on them, in the absence of independent evidence.

Tacitus's *Agricola*, written in around AD 98, is a flattering, not to say hagiographic, account of the author's father-in-law, who was Governor of Britain from AD 78 to 85, and seems to have been composed largely as an act of filial piety. Agricola is depicted as a capable soldier, responsible for defeating the last remnants of the British resistance on Anglesey and for conducting a series of successful campaigns into Caledonia. He is a thorough and wise administrator who knows how to manage a defeated people with the strictness necessary to ensure submission, but also works to end abuse and corruption by his own officials, using 'the allurements of peace' (71) as well as the threat of war in order to consolidate Roman rule. Tacitus is always admiring of Agricola: nevertheless, his admiration does not extend to the Roman state as a whole, which he finds to be corrupted from its ancient virtue; while in the Emperor Domitian he portrays a man jealous of his general's successes and too quick to withdraw him from service. This ambivalence manifests itself in a number of passages, notably in the patriotic speech Tacitus places in the mouth of the Caledonian chief Calgacus, in which Rome is characterized as a monster of greed. Elsewhere, Tacitus comments on the trappings of civilization that the Romans made available to the conquered Britons: 'And so the Britons were gradually led on to the amenities that make vice agreeable – arcades, baths and sumptuous banquets. They spoke of such novelties as "civilization", when really they were only a feature of enslavement' (72). This remark is aimed at Tacitus's own people as much as at the Britons, for the Romans had in his view also fallen into the flabbiness of luxury. Nevertheless, these asides provide a significant counterpoint to the tendency of histories of Roman Britain to stress the benefits of Roman technological and administrative innovations, and they will resurface in the children's texts dealing with the period.

Against all this, the Britons have left no written testimony at all. Our knowledge of them has to be filtered through largely hostile Roman narratives, although these are increasingly being supplemented by the findings of archaeology. This lack makes the Britons more malleable as a subject for writing. Even more than with the Romans, literary representations of the Britons may be expected to reflect the concerns and attitudes of the writer's own age, untrammelled by the constraints of historical evidence. Thus we may see Britons represented variously as 'barbarians', as nature mystics, as brave resistance fighters and as country cousins of the more sophisticated Romans, eager to be inducted into their urban and cosmopolitan way of life.

A civilizing mission: Representations of the invasion from 1900 to the 1950s

Popular histories for children in the twentieth century handle this material in many different ways. In *Our Island Story*, H. E. Marshall attempts to tell a story that will enable a modern child (of 1905) to understand and identify with Britain through its past. Her account of the Roman invasion is a self-consciously even-handed one, which stresses the contributions made by both the Britons and the Romans to the island. For their part, the Britons are brave and indomitable, to the extent that Marshall has the Romans failing to subdue their spirit throughout 350 years of occupation – a contention evidenced by the fact that the Britons, unlike their continental counterparts, did not develop a Romance language (56). Patriotic heroes of the British resistance, such as Caractacus (Caratacus) and Boadicea (Boudicca) receive a generally sympathetic press. On the other hand, the Romans were better organized as fighters, and Marshall concedes that they were the conduit for many desirable developments, most notably Christianity – a mitigation that dates back at least as far as William Camden's *Britannia* (Bradley 134). Nevertheless, she remains highly critical of an imperial enterprise motivated simply by greed. In words not dissimilar to those Tacitus put into the mouth of Calgacus, she declares that the Romans 'were a very greedy people and, as soon as they heard of a new country, they wanted to conquer it and call it part of the Roman Empire' (4). It is striking that in this book, written at the height of the British Empire, we find a more forthright condemnation of imperialist greed than is to be heard in the children's texts of 50 years later.

Marshall is equally ambivalent about the Druids, though she is less successful here in keeping ambivalence distinct from simple confusion. As Ronald Hutton has shown (*Druids*), by the time Marshall was writing there were a number of coexisting cultural niches for the Druids in popular literature, history and art. They might be depicted positively as a patriotic resistance force against the Romans, or as the wise guardians of nature and the wisdom of the ages. By others they were portrayed as a cruel and even demonic priesthood, rightfully extirpated. Marshall's ideas about the physical appearance of Druids are probably drawn from works such as Meyrick and Smith's *The*

Costume of the Original Inhabitants of the British Isles (1815), though she may also have had in mind the Edwardian Druidic ceremonies of her own day, but she has clearly not forgotten Caesar's wicker man either. The result is a picture of the Druids in which wisdom and barbarity sit in uncomfortable juxtaposition:

> The Druids were the wisest people in the land. When anyone was in doubt or difficulty he would go to them for advice. They were very solemn and grand old men with long white beards and beautiful robes [...] Some of the teaching of the Druids was very beautiful, but some of it was very dreadful, and they even killed human beings in their sacrifices.
>
> (22)

Despite this attempt to build a composite Druid from incompatible traditions, Marshall is in general content to let opposing views of both Rome and the Britons sit side by side, neither highlighting nor disguising their contradictions. This position is facilitated by her frank admission that hers is a book of stories rather than an authoritative history. Instead of insisting on a unitary truth she is able to refer her readers to a future time when they will be able to read 'the beautiful big histories which have helped me to write this little book for little people' (xviii), and decide for themselves using their mature judgement.

This kind of self-conscious openness about the provisional nature of the text's authority is largely absent from the series that may be said to have supplanted *Our Island Story* as British children's first introduction to written history from the 1950s on: the Ladybird 'Adventures from History' series. Most of these short titles focused on a single historical figure, the first seven being devoted to *Alfred the Great* (1956), *William the Conqueror* (1956), *Sir Walter Raleigh* (1957), *Nelson* (1957), *Elizabeth I* (1958), *Captain Cook* (1958) and *Florence Nightingale* (1959). The series was initially authored by Lawrence du Garde Peach – not a professional historian but a playwright and sometime writer for *Punch* magazine. He seems to have been more comfortable 'fixing' his historical narrative in the story of a single individual. *Julius Caesar and the Romans* (1959) was the first in the series to take in an historical period longer than a single life, but even here Peach anchored his book in the life of one man. That man was not in fact Julius Caesar, whose exploits are dealt with in the book's first few pages, but the more unlikely figure of Gnaeus Julius Agricola. Agricola's life story is threaded in and out of that of Britain in the first century AD. His experiences, first as a lieutenant of Suetonius Paulinus, then as commander of the XX legion and finally as governor, are presented as an ideal narrative of rule. In his various posts he learns everything there is to know about Britain, and knows it rather better than the Britons themselves. Agricola's education is more than a question of statecraft, or of watching Suetonius Paulinus as he goes about his military duties. Perhaps inspired by stories of hunting expeditions with British guides in Rudyard Kipling and Rosemary Sutcliff, Peach also invents Prince Hal-like moments for his hero: 'his way was to go hunting with British guides and hunters in the big forests which largely covered the country [. . .] It was probably over the camp fire, after a day's hunting, that Agricola really came to know and understand the British people' (26). Of course, there is nothing even in Tacitus's admiring account of his father-in-law to suggest this intimacy with 'the British people', nor indeed would Tacitus necessarily have found such fraternization commendable. For Peach, however, the seven years of Agricola's governorship were ones in which Britain 'was governed as well as it has ever been, before or since' (36). This hyperbolic claim (illustrated by a picture of Agricola sitting in judgement above a kneeling British supplicant) is of a piece with Peach's other work for the 'Adventures from History' series, which reveals an obvious admiration for 'strong leaders' – a tendency most notable in his quasi-fascistic treatment of William I.

Peach tends to present the Britons in such a way as to emphasize their distance from the world that he and his readers inhabit, while emphasizing the continuity between Roman and modern British culture. For example, he tells us that 'at the time of the Roman conquest of Britain, the people who lived in these islands were not Christians' (24–5), but neglects to mention that the same is true of the Romans themselves. The Britons north of Hadrian's Wall (the 'wild tribes') are shown in animal skins of the kind more usually associated with prehistoric peoples, as in Peach's own *Stone Age Man in Britain* (1961). By contrast, the life of people in 'peaceful Britain' (42, 46), as Peach calls the part of the island under Roman occupation, differs only superficially from that lived in the 1950s: 'thousands of people lived their lives, just as they do today, going to school, or work, or doing the housework and the shopping' (46). John Kenney's facing illustration depicts just such a scene, with prosperous shoppers going about their business in a clean, well-maintained street. For Ladybird's regular readers, the detail of a Roman housewife visiting a butcher's shop may have had particular resonance, as it appears to be closely based on an illustration from an early reader published the previous year, M. E. Gagg's *Shopping with Mother* (1958). The position of the shopper and the butcher, the woman's blond child dressed in blue, the hanging joints of meat, even the set of scales between shopkeeper and customer, all work to enforce a subliminal identification between the two scenes.[1] Peach's book is heavily reliant on Tacitus, and even includes a lengthy quotation in praise of Agricola, but while Tacitus viewed the trappings of civilization as undermining British resistance, Peach views the bourgeoisification of Roman Britain in an entirely positive light. He concludes his book with an aerial picture of a typical Romano-British town, this time emphasizing the military as the force that creates and maintains the possibility of civilized life. The citizens might see the Legions marching out down Watling St, on their way to Chester or York: 'And they would go their ways contentedly and in peace, knowing that behind the sure shield of the Legions, Britain was safe' (50).

Peach's domestication of Rome and his generally pro-Roman stance are far from unique: in fact they are typical of 1950s treatments of this period for children, both fictional and non-fictional. For an example of the former we cannot do better than turn to Lydia S. Eliott's 1953 novel *Ceva of the Caradocs*. This is the story of a great-great-granddaughter of Caractacus in the time of the Emperor Hadrian – the year being AD 122. *Ceva of the Caradocs* is not a skilful work, but its unselfconsciousness makes its ideological structure exceptionally open to view.

Ceva suffers from divided loyalties. While her immediate family has settled happily in the Roman town of Viroconium (Wroxeter) at the foot of the Wrekin in modern Shropshire, her grandfather (Caractacus's grandson), the Chief Gaelan, stubbornly persists in staying in his draughty hill fort. Ceva's birthday is approaching, when she will have to choose whether to stay with her grandfather or move permanently into town. Although she is fond of Gaelan, her own preference is clear, as she confides to her horse: 'Is it awful of me to be glad [...] that the Romans have made Britain a part of their marvellous Empire? Am I wicked, Guela, to be proud that my land of Britain belongs to Rome?' (9). Moreover, she wishes to be with her friends Julia and Lavinia, the daughters of the Roman governor, with whom she will be able to enjoy all the amenities of civilization: 'She ached to have lovely things round her, to have books to read and beautiful tunics to wear' (11). The fun she yearns for appears rather 1950ish, in fact, perhaps because Eliott makes so few concessions to period in her choice of vocabulary, referring to 'picnics' (8) and 'embroidery classes at the School of Art' (253), while Ceva's impatience at hearing of her great-grandfather's wartime privations provokes the protest: 'I'm living now, not then: and I want to live as modern girls do' (30).

Ceva's pro-Roman attitude is not universally shared. Her grandfather Gaelan (or 'naughty old Chief Gaelan', as the Roman Governor refers to him [18]) is resentful of the Romans, and indeed he paraphrases Tacitus on the enervating effect of luxury: 'The Emperor Hadrian is in Britain to take away our freedom by giving us luxury. Though he calls it bringing us civilization, it is *his* way of enslaving us' (19–20). The Druids are even more virulent in their opposition. But the Druids are shown to be charlatans, who manipulate the supposed orders of their god (the Unseen One) in order to promote an anti-Roman agenda in a way that disgusts Gaelan. Over the course of the book, Gaelan too begins to doubt the wisdom of his intransigence. Travelling home after his Druid meeting he finds himself questioning his hostile attitude to the Romans: 'Was it honest, he asked himself, to use their good roads, for instance, but to be unfriendly?' (41). True, the Romans had defeated and captured Gaelan's grandfather, Caractacus, slaughtered all his friends and put a price on his own father's head; but that was quite a long time ago, and, as Ceva argues, it would be unfair to take revenge on Hadrian and the present governor of Viroconium for what Claudius and his generals did 80 years before. Ceva believes that 'They're awfully sorry about Caractacus and about Grandfather's father. They wish it had never happened. I know they do' (31). Eventually Gaelan realizes that he has indeed been misguided. The Caradoc motto has always been 'Forward, not backward' – presumably a rallying cry to courage in battle – but Gaelan now reinterprets it as indicating that he should be looking forward towards progress in the form of Roman civilization, not backwards into barbarism.

Ceva of the Caradocs is a striking book in part because it is so unabashed in its wholesale transplantation of the mind of a 1950s debutante into second-century Shropshire, and in the declaration of its loyalties to Rome, or rather to modernity as embodied in Rome. The evils of empire, if they ever existed, are safely in the past and can be ignored, while Roman life in itself is superior in every way to the backwardness and superstition of the Britons. The Emperor is a model of good government and devotion to duty, as Ceva notes wonderingly: 'I wonder he doesn't spend his life living in [his lovely villas] and being happy himself instead of travelling from end to end of his Empire, trying to make things safe and happy for the Gauls and the Britons and lots of other people' (19). Ceva's idealistic assessment of the Roman Empire is endorsed by the book without significant qualification. Like Peach, Eliott implicitly identifies Roman life with that of her own time, but is even more emphatic in making it the beneficiary of a general principle that history tends to work in the direction of progress, that the future is preferable to the past and that this can be measured in terms of material goods and comfort (see also Hingley 144–7).

In the case of Eliott, we may wonder how far her superimposition of 1950s values onto a second-century setting was the result of a lack of historical awareness rather than a deliberate strategy. However, the following year saw the publication of a book by a writer with a far higher reputation as an historical novelist: Henry Treece. Along with Rosemary Sutcliff and Geoffrey Trease, Treece is probably the best-known British historical children's novelist of this period, and we will look in vain for Eliott's picnics and art schools in his depiction of Roman Britain in *Legions of the Eagle* (1954). Nevertheless, in other respects this book follows the pattern laid down by *Ceva of the Caradocs*, of being a pro-Roman story told from the point of view of a British adolescent.

Legions of the Eagle is set in AD 43, near the future site of Colchester. The story's protagonist is Gwydion, the son of a local Belgic warlord. Gwydion's world is about to be shattered. In the first battle against the invading Romans his adored father is killed, and Gwydion, his mother and his best friend (also his slave) Math are captured. Luckily, Gwydion is taken under the wing of a kindly centurion, Gracchus, who sends him to Gaul as company for his son Gaius. In Lugdunum (Lyon) he finds a huge contrast to the life he has been used to:

> [...] a broad, orderly town, its stone buildings shining in the sun, its clean roads bordered by regular rows of trees. The citizens strolled about in the sunshine as though they had never heard of Camulodunum, and Caratacus, and Caswallwn. Gwydion began to feel that he was a boy from some curious and primitive island, many hundreds of leagues away from civilization.
>
> (61)

Gwydion's feeling is only confirmed by events. Later, when he and Gaius return to Britain to seek Gaius's father, Gwydion is able to make the comparison with his homeland even more starkly. He looks out over Britain:

> It was a great, dark island, he thought, full of magic and of cruelty. Only here and there, along the hill ridges, did men till the land and build their comfortable houses. So much of Britain was a wilderness, where wild beasts roamed, and where people almost as wild as the beasts held their festivals of blood and suffering [...] As the boy speculated on the land of his birth, he began to wonder why the Romans had even bothered to come to Britain. What he had seen of Roman Gaul was good; it was a well-regulated land, with good roads, inns, and houses; a land where men paid their taxes in money, not in blood – and where, in return for those taxes, they were given something of value, the protection of the greatest army the world had ever known.
>
> (140)

Roman superiority emphatically extends to personal character. The kindly centurion Gracchus not only cares for Gwydion but also arranges for his mother to be made a Roman citizen and offers her a home. 'What Celt would have done that? None!' (149) as she exclaims – having apparently forgotten that she already had a comfortable home before being widowed by the invading Romans a few months earlier. Later, her conversion to the Roman point of view complete, she tells Gracchus to 'take Gwydion and teach him your ways' (156). Gaius too is 'a true Roman of the old school, who believed in telling the truth, in straight-dealing of every sort, and in honesty' (70). Treece uses crude essentialism to register cultural differences between the Romans and the Britons through Gaius and

Gwydion. When Gaius pays Gwydion a compliment, for example, he does so under his breath, 'for his education had been based on Spartan precepts, which taught that it was unmanly to make any show of the emotions'. Gwydion's response is to burst into tears: 'shaking the water from his eyes, he smiled and with a typical Celtic bravado, punched Gaius lightly in the chest' (102–3).

Gwydion is a good Celt, with the potential to be Romanized. And, indeed, he ends the novel thoroughly domesticated, as a contented yeoman farmer in Gaul. (In a later book, *War Dog* [1962], Treece would reprise the story of *Legions of the Eagle* using a dog rather than a boy as the protagonist. It is telling how little difference this makes.) However, there are also other Celts, unwilling or unable to be Romanized. Math, Gwydion's former friend, is one such. A defeated fighter against Rome, and rejected in the end by Gwydion (whom he finds sunnily playing chess with his new friend Gaius), Math is last seen setting 'his head towards those dark woods which covered the sullen face of the land' (159), and thus out of history. Math is a small, dark Silurian (i.e., he is from South Wales), and this seems to be the tribe singled out for particular distaste. As the Roman company surgeon says, slipping into full-blown *Heart of Darkness* mode: 'They are not pleasant fighters. [...] I'd rather deal with a straight slash any day than a mere prick that has been doctored by those black-faced cannibals!' (149). *War Dog* contains an even more starkly Conradian moment, in which skulls are discovered hanging on the pillars of the wooden temple in Mai Dun in a manner recalling Kurtz's jungle station, a sight that provokes 'disgust' in the Roman tribune who witnesses it (79).

The prime example of an incorrigible Celt is Caratacus himself. In contrast to the noble warrior whose dignity so impressed Claudius in Tacitus and Dio Cassius, this Caratacus has after his initial defeat become cruel, shifty and manipulative. In the final pages of the book Gwydion is delighted to hear of his capture by the Romans, assigning to him the entire blame for the bloodshed that followed the Roman invasion:

> 'Now that Rome has finally broken that man's pride and we have him prisoner and in Gaul, let us hope that the Emperor Claudius will treat him as he deserves, for all the suffering he has caused. Let us hope that Caratacus is never allowed to raise the tribes again,

> disturbing men's lives and putting innocent ones to the sword. How can men work and till the land and harvest their crops if such madmen as Caratacus are allowed to carry on their ambitious ways unchecked?'
>
> (162–3)

It seems that, in Gwydion's mind, resistance to Roman power is not only futile but can even be read as unprovoked aggression.

Both Eliott and Treece tell their stories from the point of view of British protagonists, and in both cases the story is one in which central British characters (Gaelan in *Ceva of the Caradocs*, Gwydion in *Legions of the Eagle*) come to re-evaluate their initial hostility to Rome, recognizing it as misplaced, superstitious and backward looking. Roman power is understood not just as inevitable but absolutely as desirable. Putting Rosemary Sutcliff's *The Eagle of the Ninth* (1954) into the context of these novels serves only to emphasize her achievement in producing a far more nuanced picture of Romano-British relations at the beginning of the Roman era. Sutcliff is interested in the complexity, porousness and bidirectional nature of cultural influence, in a way that recalls the Roman stories of Kipling in *Puck of Pook's Hill* (Roberts 110 *et passim*). Her major characters, Esca and Marcus, discuss their cultural differences without simply being reduced to representatives of Roman and British 'character' in the manner of Treece's Gwydion and Gaius. As in much of Sutcliff's work, the road to a wider understanding of cultural difference lies through a close *personal* relationship.

Unlike the other novels discussed so far, *The Eagle of the Ninth* is focalized through a Roman, Marcus. Marcus is a young officer recently posted to Britain, but although he is a newcomer to the island he also has a stake in the place, as his father was First Cohort of the famous Ninth Legion that was lost without trace when Marcus was a boy. Like many of Sutcliff's protagonists, Marcus is aware of straddling two worlds, and of needing to find his place in one or both – a need that becomes more acute once he is robbed of his military career by a battle wound. It is in this context that he agrees to travel north of the newly built Hadrian's Wall to recover the Ninth's lost legionary Eagle, and with it his family honour.

The early section of the book contains some familiar tropes. The Druid who foments an attack on Marcus's garrison, for example, is described as 'a wild figure in streaming robes that marked him out from the half-naked warriors who charged behind him' (40). And we have the Romanized British family, who are neighbours of Marcus's uncle, and living examples of the enervation and cultural slavery so despised by Tacitus:

> A British family of the ultra-Roman kind, a large good-natured-looking man, running to fat as men do who have been bred to a hard life and take to living soft instead; a woman with a fair and rather foolish face, prinked out in what had been the height of fashion in Rome two years ago – and very cold she must be, Marcus thought, in that thin mantle.
>
> (68)

However, the emotional heart of the book lies in the relationship between Marcus and his British slave – later, freedman and friend – Esca. By foregrounding their friendship, Sutcliff allows for a multifaceted examination of Roman and British cultures and their interaction.

Marcus and Esca's relationship offers a chance to consider both the continuities and differences between those cultures. In an early scene Esca compares the tight, symmetrical pattern embossed on Marcus's Roman dagger sheath with the natural flowing swirls of a Celtic shield boss, seeing them as indicative of two different world-views: 'You cannot expect the man who made this shield to live easily under the rule of the man who worked the sheath of this dagger' (98). For all that, Esca sees the Roman way of life as the one that will win in any struggle between the two: the straight Roman roads, the iron Roman discipline, will give them military victory, and he even grants that 'your justice is more sure than ours' (99). In other hands, this schematic representation of the two different cultures could become the foundation of a simplistic dichotomy. However, Sutcliff shades the contrast, both through Marcus and Esca's discovery of the values they share behind differing modes of expression, and also by demonstrating the diversity hidden in the homogenizing terms 'Roman' and 'Briton'. Sutcliff never loses sight of the individual circumstances, histories and personalities through which their cultural identities are refracted.

Religion affords one important example of this complex cultural topography. Whereas Treece makes the contrast between Roman and

Celtic fundamental and consistent, reflecting back in every plane the same simple difference between 'an unruly, superstitious and passionate Celtic world' and its opposite in the form of Roman 'order, decorum, rationality and civilization' (Hutton, *Druids* 120), Sutcliff refuses to allow such distinctions to stand untested. When Marcus witnesses the Feast of the New Spears amongst the Pictish Epidaii, he finds this initiation ceremony very alien, but as he speculates about the rites performed in the secret darkness of the tribe's sacred barrow, he also 'remember[s] his own hour, and the smell of bull's blood in the darkened cave of Mithras' (194). Again, before venturing into the barrow to retrieve the captured Eagle, Marcus and Esca prepare themselves with appropriate devotions: 'Marcus made his sunset prayers to Mithras, Esca made them to Lugh of the Shining Spear; but both these were Sun Gods, Light Gods, and their followers knew the same weapons against the dark' (205). On such occasions the differences and similarities between Marcus and Esca, between Marcus and the Epidaii, and indeed between Esca and other Britons, can be plotted in numerous ways, constituting an extended examination of the ways in which identities are formed, changed and revealed in new lights by lived experience.

Hunting offers another point of connection and difference between the novel's characters. It is an activity valued not only by Marcus and Esca, but also by the Epidaii and even by the supercilious young tribune Placidus, whom Marcus meets in his uncle's house. The novel casts Marcus and Esca at various points both as hunters and as quarry, and an appreciation of the chase as a physical and moral challenge is one of the areas of common experience on which their mutual understanding flourishes, so that when their death seems assured and Marcus asks what Esca had 'to win' in coming with him to seek the Eagle, Esca replies simply: 'I have been once again a free man amongst free men. I have shared the hunting with my brother, and it has been a good hunting' (255–6). Marcus echoes this, with the hunt standing metonymically for their friendship as a whole. By contrast, the jarring reaction of Placidus, a skilled hunter with whom one might expect Marcus to have much in common, to Esca's courageous killing of a mother wolf while hunting, is to upbraid him with risking a life not his own: 'Your Master, having paid good money for his slave, will not thank you for leaving him with a carcass that he cannot even sell to the knacker's yard' (82).

Sutcliff avoids pat translations from one cultural context to another, but she and her protagonists are finally more interested in human commonalities than in fundamental differences. Watching the hunter Guern (an ex-legionary who has gone native) shaving in front of his family, for example, Marcus ponders: 'How little difference there was between children the world over, [...] or fathers, or shaving, for that matter; the small patterns of behaviour and relationship that made up family life' (165). *The Eagle of the Ninth*, like all Sutcliff's historical novels, explores the ways in which these 'little differences' both do and do not matter as people from the past attempt to understand each other, and we them.

Sutcliff's investigation of cultural and racial identity in Roman Britain is far more sophisticated than that offered by Peach, Eliott or Treece, but considering these writers of the 1950s as a group we can see a number of common features. In general they are broadly sympathetic to Rome, and this sympathy rests on a number of related ideas. One is the sense that the Roman Empire brought benefits that outweighed whatever disadvantages came with being made a subject people. These include good roads, writing and luxury goods such as wine, as well as integration into a relatively sophisticated pan-European culture. Behind all this lies an assumption (sometimes articulated) that such things represent progress, and that progress is desirable. In stressing these features of Roman society it is necessary to de-emphasize the extent to which at least some of the tribes of pre-Roman Britain were already trading nations with good connections to the continent and Ireland, as well as the more onerous features of military occupation such as forced labour, taxation and the theft of natural resources. Repeatedly, too, Roman organization and teamwork are compared favourably to a tradition of heroic but futile individualism. The soldiers of the testudo may be anonymous, but they cut down the naked British warriors as surely as a tank matched against cavalry.

A general faith in technological, cultural and political progress underpins some of the sympathy of these books for the Roman enterprise. We should also note, however, that Britain in the 1950s was a place in which the ideology of empire had a far greater currency. The Roman Empire in particular was one in which the British had long seen a precursor and analogue of its own, the Pax Britannica of the nineteenth century consciously echoing the Pax Romana, as

Richard Hingley has discussed in *Roman Officers and English Gentlemen* (2000). Empire's perceived efficacy as a force for peace and stability, and particularly as a conduit for civilized values, more than justified the violence and theft involved. This equivalence is carried into the rhetoric and customs depicted in some of the fiction. When Ceva performs a dance for the Emperor Hadrian, for example, the occasion recalls the similar performances of 'tribal dance' staged for members of the British royal family on their trips into the Empire, while her effusive account of the Emperor's self-sacrifice in leaving his many palaces echoes British admiration of the royal family's workload and sense of duty.

The thought that Britain had once been in the position of the 'primitive' tribes it is now colonizing sorts well with the overall narrative of progress, and of civilization as a flame that can be passed from one culture to another and spread through the power of enlightened imperialism. Conrad's *Heart of Darkness* again provides a useful point of reference, particularly in the narrator Marlow's acknowledgement that Britain has in its time 'been one of the dark places of the earth', and his re-imagination of the first Roman incursions into the British interior in terms of his own African experience:

> Sand-banks, marshes, forests, savages, – precious little to eat fit for a civilized man, nothing but Thames water to drink. No Falernian wine here, no going ashore. Here and there a military camp lost in a wilderness, like a needle in a bundle of hay – cold, fog, tempests, disease, exile, and death – death skulking in the air, in the water, in the bush. They must have been dying like flies here.
>
> (6)

Whatever the limitations of Marlow's analogy, the British of Conrad's time certainly found themselves using some of the same justifications as the Romans for their imperial activity. Caesar's demonization of the Druids, for example, bears comparison with the self-imposed duty of the British to stamp out cruel religions and cults from their empires in Africa and India, as in the case of the Thuggees (Lloyd). But we also find a retrospective imputation of a 'civilizing mission' to the Romans: Conrad's Marlow acknowledges that, without such an idea, empire is nothing but robbery with violence, but implies (even if the story he tells undermines his implication) that its presence might nevertheless constitute a justification of the imperial enterprise. This strange attitude of self-righteous robbery is neatly encapsulated in the disgusted reaction of Henry Treece's Roman officer to the British display of captured skulls in *War Dog*: 'These folk were savages, barbarians, and no good could come of taking their land from them and trying to show them Roman ways, civilised ways' (80).

The 1950s were not of course the high-water mark of the British Empire, but rather the decade in which it became impossible to ignore the fact that Britain was no longer a first-rate international power. If, in some respects, Roman historical fiction published for children in that period afforded a retreat to a time of past imperial confidence, it is also notable that it did so by focusing on a period of British defeat, and the incorporation of Britain into a new and larger political unit, centred elsewhere. The theme of learning to embrace such a future had particular relevance at a time when Britain was seeking a new role for itself, either as part of a reconstructed European bloc of nations, or (as Harold Macmillan was fond of imagining) as the experienced 'Greek' advisors to the new 'Roman' power, the United States (Ashton 6). Books such as those by Eliott and Treece, with their emphasis on Rome's superior technology and wealth and their optimistic orientation towards the future, seem designed in part as ways of exploring how to make such a transfer of loyalty and identity psychologically possible and morally justifiable, at a time when austerity Britain was looking longingly across the Atlantic to a land of televisions, washing machines, freeways and other Agricolan amenities.

Later representations

The academic discipline of history in the decades following the 1950s took a decisive turn away from the study of individual figures in favour of broader movements within politics and society (Harnett 89–90). This was reflected in due course both in classroom teaching and in the kinds of history books produced for children. With the coming of the National History Curriculum in the wake of the 1988 Education Reform Act a new market for Roman books opened up, one designed specifically with primary school children at Key Stage 2 (aged 7–11) in mind. Some of these were children's history books, some fiction, some books designed for teachers charged with delivery of the curriculum.

In keeping with the new climate, in the late 1980s and early 1990s Ladybird published a series of short books under the general title 'History of Britain', focusing on historical periods rather than individuals. The Department of History at the University of Bristol acted as series consultants to the author, Tim Wood, and its name on the title page gave the books an air of scholarly authority that had been absent from the earlier Ladybird series. *The Romans* (1989), like other books in the series, eschews the older Ladybird format of having a page of text facing a full-page illustration, in favour of a more varied layout of the kind popularized by Dorling Kindersley amongst others, in which text and illustrations are spread across two pages, and interspersed with inset photographs and text boxes. Possibly this layout was favoured simply because it broke up what would otherwise be an intimidating block of text, but it also gave an impression of multivocality, a sense that history cannot be reduced to one narrative or point of view, and that no single version of events is finally authoritative. Indeed, *The Romans* includes a section on 'How We Know' which considers sources and the difficulty of arriving at historical truth.

Despite this, *The Romans* largely retains the pro-Roman standpoint evident in Peach's earlier contribution to Ladybird, and with it the habit of disparaging pre-Roman British societies. The main text of the double-spread 'British towns before the Romans', for example, contains some neutral lines about the Britons as traders, illustrated by a picture of a thriving and well-maintained village (8–9). However, the page also displays two lines of caption text, and these are rather less even-handed: the first reads 'Iron Age towns were dirty and smelly' and the second 'Prisoners captured in war were sold as slaves'. Given that both statements hold true for virtually any settlement or society of the period, one must wonder why these features were selected for particular notice, or why the second is reinforced by the choice of an iron slave collar for one of the three inset pictures on the same pages. Wood's remarks about the Druids are equally tendentious: 'Little is known of their religion except that they believed in many gods and they may have sacrificed humans. They had fled to Britain from Europe when the Romans had tried to stamp out their cruel religion' (11). Here Wood slides in two short sentences from an admission of uncertainty about the nature of Druidic religious practice to an assumption of their cruelty and a justification of Roman violence against them, which is implied to be a reaction to their cruelty rather than their efficacy as a focal point of resistance.

This distaste for the ancient Britons accompanies a corresponding sympathy for Rome. Two consecutive double spreads on 'British hill forts' (20–1) and 'Boudicca's revolt, AD 60' (22–3) illustrate the contrast in approach. The first shows an aerial picture of Maiden Castle hill fort in Dorset. The fort is being attacked by a force of Roman soldiers and several of the buildings within are alight, but none of the defenders or inhabitants is visible, and the distant view offered is very much that of the Roman army, with the fort depicted as a military objective rather than a habitation. Inset illustrations show catapults and the Roman tortoise formation, and the small black-and-white photograph of some vertebrae from a British body found at the site carries a clinical observation in the passive voice: 'A ballista bolt had passed through his body and lodged in his spine.' By contrast, the pictures accompanying the account of Boudicca's 'revolt' show lavish scenes of bloody destruction, including one in which naked British warriors appear to be celebrating atop a hill of Roman corpses. Here the inset picture – much larger and in full colour – shows three human skulls, which may have belonged to 'three of Boudicca's victims'. This sets the tone for the book as a whole, in which (for example) Roman military operations designed to stamp out native resistance are repeatedly described as 'keeping the peace' (25, 30). A summary section on 'The Roman Legacy' (52) finds only positive things to say about the changes brought by Rome. Some of these, however ('Roman towns showed the Britons that life could be comfortable and pleasant', 'Roman laws meant that arguments could be settled peacefully'), carry the unwarranted implication that Britain before Rome was a land without law or even pleasure.

Overall, despite some superficial gestures towards even-handedness and self-conscious reflection on the interpretation of evidence, the new Ladybird volume perpetuates the pro-Roman tenor of Peach's work. This perhaps reflects a kind of ideological inertia rather than a conscious programme – seen also in the volume's reworking of some of the earlier book's illustrations, such as one showing a supplicant Briton kneeling before the Roman judgement seat (Peach 37, Wood 24). The imbalance between the plentiful sources for Roman life and culture, and the comparative obscurity of the Britons, may also have contributed to what seems a systematic bias. In any case, Ladybird is far from unique in this respect. As one further example we may cite Felicity Hebditch's *Roman Britain* (1996), a book written in a similar format. While Hebditch generally keeps her comments factual, and interpretation to a minimum, her one explicit attempt to envision what the experience of invasion was like simply assumes a Roman subject position: 'Imagine wading into the deep, fast-flowing waters of a cold river with frightening blue men throwing spears at you!' (10). By contrast, at no point are readers asked to imagine what it might have been like for the British tribes facing invasion by the most powerful army on earth, which included war elephants in its ranks.

The National Curriculum gave an impetus not only to non-fiction books about the Roman period but also to fiction and to books designed to aid the teaching of history in primary schools. An example of the latter is the volume from Scholastic's 'Curriculum Bank' series: *History: I: Romans, Anglo-Saxons and Vikings in Britain: Ancient Greece: A Past Non-European Society* (1996). This book, from a series that contains suggested lesson plans and work sheets for teachers, encourages a participative and reconstructive style of history, in which children are asked to imagine the reality of events as they happened. Crucially, the authors are careful not to tell the history exclusively from the perspective of either Romans or Britons. In one suggested exercise, for example, the class is divided into Romans and Britons and assigned names accordingly (35–7). The exercise concerns the construction of a Roman road. The class is asked to hold what amounts to a planning enquiry, looking into the possible pros and cons of the new road from the point of view of both Romans and Britons. The worksheet provided (119) suggests some possible reactions, both positive ('Road building will provide lots of jobs') and negative ('The Romans will want to transport bigger loads of crops for their own use'). Children are encouraged to say whether they agree or disagree with these reasons, and the writers of the worksheet hope that a vigorous debate will ensue. The worksheet concludes by asking: 'How can the problem be solved?'

There are certainly virtues to this exploratory form of teaching. It shows that there is more than one side to the question, and it refrains from any explicit promotion of either the Roman or British point of view. The fact that some of the views suggested appear contradictory ('It will bring more soldiers into the area which will make life safer' versus 'More Roman soldiers will come into the area and interfere with the British way of life') acknowledges that even within the Roman and British communities there might have been room for a variety of opinions and interests. The planning enquiry format fosters thought and debate about these questions. In this way it fulfils the requirements of the history curriculum, which stresses the need for awareness about the processes of historical interpretation, as well as specific historical knowledge (Harnett 90–3).

Nevertheless, the exercise also has disadvantages. The text suggests issuing Roman names to the 'Roman' children 'such as Tiberius, Claudius, etc.' (35) – with the implication that more names will come readily to mind. The other half of the class is to be issued with Celtic names, for examples of which teachers are referred to 'the *Asterix* series of cartoons' (35). The fact that Tiberius, Claudius and the rest are to be faced in debate by Britons with names such as Getafix and Cacofonix tends to undermine the exercise's attempt to provide an even-handed exploration of the issues. More seriously, superimposing an essentially modern style of democratic debate onto a past where it could not have existed necessarily elides some important features of the historical situation. On the work sheet, the friendly framing of Romano-British relations is underscored by the inclusion of Roman and British faces smiling at each other from opposite corners of the page in a spirit of civic cooperation. In reality, of course, the Romans did not hold public enquiries about proposed road schemes, and while the book admits in the teachers' notes that 'it was the power of the conquering Romans which would have ruled the day' (36), it is not clear whether or how this fundamental fact is to be conveyed to the class. Again, some of the suggested arguments are anachronistic, such as the idea that 'Road building will provide lots of jobs', which implies a hitherto-unsuspected unemployment problem in ancient Britain. While the children are invited to disagree with the importance or relevance of the points on the worksheet, the exercise does not encourage the more fundamental critique that would expose the power relations at work, because to do so would be to undermine the premise of the exercise as a free and equal decision-making procedure. The fact that the road was primarily a conduit for Roman military power is not entirely lost here, but it is so much diluted that the exercise comes dangerously close to being what Farah Mendlesohn has described (in another context) as 'one of those appalling "imagine you are a peasant in a medieval castle" class exercises which have [...] valorized empathy over the academic extrapolation of the discipline of history' (117).

An example of fiction apparently written with the National Curriculum in mind is Stewart Ross's *Down with the Romans!* (2006). This book, dedicated to 'The Staff and Pupils of Flint High School', might well form a companion piece to a workbook such as we have just considered. The main body of the text retells Boudicca's rising in fictional terms, but this story is topped and tailed with brief historical accounts of the history of Britain, from Julius Caesar's campaigns up to AD 43, and the history of Roman Britain after Boudicca's revolt. Despite the partisanship implicit in its title, Ross's short book is a good example of the kind of balancing act assayed by some recent writers on this subject. The story it tells is sympathetic to Boudicca, but its sympathy is conditional on understanding her in a way that assimilates her to twenty-first century *mores*. Insulted by the Romans, and protective of her daughters (whose rape by Roman soldiers is hinted at), this Boudicca is nevertheless unwilling to enter a war that will inevitably cost many lives. In the end, she reluctantly musters the tribe, but warns them to 'be merciful as well as brave. Cruelty is the Roman way, not ours' (25). After the massacre at Colchester, her daughter asks her why she does not seem happier, and is told: 'All that violence and cruelty. Don't you see we're behaving just like the enemy?' (33). However, Boudicca's troops are undisciplined and headstrong, and against her wishes they run impetuously to eventual destruction at the hands of Suetonius Paulinus.

Here is sympathy of a kind, but it is sympathy predicated on introducing a wholly unhistorical motivation for the main character. Ross's Boudicca is born of a certain kind of feminist sensibility that sees women in power as admirable, but also wishes them to be gentle and pacific, and to rule in a way that does not merely echo male power. Here is a Boudicca who is apt to sigh, 'There are times [...] when I wish I wasn't queen of the Iceni' (13). Of course there is no evidence that any such sentiment ever passed through Boudicca's mind. We are left with the impression of a woman who was, in effect, ahead of her time, or at least of her tribe, which was ultimately doomed by its own hotheadedness. The other side of this coin is that the cruel Roman commander, Suetonius, is recalled by the Emperor Nero and replaced with 'a wise and kindly' governor (58), after which Britain is ruled well and peacefully for the next 300 years. The blame for the war is thus laid not on Roman imperial power generally, but on one rotten apple.

This realignment accompanies a new withdrawal of sympathy from those parts of Britain unconquered by Rome. One of Boudicca's greatest complaints is that the Romans do not treat her or her culture with respect: 'One of the guards even spat at me and called me barbarian!' (19). The book thus acknowledges the power of this word to mark cultures as alien and inferior, and Boudicca's resentment is presented as understandable. However, in the Afterword Ross describes the progress of the Roman conquest after Boudicca: 'The Romans [...] advanced into Scotland several times, winning great victories and building roads and forts. But they did not stay. Two huge walls marked the frontier of the Roman Empire and kept out the barbarians to the north' (58). Scottish readers in particular might ask why it is an insult for legionaries to call the Iceni barbarians but apparently acceptable for modern authors to apply that word to the Caledonii.

Not all modern representations of the Roman invasion are written with the requirements of the National Curriculum in mind. A more sophisticated take for older children is provided in N. M. Browne's *Warriors of Alavna* (2000), a book that appears at first to be a time-travel fantasy. Dan and Ursula, who are taking part in a school trip to Hastings, find themselves enveloped by a yellow mist, from which they emerge into an Iron Age British landscape.[2] Soon they are co-opted into the struggle of the British tribe, the Combrogi, in their fight against the Roman invaders, whom they call the Ravens. For the Combrogi, physical prowess and individual bravery are valued above all. By contrast, the Ravens have the familiar discipline of the Roman military, subsuming individuality into the mass: 'Individually the Combrogi warriors were a match for them but now the Romans had made themselves into a killing machine' (65). For all their fierceness the Combrogi are horrified when the Romans wipe out a British village – Alavna – in a My Lai-style massacre. This 'ethnic cleansing', as Ursula thinks of it (116), puts them beyond redemption.

Part of the interest of this book is that Dan and Ursula's sense of the Roman and British past is filtered through their own experience of studying history at school, although their recall is imperfect and reflects some of the inconsistencies of approach we have encountered in the present discussion. Dan remembers: 'Mrs Enright said the Romans talked about the Celts as if they were savages, but they were actually quite a developed culture – they had druids and great jewellery and stuff' (101). Later on, however, he taunts the Combrogi by adding 'I thought the Romans were the good ones, the ones who brought civilisation, law and justice' (113). We noted that Stewart Ross, in *Down with the Romans!*, reconciled the cruelty and excesses of the invading Romans with a generally benign sense of the effect of the Roman occupation by stressing that the overzealous general Suetonius was replaced by a 'wise and kindly' successor and consequent good government. Browne in *Warriors of Alavna* has a comparable problem. Her protagonists are firmly allied with an embattled tribe engaged in a defensive war for survival against an implacable and cruel invader. How can she square this with Dan's sense that 'the Romans were the good ones'? She does so through the manipulation of genre. Relatively late in the book it is revealed that this is not in fact a time-travel story at all, or not straightforwardly so. Dan and Ursula have actually been taken to an alternative reality, in which the Roman army – Ravens rather than Eagles – are crueller than their real-life counterparts. Indeed, the solution to the Combrogi's problems comes in the end through Ursula's ability to call a Roman legion from her own history into theirs, to fight on the children's side. This is the Ninth Legion itself, whose disappearance Ursula remembers reading about in the work of, probably, Rosemary Sutcliff: 'There was a book written about them. It was a story, I forget what it was called, we read some of it in class, but the thing was, there really was no record of what happened to them' (253).

This device allows Browne, like Ross, to reconcile the Janus faces of Rome, as both a brutal and a civilizing force, not by suggesting that these qualities may coexist in the same person or even the same action, but by assigning them to different groups. Everything savage in Roman behaviour is put at the door of the fictional Ravens, allowing the historical Romans to be respectable – good cops, who quickly sort out their rogue alternative-history equivalents. 'No legion known to me fights under the banner of a carrion bird,' as the Legate of the Ninth sniffily observes (277). The question of whether Roman soldiers (or indeed British ones) might historically have carried out massacres such as that at Alavna thus becomes moot.

In their very different ways Ross and Browne present a 'balanced' view of the Roman invasion, but one in which the effective answer to corrupt imperialism is not armed resistance but rather imperialism of a more enlightened stripe. Nor are they alone in this. In *The Time-Travelling Cat and the Roman Eagle* (2001), for example, Julia Jarman tells of a British insurrection sparked by a junior Roman officer's rash decision to destroy a sacred grove; but this act is ultimately countermanded by the intervention of the wise governor Agricola, who thus saves the situation and restores order (140). Again, high-handed government is set right not from below but from above, by a higher *Roman* authority.

However, some books in the last few years have taken a decidedly negative view of both invasion and the Romans themselves. For convenience we may broadly describe these negative accounts as falling into two categories: the political and the ecological. Representative examples of the former are Pauline Chandler's *The Mark of Edain* (2008) and Jim Eldridge's *Roman Invasion* (2006), which is part of Scholastic's 'My Story' series. *The Mark of Edain*, like many earlier books featuring British children at the time of the Roman invasion, from G. A. Henty's *Beric the Briton* (1893) to *Ceva of the Caradocs* and *Legions of the Eagle*, carries its British protagonists deep into Roman territory before describing a return to British soil. *The Mark of Edain* tells of Aoife and her brother Madoc, the niece and nephew of Caratacus, whom we find first as slaves in Rome, then caught up in the Claudian invasion as valuable hostages. However, while earlier stories on this pattern generally used their protagonists' continental tour in order to complicate or even reverse a rather insular world-view and teach them the worth of Roman culture and values (Johnson), here this is not the case. The novel makes the customary concession to the Roman army's organizational abilities ('Every man followed orders in a rigid pattern of activities: weapons practice, equipment inspections, recreation, discipline, punishment'), but this is seen as dehumanizing rather than admirable, and the invasion is likened to the inexorability of 'an attack of locusts' (96). Individually, the Romans are cruel and, in their inability to control the two British children supposedly in their power, remarkably incompetent. In Eldridge's text, too, the narrator – another nobly born British hostage – finds no kindness in his Roman captors, but only in the company of the Greek road surveyor to whose care he is assigned, and who is a former victim of Roman brutality in his own country.

A striking feature of both these books is that the primary cultural loyalty of the children lies not with their own tribe, nor even with the Britons in general, but with a much more broadly conceived Celtic world, which is considered as a fraternal community of nations. Thus in *The Mark of Edain* Madoc proudly cries as he and Aoife walk through the streets of Rome, *'I AM CELTOI!'*, an ejaculation glossed helpfully if mystifyingly by his sister as 'the name given to them by the Greeks' (8). The narrator of *Roman Invasion* too is inspired by pan-Celtic nationalism: 'We Britons are Celts from the great Celtic race, whether Brigante or Trinovante or Caledonian, or from across the water to the west where the Isles lie' (50). Indeed, despite the long history of intertribal warfare amongst the Britons, he fears that the goddess Bridget will strike him dead for the 'sin' of killing a warrior from the neighbouring Brigantes tribe (78). Historically there is no evidence that any sense of a Celtic 'race' existed at this time, and in fact the Britons are not even referred to as Celts in ancient literature. The concept does, however, cast the Roman invasion in a still more unfavourable light, as an attack not on a rabble of squabbling petty kingdoms but an attempt to snuff out an ancient and widespread culture. As Eldridge's hero puts it:

> We were Britons! We must not let our whole culture be crushed out of existence by these invaders. Everything we were, the way we spoke, the way we dressed, our gods and goddesses, our music, our houses, the way we prepared our food, the way we buried our dead and honoured our heroes, all of these had been our way of life for thousands of years.
>
> (101–2)

Both Chandler's and Eldridge's books take an anti-Roman position rooted in patriotic resistance to a foreign oppressor. By contrast, in Beth Webb's *Fire Dreamer* opposition to Rome is founded more on ecological and religious considerations. *Fire Dreamer* is the second of a series of novels about Tegen, a trainee Druid (although a girl) living just after the Claudian invasion. Webb's book has a complex weave of magic and politics; and, like Browne's, it is an historical fantasy. In reality the practices and beliefs of the ancient Druids are, as we have seen, known in only the sketchiest way, and most of the information we have about them is both fragmentary and tendentious. Modern Druid rituals are largely a twentieth-century invention, but in order to create her Druids Webb relies heavily on the beliefs and rituals of the contemporary Druid movement. One of the book's dedicatees is 'Bruce Johnstone-Lowe of the British Druid Order', and in interview she has written that she is 'advised by Modern Druids' who inform her about 'fire rituals, walking fire spirals that take you from this world to the next' ('Interview'). Her website contains many pictures of 'real-life druids' in and around Glastonbury, several of whom seem to have attended her book launch (*Beth Webb Site*).

Webb's book is notable for the extent to which her characters have internalized the ethos and arguments of modern ecology in some of its more mystical forms. Indeed, both Eldridge and Webb have their characters express themselves in terms that seem decidedly twenty-first century. 'The Romans weren't known for being caring to people with disabilities' (26), muses Eldridge's British protagonist, while Webb has a young Druid ask her heroine: 'Don't you think there are times when ethics become situational?' (140). Even the villain of her piece declares of the Romans, 'I am as angry at their cultural insensitivities as anyone else' (181–2). Webb's characters are also keen to stress the multiculturalism of Iron Age Britain as a place that welcomes international trade and whose inhabitants will 'gladly marry a stranger' (16). Most strikingly, the arguments of Webb's Druids against the Roman invaders rely heavily on New Age beliefs that reflect modern preoccupations and attitudes more obviously than those of first-century Britons: 'We see our land as sacred – it is the body of the Goddess married to the Green Man [...] But these invaders treat it as if it was just – well, *land* – something people can *own* and use and do what they like with – like a slave' (29).

While anachronistic thoughts and language are perhaps inevitable in any historical work, and Webb is quite open about her intention to use Tegen as 'a character that modern readers can relate to' ('Interview'), it is always instructive to see what *kind* of anachronism is in place, especially in light of the contrast with the earlier books we have considered. In this case, one of the aspects of Roman rule that was regularly admired in older children's literature was their construction of cities and roads. These large-scale projects were praised in terms of their ability to deal with the landscape as an engineering challenge. In the world of *Fire Dreamer,* and in a more environmentally concerned age, we may suspect this willingness to mould nature to human requirements as arrogance. And, since Druidism is often depicted as a nature religion, lack of respect for it is conflated with lack of respect for nature. Thus in *Fire Dreamer,* the Druid Owein complains: 'These *barbarians* with their roads that slice in straight lines through our fields and sacred places – they are *raping* the Land!' (16: emphasis in the original). Similarly, as we have noted, the cause of contention in Jarman's *The Time-Travelling Cat and the Roman Eagle* is the Roman plan to build a road through the middle of a sacred grove. In this way, such books often echo the arguments and rhetoric of anti-road protesters in modern times, at such places as Twyford Down in the 1990s, and more recently the campaign against the proposal to drive a motorway through the prehistoric network of sites near the Hill of Tara in Ireland (a project that has been called 'rape' by its opponents [Tsarion]). It may also be that the Roman capacity for organization and for subsuming oneself into a larger unit are held in lower regard in an age when individualism and nonconformity have acquired greater cachet than was the case in the post-war years. The ability of a Roman army to act as a single fighting machine is seen as sinister rather than admirable, and its 'cultural insensitivities', like its natural ones, as the effect of wilful indifference. The ability to erect camps and cities on a similar plan in all parts of the empire, for example, anticipates the efficiency of modern mass production, but whereas this may have seemed presciently forward-looking to a society still enamoured of that industrial model, its implications are less attractive in an age of multinational corporations and coca-colonization.

Attitudes to multinational businesses are also relevant to what has been perhaps the most important change since the 1950s for our present purposes: the end of the British Empire and the subsequent rise of postcolonial literature and studies. The Empire has written back, and authors today cannot but be far more sceptical about the idea of military forces with a civilizing mission. The Roman invasion and colonization of Britain has offered itself as one of a very few historical sites on which British people can view the question of Empire from the point of view of the colonized. However, while postcolonial studies have created analytical tools and a vocabulary for the discussion of invasion, Britain's own colonial history has made it hard for British writers to assume that perspective innocently, without some foreshadowing knowledge of the part Britain itself would come to play in the story of empire, and of how the example of Rome would be co-opted into that story. The question of reader identification with which we started this chapter can thus be recast as a choice between reading strategies: one in which the Romans are read historically, *in propria persona*; and another in which the shadow of allegory hangs over them, making them the British *in potentia*.

These issues are already far from straightforward, but it is easier to paint the Roman invasion in moral primary colours than is the case for later periods in the history of Roman Britain. Notably, recent historical fiction for children set in Roman Britain has tended to avoid later settings. Whereas Kipling set his Roman stories in the fourth century, and Treece and Sutcliff both attended to the later periods of Roman occupation as well as to the invasion itself, in the last decade the focus has been more exclusively on the period of conquest. Again, this may reflect the ideological preoccupations of the time: Kipling famously saw in Hadrian's Wall and Britain generally an analogue for the Northwest Frontier (Roberts 114), while in Sutcliff's *The Lantern Bearers* (1959) and Treece's *The Eagles Have Flown* (1954), both set immediately after the withdrawal of the legions, the problems of decolonization are rehearsed. It is, however, curious that so little attention has been paid by more recent writers to the processes of integration and assimilation, matters of obvious relevance in multicultural Britain.

One quality that sets Sutcliff apart from the other writers we have considered in this chapter is the intelligent and undogmatic attention she pays to precisely these questions. Her sense of the *movement* of history over many generations is given expression in *The Eagle of the Ninth* and also in its sequels; and while she broadly subscribes to the assumption of her contemporaries, that history leads (albeit unsteadily) in a progressive direction and that 'civilization' denotes a set of values worth preserving, the process by which this preservation happens is more likely to involve assimilation than the replacement or erasure of cultures. Her pragmatic and supple view of cultural interaction has made her not only a more subtle writer but a more ideologically adaptable one, and it is not surprising that she, alone of the children's historical writers of her generation dealing with this period, has remained continually in print.

History's vulnerability to ideological manipulation – indeed, the inevitability of such manipulation – is a theme to which we will be returning in various forms throughout this book; but the Roman invasion, standing at the very beginning of recorded British history, offers an ideal way to illustrate some of the complexities involved. Moreover, by considering texts from two decades some 50 years apart we have been able to make the ideological forces in play more visible than might have been the case had we confined ourselves to a shorter span. In Chapter 3 these questions will continue to be relevant as we focus our attention on Arthur, a figure who has been claimed for many ideological and cultural purposes. However, the primary emphasis in that chapter will not be on these rival claims, but more fundamentally on Arthur's own claim to be an historical figure at all.

3
Once, Future, Sometime, Never: Arthur in History

> It is of this Arthur that the Britons fondly tell so many fables, even to the present day; a man worthy to be celebrated, not by idle fictions, but by authentic history.
>
> William of Malmesbury *Gesta regum Anglorum* (c. 1125)

The claim of Arthur to a place in a book devoted to the representation of the past in texts for children is a debatable one. Arthur's historical status has been much disputed over the years, with scholarly consensus at the time of writing inclined markedly towards disbelief. He has been pictured as a local king, a quasi-Roman figure attempting to maintain the ways of empire, the leader of a roving band of elite cavalry, an amalgam of several individuals fitting the above descriptions – or else as the product of myth, poetry, ambiguous manuscripts and nationalist longing, 'a copy which has no original' (Fulton, 'Introduction' 1). It is not our intention to arbitrate these claims, although we shall be considering some of the reasons behind them and the ways in which fluctuating scholarly opinion about Arthur has affected his representation in children's books. For the purposes of this chapter, Arthur's questionable historicity is precisely what makes him interesting. He belongs to a small group of people – Robin Hood being the other most prominent – who stand in the liminal space between history and legend. Although they suffer from a lack of firm supporting evidence, they are nevertheless tied irrevocably to certain places and times, and are stubborn in maintaining and renewing their presence in the public consciousness of British national history.

One reason for Arthur's persistence may be that the period when he is supposed to have lived, in the generations after the final Roman withdrawal from Britain in the first half of the fifth century, really is a Dark Age in terms of our knowledge: 'for the history of Britain for the centuries immediately following 410 we are largely dependent on insular sources: and for over a century this means just one text' (James, *Britain in the First Millennium* 94). The gaps in the historical record are easily large enough to accommodate a person who might have gained renown and a vigorous afterlife in oral tradition, without having left any trace in the sparse written accounts. Arthur is more than a convenient figure with whom to plug an historical hole; however, he has become an essential and wonderfully flexible national symbol. To the Welsh he may be a leader of the Britons against the Saxons; but he is no less iconic for the Saxons themselves, who have appropriated him as an honorary Englishman. (Oddly, he appears to have less of a presence in Scotland, despite much of the evidence for his existence placing him in that country [Hutton, *Witches, Druids and King Arthur* 40].) He is also a vibrant and perennial cultural export, the Matter of Britain having inspired as many Continental writers as British ones. The legend, incorporated into the 'rex quondam, rexque futurus' formula, that Arthur is not dead but awaiting a time when Britain will need him once again, even provides him with a foothold outside of history itself – a fact that children's writers have readily exploited, as we shall see.

Where does this leave writers wishing to represent Arthur, or the age of Arthur, in children's books? Clearly there is a generic question at stake here: if Arthur is an historical figure, then a book featuring him may be an historical novel; but if he is understood to be mythical, his presence will serve to indicate that we are in the realm of fantasy. Rebecca Barnhouse works on just this principle in her study of medieval historical fiction for young adults, *Recasting the Past* (2000). Barnhouse distinguishes realist historicals from fantasies by suggesting that only fantasy includes magical elements, and as an example cites the opening of Katherine Paterson's version of the Parzival legend, *Parzival: The Quest of the Grail Knight*:

> The medieval poem [*Parzival*], like most medieval romances, is a fantasy, with its long-ago, far-away setting and its insistence on magic. Paterson's version, too, is fantasy, and the opening words

> define it as such: 'In the ancient days, when Arthur was king of Britain'.
>
> (85)

For Barnhouse, clearly, King Arthur is so quintessentially a creature of fantasy that his name is enough to place Paterson's book within that genre. This degree of certainty may seem excessive, but it has a venerable precedent: Chaucer's Wife of Bath, too, begins her tale of the loathly lady by signalling that her story is fantasy, not history, and she does so by invoking Arthur:

> In th' olde dayes of the Kyng Arthour,
> Of which that Britons speken greet honour,
> Al was this land fulfild of fayerye.
> The elf-queene, with hir joly compaignye,
> Daunced ful ofte in many a grene mede.
> This was the olde opinion, as I rede;
> I speke of manye hundred yeres ago.
> But now kan no man se none elves mo [...].
>
> ('The Wife of Bath's Tale', ll. 857–64)

The Wife of Bath nominally sets her stories in 'th' olde days'; but her introduction evokes not an historical past but a magical otherwhen in which Arthur's reign coincides with that of the Queen of Fairies. Such faux-references to a non-historical past are a common characteristic of oral storytelling, encapsulated in the phrase 'Once upon a time' and its many variants, and in this case the point is underscored by the Wife's wry observation that she and her listeners live in very different times, in which 'now kan no man se none elves mo', although mendicant friars are thick on the ground.

To the metropolitan Chaucer, whose primary literary models were classical and continental, Arthur may have been a superstition fit only for the 'Britons' (i.e., the Welsh, Bretons and Cornish). However, by Chaucer's time Arthur already had a long and complex history, and in this his non-existence was not always assumed. It is impossible to do that history justice here, but a few key documents must be mentioned. The earliest is the *De Excidio et Conquestu Britanniae* ('Of the Destruction and Conquest of Britain') attributed to the monk Gildas, who lived in the fifth or sixth century. This work consists in large part of denunciations of contemporary British kings for their moral failures, and is the 'one text' from the century after the Roman withdrawal alluded to above. Gildas gives a brief account of the previous 50 years, telling the story of how the Saxons were initially invited into Britain by a native tyrant before turning to conquer the island for themselves. In this ambition the Saxons were resisted by a figure Gildas calls Ambrosius Aurelianus, who eventually defeated them in a series of battles, including one at Badon Hill. Arthur's absence from Gildas's account is notable, and has been explained in many ways (including of course his non-existence), but Gildas does at least offer a context for an Arthur-type figure, under whom the British were for a time united against the invading Saxons.

Gildas's work is primarily a polemic, but other texts are historical in nature. The *Annales Cambriae* give a year-by-year description of events in Britain during the period when Arthur was supposed to have lived. Crucially, the *Annales* include references to Arthur for 516, the year of the victorious Battle of Badon, and 537, identified as the year of the Battle of Camlann, at which both Arthur and Medraut died – although whether they were fighting against each other or on the same side is unclear. The *Annales* as we have them date from the tenth century, and while they are likely to have drawn on earlier documents, it is uncertain how much earlier. The date of the ninth-century *Historia Brittonum*, by the writer known as Nennius, is more certain. This text provides a list of 12 victories associated with Arthur, including the victory at Badon. It is Nennius who first describes Arthur as *dux bellorum* (battle leader), a phrase that has come to vie with that of 'king' in recent fictional representations; and it is Nennius too who gives us the earliest evidence that Arthur was becoming a figure of folklore, referring in a list of British 'marvels' to a cairn associated with him and a hoof-print said to have been left in a stone by his horse.

Arthur thus appears to have had a dual life as a folkloric figure and an historical one from a very early date. Indeed, in the work of the influential twelfth-century chronicler Geoffrey of Monmouth it is impossible to keep literary and historical traditions distinct. Geoffrey's *Historia Regum Britanniae* (c. 1136) purports to be a history of the kings of Britain, and much of his material is clearly based on earlier sources such as those we have mentioned. For example, he takes from Gildas the story of the tyrant who invited the Saxons to Britain, giving him the name Vortigern. However, Geoffrey also includes much magical and mythological material, and a large proportion of his account of Arthur is devoted to a propagandistic description of the continental campaigns that supposedly followed his establishment of authority in Britain. The prominent place of Arthur within twelfth-century chronicle histories of Britain was maintained in such post-Geoffrey works as Wace's *Roman de Brut* and Laȝamon's *Brut*, and his historical credentials were underscored further in 1191 through the announcement by the abbot and monks of Glastonbury Abbey that a tomb had been discovered there, the inscription of which declared it to be that of Arthur and Guinevere. This proved a lucrative draw to pilgrims, who presumably would not have been tempted to pay homage to the remains of a man they believed to be mythical.

By this time, however, William of Newburgh was already declaring Geoffrey a charlatan (Thorpe 17), and in France Chrétien de Troyes had written the French romances that would mark the Matter of Britain's decisive turn from history into imaginative literature. In Chrétien's work and in that of his successors, from Malory's *Le Morte D'Arthur* (1485) to Tennyson's *Idylls of the King* (1856–85), the realm of Arthur would be detached from the post-Roman context that Geoffrey and earlier tradition had given it, and placed in a world of chivalry, quests and enchantment effectively outside history – an orientation reflected in the Wife of Bath's use of Arthur's reign as a synecdoche for the fantastic. When children's writers began to pay attention to Arthur in the nineteenth and twentieth centuries, the chivalric picture of him – usually filtered through Malory, with Tennyson and the pre-Raphaelites being influential modern exemplars – was not only the default view of Arthur but also the only one with any significant literary currency. With the important exception of T. H. White, the standard treatment of Arthur by early and mid twentieth-century children's authors was in the form of adaptations and retellings of the medieval chivalric legends, such as Roger Lancelyn Green's popular *King Arthur and His Knights of the Round Table* (1953).

Developments within the academy in the 1950s were, however, about to change the nature of Arthurian studies, and thus to transform Arthur's fictional potential. Ronald Hutton's essay 'Arthur and the Academics' succinctly charts the changing attitudes towards the idea of an historical Arthur amongst archaeologists, historians and literary scholars, from the 1950s through to the early twenty-first century (*Witches, Druids and King Arthur* 39–54). The picture he paints is one of a rising tide of faith in an historical Arthur through the 1960s, which virtually congeals into orthodoxy in the early 1970s before converting to extreme and perhaps excessive scepticism from the middle of that decade. This change was not due to any significant new textual discoveries. Indeed, the documents available to modern scholars had for the most part been equally available to Geoffrey of Monmouth; but in the 1950s and 1960s, in combination with the promising results of excavations at Tintagel and South Cadbury (one of the traditional candidates for the site of Camelot), they seemed to offer archaeologist-writers such as Geoffrey Ashe and Leslie Alcock a new and exciting perspective onto a sub-Roman Arthurian world. Already in the 1940s Trelawney Dayrell Reed had produced a book on *The Battle for Britain in the Fifth Century* (1944) that was to influence both Rosemary Sutcliff and (judging from internal evidence) Henry Treece in their historical recreations of Arthur's story.[1] From 1966 South Cadbury, excavated by Alcock, was producing evidence that it had been a royal residence of the right date for Arthur, and while Arthur himself might always be shadowy, he was beginning to seem far more than a figure of fantasy. The man revealed in books such as Ashe's *Caesar to Arthur* (1960) and Alcock's *Arthur's Britain* (1971) was not, of course, the king of medieval romance but a figure in a grimmer if no less heroic mould: he was a regional king who managed to forge a British alliance against the Saxon threat; or else a roving war leader (Nennius's *dux bellorum*), an elite cavalryman in direct descent from Roman military tradition, leading his *comitatus* into battle wherever there was need. The magical elements of the Matter of Britain could be discarded or else explained as romantic stories spun from this coarser cloth. When Rosemary Sutcliff came to write the 'Author's Note' to her Arthurian novel *Sword at Sunset* (1963), she did so in the confidence that she was helping to excavate the truth that lay under the many accretions of medieval and Victorian fantasy. Beneath the yellowing varnish of Tennyson, Malory and Chrétien de Troyes, lay the stark reality of a sixth-century warrior:

> [...] of late years historians and anthropologists have come more and more to the belief that the Matter of Britain is indeed 'matter

> and not moonshine.'[2] That behind all the numinous mist of pagan, early Christian and mediaeval splendours that have gathered about it, there stands the solitary figure of one great man. No knight in shining armour, no Round Table, no many-towered Camelot; but a Romano-British war-leader, to whom, when the Barbarian darkness came flooding in, the last guttering lights of civilisation seemed worth fighting for.
>
> (vii)

A similar air of having revealed the 'true' Arthur in place of a fanciful legend also pervades Patrick Dromgoole's preface to Terence Feely's *Arthur of the Britons* (1974), a book produced to accompany the HTV children's television series of that name, of which Dromgoole was Executive Producer:

> Historians know little that is factual about this period in our history but upon one thing they are agreed: the legendary picture of Arthur is a fantasy. The truth was different. Camelot was an unlovely encampment of log and thatch within cunning defences.
>
> (7)

This sounds decisive – although the scope of the unanimity Dromgoole claims is unclear. Does it extend only to the proposition that Arthur was not the legendary king of tradition, or as far as the vision of Camelot as an 'unlovely encampment' à la Alcock's South Cadbury? If the latter, the consensus to which he refers was in the process of breaking down. Hutton identifies 1973 as the high-water mark of belief in an historical Arthur, quoting a text book from that year that claims 'general agreement' that he was 'a genuinely historical figure' (D. J. V. Fisher 9–10, qtd. Hutton 49); but a new and more sceptical movement was growing within Early Medieval historiography, spearheaded by the revisionist academic David Dumville. The claims of the Arthurians were shown to have outrun the evidence, and in the retrenchment that followed Arthur's name became synonymous with a romantic and unscholarly approach to an extent that effectively frightened mainstream scholars from his banner. Even Rosemary Sutcliff, when she returned to the Arthurian legend in a Malory-inspired trilogy in the late 1970s, was more muted in her advocacy. She reworked the passage from the 'Author's Note' for *Sword at Sunset* for this new work, but made some changes in the process. Where she had previously asserted that 'historians and anthropologists have come more and more to the belief that the Matter of Britain is indeed "matter and not moonshine" ', she now wrote: 'Many people believe, as I do, that behind the legends of King Arthur as we know them today, there stands a real man.' Next to the earlier, confident declaration of consensus this seems closer to a statement of personal faith.

Scepticism continues to be the new orthodoxy respecting historians' attitudes towards Arthur, but this may have been to literature's advantage. This intricate and shifting history means that the responses of writers to the Arthurian corpus over the last 50 years have had to be equally complex and in many cases ingenious as they addressed themselves to the challenges posed by writing about Britain's most famous yet least evidenced monarch. Are stories about Arthur best understood as history, fantasy, traditional story or something else again? Should writers seek clarity even at the price of excluding some aspects of the Arthurian tradition, or embrace pluralism with all the attendant risks of self-contradiction? Each writer's approach is unique, but it still may be useful to outline the approaches that have been adopted. Here, then, is a preliminary categorization of ways of writing about Arthur in modern children's books:

- to treat Arthur as an historical figure of the post-Roman era and tell his story in those terms;
- to stay within the general tradition of Malory and other post-Chrétien writers, in which Arthur is a high-medieval figure in a world of chivalry and magic;
- to establish an ahistorical time, divorced from any particular period although drawing on all, in which to situate Arthur;
- to find a way of acknowledging Arthur's dependence on different periods, whether by using double-narratives, magic, time-travel or by drawing analogies between different times.

This list is not exhaustive and neither are its categories entirely distinct; but it will serve as a starting point from which to explore the territory.

Reconstructing an historical Arthur

In Chapter 2 we discussed Rosemary Sutcliff's *The Eagle of the Ninth*. This was the first in a series of books following the fortunes of one Roman family in Britain, a series that ended with *The Lantern Bearers* (1959). In that book, Aquila, a distant descendant of the Marcus who was the protagonist of *The Eagle of the Ninth*, is a member of the last legion to be posted in Britain. When that legion is recalled Aquila deserts and stays behind, and what follows is an account of his experience of Britannia's unravelling. Aquila's family is massacred, and he spends some time as a Saxon slave before escaping and making his way to Wales and the stronghold of Ambrosius Aurelianus. Sutcliff draws a complex picture of a society in transition, with some sheltered pockets still managing to maintain Roman manners, but for the most part (and especially around the coasts) inexorably reverting to pre-Roman Celtic tribalism under the onslaught of Saxon and Irish raiders. Arthur, under the name Artos or Artorius, is Ambrosius's nephew, and is seen initially as a child at his camp in Snowdonia: 'a small boy and a hound puppy very intent on a hole under a brown tumble of last year's fern' (120). By the time the book ends, some years later, Artos is a successful young warrior and his dog Cabal is full grown, but, although Artos gains in prominence, *The Lantern Bearers* is the story of the broken and embittered Aquila, and his eventual winning of a kind of peace both for himself and, temporarily, for the country. Near the novel's conclusion he and his friend Eugenus agree that they 'stand at sunset' (250) and that the Saxons' eventual triumph is inevitable, but they look forward to a time beyond even that, when the light will return to Britain. Aquila asks: 'I wonder if they will remember us at all, those people on the other side of the darkness' (250–1). Eugenus looks down the colonnade to where Artos is standing with some of the other young warriors:

> You and I and all our kind they will forget utterly, though they live and die in our debt [...] Ambrosius they will remember a little; but *he* [Artos] is the kind that men make songs about to sing for a thousand years.
>
> (251)

Sword at Sunset was published for adults, but as Sutcliff herself pointed out, the move between adult and children's writing can represent 'quite small gear change' (qtd. Trease, 'The Historical Novelist' 5), and the book is clearly a sequel to *The Lantern Bearers* and the Roman series, mentioning many of Sutcliff's invented characters such as Aquila, as well as such Arthurian stalwarts as Ambrosius. The major change, other than the inclusion of rather more sex, is the shift to Artos's own voice, for *Sword at Sunset* is a first-person account of Arthur's life. As modelled by Sutcliff in *Sword at Sunset*, Artos is the leader of a post-Roman resistance against the Saxon (and other) invaders. Working initially under the fatherly aegis of Ambrosius as Count of Britain, Artos is a practical soldier, a cavalry specialist who takes the battle to the enemy wherever there is need. Here is the Arthur of South Cadbury hill fort, of hard camps and bloody battles at a time of national emergency. Sutcliff retains the adultery plot which stands as the courtly-love centrepiece of medieval treatments, but gives it to Bedwyr rather than Lancelot ('a later French importation' as she puts it in her 'Author's Note' [vii–viii]). Sutcliff acknowledges 'authors of many books from Gildas in the sixth century to Geoffrey Ashe in 1960' (viii) in the book's making, and concludes that 'almost every part of the story [...] has some kind of basis outside the author's imagination' (viii). This historical underpinning is for her clearly more than an incidental fact: it validates the whole enterprise, making the book as much an historical reconstruction as a work of fiction.

Its emphasis on how things might have 'really happened' means that *Sword at Sunset* is a resolutely non-magical book. Sutcliff deals with the magical aspects of the Arthurian legend largely by ignoring them, but she does offer some hints about the ways in which the name of a great man such as Arthur might have come to collect legends about it. For example, when Artos is mortally wounded at the end of the book, his closest comrades remove him from the battle and the sight of his own men. For reasons of morale, the dying Artos gives orders that news of his death should not be announced: 'Nobody save yourself and the brown Brothers here must see my body once the breath is out of it, and no one must know the place of my grave. So they will maybe fight on with a better heart' (478). Thus the seeds of the legend that Arthur did not die are planted. In naming Constantine as his successor, he even triggers the 'rexque futurus' motif, adding the rider: 'Until I come again' (479). Finally, when Constantine asks how he will know Artos is dead, his answer suggests a non-supernatural explanation of the traditional story of Bedivere/Bedwyr's return of Excalibur to the Lady of the Lake:

> 'There is a wild-fowl mere only a few miles north of this place, and eastward of it the land rises. Set a watcher there among the alder woods – one that you can trust – and when I am dead, Bedwyr shall bring my sword and throw it into the mere. That shall be your sign.'
>
> (480)

This technique of euhemerism, or the attribution of mundane origins to supernatural stories, is one way of incorporating the supernatural Arthurian tradition without incorporating the supernatural itself. For Sutcliff it is useful in providing 'points of contact' between two traditions, but it is absolutely central to Philip Reeve's post-Roman treatment of the Arthur legend, *Here Lies Arthur* (2007). Reeve's title is a play on the words of the Glastonbury tomb, as rendered by Malory: 'Hic Iacet Arthurus, Rex Quondam Rexque Futurus'. Arthur lies here, but Arthur – or the myth associated with Arthur – is also a lie. The idea of Arthur as a fraud goes back at least as far as the tomb itself, the 'discovery' of which by the Abbey monks was suspiciously fortuitous, coming just at a moment when their waning revenues needed the kind of boost that a vigorous pilgrim trade could provide. Reeve will have been aware too that Sir Thomas Malory, who put the Arthurian matter into its classic English form with an emphasis on the ethos of chivalry and spiritual purity, was in his personal life a kidnapper and rapist whose principal recreation seems to have been robbery with violence.[3] Fittingly, *Here Lies Arthur* is a book that explores the ways in which legends can be constructed from distinctly unpromising material, and the uses to which they can be put.

Speaking before the book's publication, at the IBBY Conference in Roehampton in 2006, Reeve emphasized the role of political 'spin' in its genesis, particularly as practised by modern politicians such as Peter Mandelson and Tony Blair. Reeve's Arthur is a local warlord based in what is now south-west England. This Arthur is neither worse nor significantly better than the other warrior leaders with whom he shares the territory and whom he spends most of his life raiding and fighting. His world is violent, ignorant and superstitious, and his main aim is the accumulation of treasure, land and cattle. All that distinguishes him from his rivals is the support of a skilled spin doctor in the person of Myrddin (Merlin). Myrddin, a true politician, has a more strategic goal: he plans to build up Arthur and make him a rallying point around whom the British will be able to unite against the Saxon invaders.

Here Lies Arthur is told from the point of view of a peasant girl, Gwyna, whom Myrddin takes into his service. At the beginning of the book Myrddin uses Gwyna in order to construct a marvel. A strong swimmer who can hold her breath for minutes at a time, Gwyna is told to hide in the middle of a lake, and, when Arthur approaches, to hand him a sword from beneath the water. It is an extremely successful moment of theatre, which fools not only the watching warriors but even Arthur himself into imagining that he has been supernaturally favoured. Such elaborate acts of fraud are rare, however. Mostly Myrddin works by means of language. When Arthur enters a settlement, Myrddin makes sure it is to cries of 'Make way for the *Imperator* Artorius! Make way for the *Dux Bellorum* of the island of Britain! Great Arthur will protect you from the Saxons!' (46). After each battle, Myrddin spins the deeds of Arthur and his men into tales of superhuman valour, or invents magical stories about him that hover in a comfortable place somewhere between belief and an enjoyment of fiction:

> In the silence as the story ends, I look about. I see their faces, and I feel the same look on my own. An enchanted look. It's not that we believe the story. We all know no green man really came here, or walked about with his head held in his hand. But we feel we've heard a kind of truth. Even Arthur feels it, lounging in his big chair with Cunaide at his side and his hound Cabal at his feet. For a moment, the real Arthur and the story Arthur are one and the same, and we know that we are all part of the story, all of us.
>
> (58)

This state of negative capability offers Gwyna, and perhaps her readers, an alternative to the rigid binary of fact and fiction, at least as long as they are able to refrain from reaching after a more detailed account of exactly what 'kind of truth' Myrddin's story represents. Myrddin's spin-doctoring is effective in that he is aware of the stories people tell each other and themselves, and of their reasons for telling them – of their need for reassurance and for a version of reality that confirms and reinforces their sense of their own place in the world and the identity of their group. Sometimes, indeed, he does not need to invent so much as present events in a way that will allow his listeners' mythmaking predispositions full rein. For example, he advises Arthur to engage the Saxons in battle near the hill of Badon, where Ambrosius won a major victory in the previous generation:

> What if Arthur could meet them there, where his father Uthr and Ambrosius Aurelianus won their great fight all those years ago? A new victory at Badon would add far more to Arthur's legend than a skirmish beside some fading town most men have hardly heard of.
>
> (95)

The victory is won easily enough and, as Myrddin had foreseen, 'It wasn't long before people who hadn't been there started to get Arthur's little victory over the robber-band confused with that other battle of the Hill of Badon, the big, important one that old Ambrosius had won' (101). Myrddin's plan shows a shrewd understanding of oral tradition, while also incidentally allowing Reeve to reconcile the accounts of Badon given by Gildas (who ascribes the victory to Ambrosius) and Nennius and the *Annales Cambriae* (for whom it belongs to Arthur). *Here Lies Arthur* is full of such understated strokes. When Myrddin eventually dies, Gwyna buries him in the hollow of an old oak tree, watched by his servant boy. No more is made of this fact, and it is left to the reader to see how this act might grow in time into the legend of Merlin's entrapment within a tree by Nimue/Vivien, in return for his teaching her magic.

Reeve also demonstrates that spin has only limited traction on the world it attempts to manipulate. In the end, Myrddin cannot turn Arthur into a national leader by means of rhetoric. He remains what he has always been at heart, a local warlord who cannot resist raiding his neighbours when Myrddin is away. Goaded by his spin doctor to build a feasting hall in the ruins of Aquae Sulis worthy of that city, with baked tiles and glazed windows, Arthur attempts to oblige, but somehow his building turns out more like a round house, and it is not long before the awkward hybrid falls to ground, an eloquent symbol of the ultimate futility of Myrddin's vision. Reeve writes in his 'Author's Note': '*Here Lies Arthur* is not a historical novel, and in writing it I did not set out to portray "the real King Arthur", only to add my own little thimbleful to the sea of stories which surrounds him' (291). Reeve may feel that an historical novel is not something that can be written about so dubiously historical a figure as Arthur, or this may simply be self-deprecation; but for all its modern interest in the arts of spin *Here Lies Arthur* is also a richly imagined and well-researched Arthurian novel, which sets its action within a plausible post-Roman context. Perhaps its greatest achievement is that a book that appears at first to be using the Arthurian period almost as a cipher for the present day and as a vehicle for a cynical view of power politics, is nevertheless so moving and sympathetic in its portrayal of this doomed world and its inhabitants. In the context of the present discussion it is especially valuable for its investigation of the relationship between history, propaganda and wish fulfilment, and the function of stories in maintaining a sense of personal and group identity. Although it ends by apparently dismissing the Arthurian mythos as 'all tricks and stories' (286), the novel's total effect is a good deal more subtle than this downright conclusion might suggest.

Fashioning a chivalric Arthur

In *Sword at Sunset* and *Here Lies Arthur* Sutcliff and Reeve both chose, in very different ways, to visit the Arthurian legend from the perspective of twentieth-century archaeological and historical theories about what a post-Roman Arthur might have been like. This does not mean, however, that the literary approach exemplified by Roger Lancelyn Green earlier in the century has been superseded. There continue to be regular updatings and retellings of Arthurian legends. In the late 1970s Sutcliff herself returned to Arthur in three novels for children: *The Sword and the Circle* (1981), *The Light Beyond the Forest* (1979) and *The Road to Camlann* (1981). This time, like Green a quarter of a century before, she chose to put into novel form the legend as related by Malory – eked out with material drawn from other sources such as Geoffrey of Monmouth, *The Mabinogion* and the Gawain poet. The result is a very different book from *Sword at Sunset*, and in fact most of the incidents in the later trilogy have no direct parallel in Sutcliff's earlier work, although where they do coincide they serve to illustrate some of the more fundamental differences between the texts.

In *Sword at Sunset* Artos fathers Medraut upon his half-sister Ygerna, who seduces (and possibly drugs) him before revealing her identity. This is explicitly an act of personal revenge for her own abandonment by their father Uthr, who left her and her mother to shift for themselves on a desolate Welsh smallholding while Arthur, as his son, was brought up in relative privilege in the court of Ambrosius (*Sword at Sunset* 33). In the later trilogy Arthur is again unknowingly seduced by his half-sister, although this time (as in Malory) Mordred's mother is Margawse – who shares Arthur's blood through their mother Igrayne rather than through Uther. In this world Arthur is more conventionally noble, and he is largely excused by the narrative. Margawse is twice his age (*Sword and the Circle* 49) and, as the wife of King Lot of Orkney already has four sons and a secure social position, quite different from the embittered Ygerna. Malory notes that Arthur does not realize Lot's wife is his sister; but in Sutcliff he is ignorant even that she is married, reducing his guilt still further. Her malice, by contrast, is very conscious and much pondered. Margawse is simultaneously presented as inscrutable ('Why she did it, there can never be any knowing'), wilful ('she had never cared for any law, save the law of her own will'), vain ('she had never loved King Lot and dreaded growing old') and manipulative ('Maybe she thought it might help her in her spying') (*Sword and the Circle* 50). Vengeance is still ascribed as a possible motive, but although Margawse might easily have been made to resent Arthur because of her father Gorlois' murder and usurpation by Arthur's father Uther, her revenge is given a racial rather than a personal cast: 'Maybe it was just revenge, the revenge of the Dark People, the Old Ones, whose blood ran strong in her, upon the Lords of Bronze and Iron, and the People of Rome, who had dispossessed her' (50). In Sutcliff's second version of the story, then, not only are the names given their Malorian rather than their Welsh/Latin forms, but the ethos is one in which the morality of characters, and hence the blame, is more starkly apportioned. Arthur must suffer for his sin, and the tragedy of Mordred must be played out, but that sin is presented as the almost-innocent blemish of a young man seduced by a sophisticated and unscrupulous older woman.

Also in this tradition sits Michael Morpurgo's *Arthur, High King of Britain* (1994). Morpurgo gives his text a frame story, in which an unnamed modern-day boy, living on the Scilly Isles, is cut off by the incoming tide and rescued by Arthur, who with his dog

Bercelet has been hidden in a cave for 1400 years under the watchful eye of the Lady Nemue and her companions. As the boy recovers and his clothes are dried, Arthur recounts the story of his own life. In Morpurgo's version of Arthur's seduction, the relative sexual maturity of Margawse is again stressed ('she was twice my age' [53]),[4] and she appears to him simply as a stranger who enters from the storm one night and creeps under his bedclothes, before disappearing by morning. (In Malory, she stayed for a month.) This time, Merlin lets Arthur off even more lightly: 'There is no blame on you. You are a man like any other. You were enchanted, bewitched. Morgana Le Fey planned it all' (74).

Although Sutcliff and Morpurgo make some significant modifications to Malory, as in their rendering of this episode, in general they stay close to their source texts, at times producing something closer to a loose translation than a retelling, let alone a root-and-branch re-imagining. Their versions of the story of Gawain and the Green Knight, for which the source text is the Pearl manuscript rather than Malory, are cases in point. There is not room here to show this at length, but the following short passage is not untypical. We have placed the original and a modern translation before the versions by Sutcliff and Morpurgo:

> '[...] in fayth I þe telle,
> Hit arn aboute on þis bench bot berdlez chylder.
> If I were hasped in armes on a heȝestede,
> Here is no mon me to mach, for myȝtez so wayke.'
>
> (*Gawain and the Green Knight* 1.13)

> '[...] in faith I tell thee there are but beardless children about on this bench. If I were hasped in arms on a high steed there is no man here to match me, their might is so weak.'
>
> (*Gawain and the Green Knight* [trans. W. A. Neilson])

> 'That is as may be', said the Green Knight, 'but for the most part I see here only beardless bairns who I could fell with one flick of a bramble spray!'
>
> (Sutcliff 152)

> 'Looking about me, I see nothing but a bunch of beardless little boys. Are you quite sure I have come to the right place?'
>
> (Morpurgo 135)

Not only is the sense largely preserved, but both Sutcliff and Morpurgo even replicate the poem's alliterative measure to the extent of converting 'aboute on þis bench bot berdlez chylder' to 'beardless bairns' and 'but beardless little boys', respectively, with Sutcliff contributing 'fell with one flick' into the bargain. Morpurgo's Knight is perhaps a little too urbane with his ironic 'Are you quite sure I have come to the right place?', but here and throughout their renderings of this story both writers clearly have *Gawain and the Green Knight* open before them as they write. This is not because either author lacks imaginative power, but it does indicate the kind of project they see themselves as engaging in, which is one of transmission as much as of creation. 'I have followed Malory in the main,' wrote Sutcliff, 'but I have not followed him slavishly – no minstrel ever follows exactly the songs that have come down to him from the time before' (8). For Sutcliff and for Morpurgo, the heroic tales of Arthur must be perennially remade, and the link between the past and the present (represented in Morpurgo's case by the nameless boy listener to Arthur's tales) constantly re-forged. But this past is the literary past, the past of the heroic tradition of the Matter of Britain, rather than a past to which dates can be unproblematically assigned.

Arthur and 'story-time'

Sutcliff and Morpurgo effectively abstract Arthur from history in their versions of his story. Morpurgo's Arthur talks about having been trapped in his cave for almost 1400 years (257), but the tale he tells is not that of a sixth-century king, and he admits that time runs differently for him: 'We live in time, but we do not move with it. Here in this place, we are beyond the reach of time' (259). In effect, Arthur lives not in history but to one side of it, in the temporal no-man's land that Diana Wynne Jones has defined as 'story-time'. Jones describes this concept in her essay 'Inventing the Middle Ages':

> [...] when I was eight, I started reading Malory in the edition my mother had used as an undergraduate – my parents did not really believe in books specially for children, so the language was a bit of a struggle, and the small print, but I read with enormous enthusiasm. Things like 'How Sir Launcelot slew three Giants and set a Castle Free' really turned me on. I had got to the middle of

> Tristram and Isolt, when my mother told me sternly that I must remember that knights didn't *really* wear armour in King Arthur's day. This totally bewildered me. 'How did they *manage* then, when they were fighting?' I wondered, and pondered deeply. My ponderings led me to locate that sense that everyone acquires, that there is a 'story-time' which has nothing to do with history. 'Story-time' is when things bizarre or adventurous or enchanted can happen, as in the 'Once upon a time' of fairy stories. So of course the knights could wear armour: they were in this 'story-time' and it didn't matter.

It is not quite true that 'story-time' has 'nothing to do with history', even though it cannot be fully accommodated within it. The knights of Malory (and of Morpurgo) are high-medieval warriors wearing plate armour of a kind unavailable in post-Roman Europe before the late thirteenth century, and this has implications for a story in which Arthur claims to have been in a cave for over a millennium and to have fought against the invading Saxons. These artefacts and claims are historically contradictory rather than ahistorical, and it is precisely their contradictory nature that marks them out as belonging to story-time. Arthur lends himself to story-time particularly well, having associations with so many epochs. As a possibly historical figure he belongs to the fifth or sixth century; as a chivalric figure he is medieval; as a prophetic figure he belongs to the present and the future. Various writers, rather than narrow the focus of their treatments by choosing one of these periods to the exclusion of others (as Sutcliff does in *Sword at Sunset*, for example), have chosen to incorporate this multiple temporality as an explicit element within their work.

The earliest and in many ways boldest writer to attempt this within children's fiction is T. H. White in *The Sword in the Stone*, a book that was first published in 1938, and later incorporated in a heavily revised version into *The Once and Future King* tetralogy (1958).[5] White is aware that there is no period in history during which the story he wants to tell – a story that draws on the high-medieval chivalry of Chrétien or Malory – can be set. His implied medieval setting is already occupied by historical medieval society. Rather than ignore this fact White embraces it, adopting a combination of incompatible strategies to mark out a medieval story-time in which to develop his narrative. The first of these strategies is to set the book in Norman England, and this is where White generally places it in terms of architecture, technology, clothing and social structure. The book begins with an introduction to the routine of Wart (the young Arthur) and his step-brother Kay:

> On Mondays, Wednesdays and Fridays it was Court Hand and Summulae Logicales, while the rest of the week it was the Organon, Repetition and Astrology. The governess was always getting muddled with her astrolabe, and when she got specially muddled she would take it out of the Wart by rapping his knuckles.
> (13)

There are some anachronisms built into even this opening paragraph. It is highly unlikely that the sons of a country knight would be taught Aristotle, and certainly not by a governess. Nevertheless, these sentences orientate us relatively unambiguously towards a medieval England, and in general terms that identification is maintained throughout the book, with an early thirteenth-century date being implied at more than one point.[6] In some instances the revised version of the text makes this medieval setting even more explicit than the original: for example, the phrase 'The villeins were slaves if you chose to look at it in one way' (227) becomes, in revision, 'The Saxons were slaves to their Norman masters if you chose to look at it in one way' (129).

White appears to take pleasure in undermining this historical setting, however, and freely uses anachronism to disrupt the illusion (such as it is) of historical mimesis. The opening pages of the book present Sir Ector and Sir Grummore speaking in the accents of twentieth-century fox-hunting men (except that they are talking about an evil knight called Sir Bruce Saunce Pité rather than a fox), drinking port and discussing whether to send Ector's children to Eton (15), while later in the book Sir Ector is said to be 'an old tilting blue' (106). These superimpositions of twentieth-century language and culture onto the Middle Ages are explained in a sentence inserted into the revised text: 'It was not really Eton that he [Grummore] mentioned, for the College of Blessed Mary was not founded until 1440, but it was a place of the same sort. Also they were drinking Metheglyn, not Port, but by mentioning the modern wine it is easier to give you the feel' (8–9). Although this invocation of the principle of accommodation appears reasonable, in practice it is carried through very inconsistently, and the figure of Merlin in particular provides an alternative way of considering the book's anachronisms:

> I unfortunately was born at the wrong end of time, and I have to live *backwards* from in front, while surrounded by a lot of people living forwards from behind. Some people call it having second sight.
>
> (53)

Merlin's condition means that he possesses knowledge and indeed objects belonging to later periods than the story's supposed era. At one point, for example, Merlin addresses his magic (which has supplied him with inappropriate headgear): 'I don't want a hat I was wearing in 1800. Have you no sense of time at all?',[7] adding 'This is an anachronism... a beastly anachronism' (162). In his duel with the witch Madam Mim he even takes a leaf from H. G. Wells's *The War of the Worlds* (1898) and kills her by becoming a series of 'microbes, not yet discovered' (105).

For all his playing with time sequence and anachronism, however, White sometimes chooses to push the setting of the story to a far remove, emphasizing its temporal distance and the irrecoverable nature of the Wart's world. He does this by describing Sir Ector's home, the Castle of the Forest Sauvage, as it appears in the twentieth century, a ruin preserved complete with safety railings by 'the Society for the Preservation of This and That' (64). He invites his readers to wander around the site and to recreate in their minds the way that it might have appeared in the Wart's day, in a different age though the same geographical space. 'If you are a sensible person, you will spend days there, possibly weeks, working out for yourself by detection which were the stables, which the mews, where were the cow byres [...]. Then it will all grow about you again' (65). This is an intellectual and empathetic exercise, but although it allows for the reconstruction of the castle it also necessarily focuses our attention on the length of time between Then and Now, even as the anarchic play with time sequence elsewhere in the novel seems designed to distract us from that contemplation.

Finally, *The Sword in the Stone* is also a novel of Merrie England, and as such is the natural home of such archetypal characters as Robin Hood (known here as Robin Wood), who shares its greenwood with Little John and Maid Marian, as well as the fairy-tale witch Madam Mim. In this mode the book's relationship to history changes yet again: it becomes a timeless pastoral in which natural and social cycles, marked by such events as haymaking and Christmas, are repeated continually, as the ploughs go to and fro from year to year.

Arthur in double vision

Aaron Isaac Jackson has argued convincingly that 'White's narrative is a hybridized and metalinguistic construct that incarnates the fragmentation English identity underwent during the period of its composition' (44). Whatever its fragmentary nature owes to the historical moment of its writing or to the modernist aesthetic, however, it is also the case that a degree of fragmentation, or at least a multiplicity of perspective, is the general condition of modern treatments of Arthur, simply because of his doubly ambiguous position as a figure neither wholly fantastic nor reliably historical; and (within history) neither truly medieval nor verifiably post-Roman. All the writers we have discussed so far have been attempting, as Tom Shippey has put it, 'to reconcile two different imaginary worlds' in their renditions of the Arthurian story: 'the post-Geoffrey of Monmouth tradition (knights in armor, Arthur and Guinevere, Lancelot and Mordred, Excalibur and the Grail), and the Fall of Empire image (deserted towns, language change, meager and unreliable records)' (454). These do not exhaust the possibilities offered by Arthur, however. A consideration of two more texts, by Kevin Crossley-Holland and Catherine Fisher, will indicate something of the variety of approaches that have been taken to the problem of Arthur's 'doubleness'.

Kevin Crossley-Holland, in his 'Arthur' trilogy (2000–3), beginning with *The Seeing Stone*, tackles Arthur's dual nature in an unusual way. His books tell the story of Arthur de Caldicot, the younger son of a knight in the Welsh Marches, living at the turn of the thirteenth century. Arthur's social position, no less than his name, underlines the parallels between his life and that of Malory's Arthur. His older brother Serle bears a passing resemblance to Kay in his complacent assumption of superiority as the favoured heir. Most telling of all, one of the cottages on the estate is occupied by an enigmatic Welshman who goes by the name of Merlin, and about whom rumours abound, including one that his mother was a nun and his father an incubus (72). The question naturally arises whether this is *the* Merlin, perhaps in one of his time-travelling incarnations, or whether the rumours are the result of simple confusion between the village eccentric and his more famous namesake, whom Geoffrey of Monmouth provides with precisely that parentage. Crossley-Holland's narrative leaves that question open, but it is Merlin who gives Arthur a piece of obsidian (the 'seeing stone' of the book's title) that does indeed seem to hold supernatural powers. Arthur finds that when he stares at the stone he is able to see episodes from the story of another Arthur, whose father is Uther Pendragon. In this way Crossley-Holland is able to intersperse chapters recounting the traditional legends of King Arthur with the more quotidian life of Arthur de Caldicot.

Crossley-Holland has written that he made several attempts to find a way into the Arthurian corpus before he hit on this method of producing 'two stories in tandem' (Official Web Site). The structure of his book allows and encourages comparisons to be made between the two Arthurs' lives, but without forcing the issue of the legendary Arthur's historicity. Stripped of the visions Arthur de Caldicot has in the seeing stone, the book is a realist historical novel; equally, the visions on their own make a coherent retelling of the Arthurian legend. There is little formal connection between the two, although (as Crossley-Holland notes on his web site) the legends 'anticipate and reflect [Arthur de Caldicot's] own eagerness and ideals and anxieties and passions and sorrows'. As the narrator of this journal-like novel, medieval Arthur models the reading process for Crossley-Holland's readership, straddling the legendary and the mundane and becoming, as well as a realistically portrayed medieval boy, a kind of Arthurian Everyman.

White had set Sir Ector's castle in England, but close to the border with Wales, which is throughout *The Sword in the Stone* a mysterious and dangerous land whose people, armed with bows and arrows, move silently through the forest, leaving no trace. In his description of the modern-day castle, for example, White writes:

> The little people [...] will hurry about in the sunshine, the sheep will baa as they always did, and perhaps from Wales there will

> come the ffff-putt of the triple-feathered arrow which looks as if it had never moved.
>
> (51)

Whether or not Crossley-Holland had White's example in mind, it is notable that he too places his Caldicot in the Welsh Marches, basing it on the thirteenth-century fortified manor house Stokesay Castle in Shropshire. He explains his reasons on his web site:

> I knew the setting should be the magical Welsh Marches so rich in Arthurian association, here secretive, there expansive, looking east to plainspoken England, looking west to dreaming Wales.

The choice of setting reflects the fact that Arthur is both a Celtic and an English hero, both the leader of a resistance movement against invasion and an *imperator* who (in Geoffrey of Monmouth's imagination at least) subdued most of Europe. Crossley-Holland's own Arthur too is a product of both worlds. Caldicot is an English manor, and Arthur's father (like Sir Ector) is a conscientious man who takes his social position and duties very seriously. But his mother and several of the servants are Welsh, and share a Welsh outlook to which secrets, hidden stories and a history of oppression are central. Here, then, the historical and the magical are mapped loosely onto traditional national characteristics, with Arthur de Caldicot being positioned as a person who combines the positive qualities of both nations.

Catherine Fisher's *Corbenic* (2002) is another Arthurian novel that sits on the border between plainspokenness and dreams, and although in her book these qualities are not so straightforwardly rendered in terms of national character, *Corbenic* too threads its course along the boundary between Wales and England, featuring scenes in Chepstow, Ludlow, Caerleon, Bath, Abergavenny and Glastonbury. The protagonist of this modern rendering of the Perceval legend is Cal, a boy who has left his mentally ill, alcoholic mother and is travelling from his home in North Wales to live with his uncle in Chepstow when he mistakenly disembarks from the train at a station called Corbenic. (Corbenic appears to be located between Craven Arms and Ludlow, which, whether coincidentally or not, is just where Stokesay Castle stands within sight of the railway line.) There, Cal takes refuge in the Castle Hotel, which is run by a Fisher King figure named Bron. Like Perceval in the legend Cal witnesses the grail procession, but like him too he fails to ask the required question that would heal the Waste Land, instead denying that he has seen anything at all. Apart from this hallucinatory passage, most of the novel takes place in modern Britain. Crossley-Holland's Arthur found in the seeing stone a legendary analogue for his own coming of age, but the connection between Cal's experience at the Grail castle and his personal situation is more complex. Cal's psyche is another Waste Land and, like Perceval, he must heal it by making good his mistakes, seeking a second chance to repair the damage that his relationship with his mother has done to them both.

Corbenic is not an historical or time-travel fantasy in any straightforward sense: the 'castle' visited by Cal belongs to another reality rather than to the past: it is 'a state of mind' (97). However, it belongs in this discussion as an example of a book that, like *The Seeing Stone*, exploits the duality of the Arthurian myth. Arthur himself is not a central figure in this version of the grail myth, but in Chepstow Cal encounters the Company, a group who perform re-enactments of Dark Age battle. Arthur is their leader, and others in the Company include Arthur's wife Gwen, the half-mad vagrant Merlin, supercilious Kai and Hawk (Gwalchmei). Although they dress in modern clothes, Arthur and his followers stay 'in role' even when not performing, and Fisher leaves it ambiguous whether they are merely particularly dedicated re-enactors, or (as they claim) immortal warriors who have lived through the centuries since Arthur's supposed death. When questioned by Cal, Kai is scornful of legends that have Arthur's band sleeping in a cave under a hill until their country needs them:

> 'Ah, the dear old cave. Trouble with that was, people always need us. They need someone to fight their nightmares for them, the dragons, the black knights. They need dreams to dream, quests to follow.'
>
> (120)

Is this a claim to immortality within history, or to an archetypal status within a reality that sits at an angle to historical time? In the world of this text, both time and space are liable to distortions and lacunae. At one point Cal finds himself in a dream-like landscape and decides that 'This was not Wales. This was not England. He had fallen into the crack between them' (169). It seems that the Arthurian mythos can inhabit the space 'between' Wales and England just as it can exist *in* either country. Similarly, it can belong to the past or the present, or it can fall into the 'crack' between times. Whether in terms of history, geography or along that third axis running from realism to fantasy, Arthur remains the most flexible, least fixable of characters. This is of course one of the reasons for his perennial appeal to writers, and also why he eludes any attempt finally to rule him in or out of the ambit of the historical novel.

Arthur's status is likely to remain a matter of controversy amongst historians and archaeologists, but he continues to haunt scholarly discourse in those fields. Whether believed in or not, Arthur also dominates the fictional landscape of Britain between 450 and 550, to the extent that there are very few children's books that have attempted to tell that century's story without him.[8] As Dan Nastali has noted, 'the very darkness of the age permits a writer more options than he might wish when portraying Arthurian Britain' (7), but none of those options seems to involve imagining a Britain that is not Arthurian at all. The crucial hundred years following the Roman Empire's effective abandonment of Britain are in large part an historical vacuum. As yet, no one has found any story but Arthur's with which to fill it.

4
'She Be Faking It': Authenticity and Anachronism

Historical fiction is haunted by the demand for, and the impossibility of, authenticity in its representations of the past. The concept of authenticity covers a lot of semantic territory, encompassing not only the criterion of factual accuracy – that is, of telling it like it is (or was) – but also the questions of *who* is doing the telling, and *how* and *why*. Any modern representation of the experiences of those who lived in the past must necessarily be a ventriloquistic performance, given in terms designed to be understood by a modern audience. The dead are not here to speak for themselves, or to comment on or correct the words of others, a fact that can only add to the responsibility of the historical writer even as it makes that responsibility harder to fulfil. The ethical obligations and constraints are especially acute where authors are writing for an audience, such as children, unlikely to have an extensive background knowledge against which to measure any account of the past. How do these duties, both to the subjects and the readers of historical texts, intersect with the possibly competing aims of entertaining and engaging those readers?

Rebecca Barnhouse, in her book on children's historical fiction, *Recasting the Past* (2000), takes a relatively uncompromising approach to this question. She begins her introduction by quoting Celia Keenan's summary of the views of Katherine Paterson: 'being true to the past means being true to a time when moral and social sensibilities were different from today's' (ix). As Barnhouse makes clear, 'being true to the past' is at least as much about good faith as about accuracy. Barnhouse's idea of historical writers' obligations, as it emerges over the course of her book, comprises a requirement not only to conform to the facts as they are known but also to respect the lives of past peoples, and to acknowledge that they were as real and possessed as much intelligence as those alive today. The other main component of her position is that, while historical writers have a duty not to misrepresent the past, they must also respect the needs of modern readers, who deserve access to a history that is honest, rather than distorted to fit the *mores* and priorities of the present. This threefold obligation – to historical accuracy, to the people of the past and to present-day readers – constitutes the main measure by which Barnhouse judges historical fiction.

As this suggests, Barnhouse is hostile to anachronistic writing not only when it is due to authorial ignorance or indifference to the past but also when it is employed as a strategy to engage modern readers by presenting them with people, beliefs and reactions to which they can be expected to 'relate'. A medieval character who espouses universal suffrage, for example, may be expressing admirable sentiments from a modern perspective, and ones that most readers will share and approve. However, in Barnhouse's view this will be at the expense of respect for historical verisimilitude and for the actual people of the past, whose complex realities deserve to be seen in their own terms, while also making a restricted estimate of the intelligence and sympathetic range of modern readers. As she says of authors who employ this kind of strategy:

> [...] not only do they underestimate the cultural differences between medieval and modern society, they also underestimate their readers' ability to comprehend and learn from such differences, condescending therefore to both the past and the present. (10)

Two of Barnhouse's examples will serve to illustrate her method. In Frances Temple's *The Ramsey Scallop* (1994), a story about a pilgrimage to Santiago de Compostela in 1299, the legend of Roland and Oliver is told by one of the pilgrims. The doomed Roland, far from being admired as the epitome of heroism, is seen by many of the company as having recklessly endangered his own life and those of his companions. For Barnhouse this reaction implausibly superimposes the twentieth-century attitudes of a society disenchanted with war onto the conventions of a medieval epic romance. To this extent, the medieval characters become merely the anachronistic mouthpieces of their author's anti-war sentiments. Similarly, Barnhouse notes that, in Karen Cushman's thirteenth-century story *Catherine, Called Birdy* (1994) (a book she generally admires), Birdy's friend, the goat boy Perkin, has ambitions to learn to read. However, Barnhouse considers that the high value placed on literacy by modern writers and educationalists is here being projected onto a society in which reading was simply a specialist skill, like weaving or blacksmithing, rather than being seen as a universal key to knowledge and self-development. Perkin is thus, in this respect, an anachronistic figure.

> These characters become role models for today's adolescents; just as [...] Perkin and Birdy value books as a means to gain knowledge, so ought their audiences. By this unintentional didacticism, the writers commit anachronism instead of giving us the real Middle Ages.
>
> (10)

In ignoring the facts of the past, Barnhouse complains, writers 'allow their didactic tendencies to overshadow historical accuracy' (1). It is worth pausing here to point out that Barnhouse's use of the word 'didactic' is an idiosyncratic one. Here and throughout her book Barnhouse uses 'didactic' to refer not to the general desire to write literature that educates its readers about history, but to a specifically *ideological* didacticism, which appropriates history as a tool through which to promote modern values, often at the expense of historical accuracy. To didacticism in its broader sense of a project to inform readers about the past and expand their imaginative sympathies, however, Barnhouse is very much committed:

> Writers who create memorable, sympathetic characters who retain authentically medieval values teach their audience more than those who condescend to readers by sanitizing the past. Trusting readers to comprehend cultural differences, presenting the Middle Ages accurately, and telling a good story results in compelling historical fiction that, like medieval literature in its ideal form, teaches as it delights.
>
> (86)

Behind this Horation *dulce et utile* formula lies a conception of the child reader as one who does not identify in an unthinking way with the fictional protagonist, but is able to register differences as well as similarities, and to do so without the need of an obtrusive narratorial voice or an unrealistically 'modern' character identifying those actions or attitudes appropriate for approval. As Barnhouse puts it: 'The convictions readers come to on their own, may be stronger than the opinions they are fed pre-digested. Don't readers deserve this measure of trust?' (16).

The confidence in children's emotional and intellectual sophistication implied by Barnhouse's approach is attractive, as is her commitment to accuracy and her passionate rejection of presentism.[1] Nevertheless, there are practical difficulties in her application of her criteria, which may turn out in any case to be rather too procrustean to account adequately for the many different ways of representing the past in fiction. One problem is Barnhouse's tendency to homogenize particular periods and cultures. In vetting texts for evidence of anachronism, Barnhouse compares fictional accounts against her own informed sense of what the past was actually like. This is necessarily a subjective measure, and in Barnhouse's case tends to militate against the possibility of statistical outliers. When Barnhouse criticizes Cushman's depiction of the book-hungry Perkin, for example, she suggests that Cushman 'is providing modern audiences with role models who value books' (9), rather than giving a plausible rendition of what such a boy might have been like. However, while Perkin's hunger for literacy may not be typical of a boy of his class and time, it is far from unheard of: there are numerous recorded cases of literate clerks being drawn from the peasantry (Orme 49). Cushman is not making broad sociological claims about medieval society but depicting individuals, and that a curious boy such as Perkin might have wished to learn to read does not stretch credulity. Indeed, in a later discussion of Mary Stolz's *Pangur Ban*, Barnhouse writes approvingly of the portrayal of the Irish peasant boy Cormac, who 'longs for the monastic life because it offers the chance to learn things and make books, not just to plow fields and mend fences' (35). Why Cormac's interest in learning is historically acceptable but Perkin's an anachronism is unclear, and such inconsistencies are a general problem with Barnhouse's application of her method, as is her tendency to approve only that which is safely representative and typical rather than that which is individual or unusual. Novels often involve unusual events and individuals, a fact that Barnhouse's regression-to-the-mean approach is ill-equipped to take into account.

Similar objections apply to her criticism of the discussion of the *Chanson de Roland* in *The Ramsey Scallop*. The pilgrims who find Roland's style of derring-do less than admirable are seen as unhistorical in their dislike of male-dominated heroic tales. Barnhouse complains of Temple's approach:

> [Temple] has Nora say: 'In stories the men are heroes because of what they do, but if the women are heroes at all, it is because of what they think or because of what happens to them' (175). This analysis by medieval people of an oft-told tale seems better suited to an audience of a later age [...] Temple comes dangerously close to implying that the story – so popular in the Middle Ages – is childish, and therefore, so were those silly medieval people.
>
> (30)

It is always a dangerous critical move to read a fictional character as the author's spokesperson, but Barnhouse's point is problematic in other ways too. First, as with the case of Perkin, there is the danger of inconsistency. To revert to *Pangur Ban*, Barnhouse finds nothing to object to in young Cormac's distaste for the heroic tales of Cúchulainn and the *Táin*, even though these stories are at least as central to his medieval Irish culture as the *Chanson* is to that of Nora and the other pilgrims. Second, the historical record has little or nothing to say about what women of Nora's class thought about heroic epics, and one of the attractions of historical fiction of Temple's kind is the imaginative opportunity it provides to recreate such silenced voices. How can we be sure that these views really are atypical, let alone anachronistic? This evidential problem is partly recognized by Barnhouse, who quotes Chaucer's Wife of Bath to the effect that if women had written the stories, then we would have a very different literature (32). But, Barnhouse warns, the Wife of Bath (like Christine de Pisan and a few others who speak out on behalf of women) is exceptional, and to be treated with great caution as a model for fiction. Again, the rule of regression to the mean implies that even genuine medieval examples of 'feminism' must be disregarded. Barnhouse admits that 'for the sake of the plot, the novelist must take some liberties' (48), but offers no systematic way of deciding how many, or how great.

Some of these criticisms are more serious to Barnhouse's project than others. The problem of inconsistency may be considered as lying less with her method itself than with its application, and might be addressed without undermining her core assumption that historical fiction derives its authority from its ability to convey the material and mental realities of past times. The more serious problem of 'regression to the mean' might be solved by recognizing unusual events and attitudes simply *as* unusual rather than as 'wrong', if their unusualness is sufficiently acknowledged and accounted for within the fiction. Barnhouse herself, in her novel *The Book of the Maidservant* (2009), depicts the far-from-typical figure of Margery Kempe in this way with considerable success, and this does not involve departing fundamentally from her own conception of historical fidelity. *The Ramsey Scallop* finds room for a sceptical critique of heroism in its pilgrim party that may not be 'typical' of the Middle Ages but that is far from inconceivable, especially when we recall that the pilgrim party includes an astutely-drawn young man who has returned from the Crusades disillusioned with the reality of war. Such a psychological state certainly existed in the Middle Ages, as is shown in the reaction of many crusaders to the constant failure of their campaigns, and to the disparity between the ideal of winning souls for Christ and the actuality of cruelty and bloodshed (Sibbery).

Other examples of this type of accommodation are not hard to find. One is that of Eleanor Hungerford, the heroine of Marie-Louise Jensen's *The Lady in the Tower* (2009). This novel is set in 1540 and the years immediately preceding, and Eleanor is that unlikely creature, a Tudor girl who has been taught to joust and use a sword. These are certainly not everyday female accomplishments, but Jensen does not present them as such. Eleanor herself notes:

> I knew very well how fortunate I was to have been allowed to continue riding lessons with the boys once they began training to tilt. My mother considered that it would be more appropriate for me to improve my stitching and learn to read and write better. Luckily, Father had overruled her, saying I might continue riding

> lessons for at least a few more months. He was proud of my riding skills and despised book learning of any kind.
>
> (3–4)

Jensen is clearly aware that men of Eleanor's father's class might be ambivalent about the benefits of learning, and not only for girls: such inkhorn pursuits might be seen as unfitting for a knight.[2] There is no suggestion that Eleanor's riding lessons will persist much longer, however, and it is only the subsequent breakdown of her family after her father has imprisoned her mother that enables her to continue her training. In 1540 she writes: 'I stay out of sight [...] I doubt my father has caught sight of me in two years' (15), while the prospect of his renewed interest in her existence spells the end of such boyish pursuits: 'My father's arrival would mean less freedom within the castle and the end of jousting practice for me. Although it had been he that allowed me to begin learning, I'm quite sure he would be shocked if he knew I had continued all these years' (18).

Kevin Crossley-Holland's peasant girl Gatty, who features in his Arthur trilogy and is the protagonist of the subsequent novel, *Gatty's Tale* (2006), is another medieval character whose atypical experiences and attitudes are accounted for in realistic terms. Like the maidservant Johanna in Barnhouse's *The Book of the Maidservant* and Nora in *The Ramsey Scallop*, Gatty goes on pilgrimage, in her case to Jerusalem. Pilgrimage did, of course, hold a very important place in medieval life, and there is no need to look for an 'explanation' for its regular use in fiction set in the period. However, it has a number of features that are relevant to our consideration of authenticity and anachronism. These include the opportunity to bring people of diverse classes into close proximity, in what was generally a highly stratified society. This advantage has been exploited by writers from Chaucer onward, and the knight in K. M. Grant's recent novel *Belle's Song* (2010) (which features Chaucer as a character) makes the point explicit: 'God doesn't stand on precedence and, during a pilgrimage, nor should we' (43–4). This freedom of mixing, both of social classes and between the sexes, is particularly important for girls and women, who may be enabled to play a more active and less confined role in the context of a pilgrimage than would generally have been available to them within medieval society.

The opportunity to encounter a greater diversity of people extends beyond the pilgrim party itself. In the course of her journey from her small village to London, then Venice and eventually to Jerusalem, Gatty encounters a wide range of people, including Saracens. As Crossley-Holland observes: 'Gatty gets to hear what [the Muslims are] thinking, what they're talking about, and contrary to having horns and tails, she discovers they are immensely learned in astronomy, medicine, music, mathematics, architecture [...] and Gatty sees that it won't do, to accept hand-me-down information and truths'. In writing of medieval life, Crossley-Holland has noted, it is 'not very difficult to find out what people ate, what they wore, what they talked about; a damn sight more difficult to discover what their mindset was' (Crossley-Holland, 'Kevin Crossley-Holland'). Pilgrimage is one way of allowing a medieval character to develop an understanding of people with different religions (amongst other mindsets) in a way that may not be 'typical', but is a plausible result of having met them for themselves.

Finding a place for anachronism

Barnhouse's approach to the question of authenticity, at least in this modified form, provides a useful basis for our own enquiry, but it is still predicated on the rigid assumption that anachronism is to be deplored. In this section we question this assumption, arguing that there may be good reasons for the presence of anachronistic elements in historical fiction – a presence that is in any case inevitable. First, however, it will be useful to consider the concept of anachronism rather more closely, and to distinguish some of the circumstances that give rise to its use, as well as the various ways in which a text can be said to *be* anachronistic – whether in its portrayal of beliefs, of language or of material culture. The simplest type of anachronism conceptually is that caused by authorial ignorance, in the form of inadequate research or insufficient familiarity with historical patterns of speech. However, Barnhouse's disapproval is more usually directed at texts in which modern attitudes and beliefs are attributed to characters in the past – for example, as a strategy to smooth the path of sympathy and identification by creating central characters to whom (in the words of Beth Webb) 'modern readers can relate' ('Interview'). Untainted by such unappealing historical traits as a belief in the inferiority of women or the justice of slavery, such protagonists may thus demonstrate the superiority of modern values. The use of these anachronistic characters relieves modern authors of the necessity of seeming (through their sympathetic protagonists) to endorse unwelcome attitudes.

Anachronism may be deliberately introduced for numerous other reasons besides smuggling ideologically acceptable points of view into the narrative. These include aiding comprehensibility and accessibility (in terms of language, for example), and comic effect. Again, just as authors may select particular milieux (such as the medieval pilgrimage) that cater to their purpose of, say, representing a wide range of medieval people and places, so they may select for other purposes – and the distinction between selectivity and anachronism is not always a very clear one. Mary Hooper, in her novel about the Great Fire of London, *At the Sign of the Sugared Plum* (2003), constructs a heroine out of materials not impossible for the time depicted, but evidently tailored to the tastes of a modern readership. Young Hannah, on her arrival in London from the countryside, is particularly excited by the prospect of what she may find in the shops, and the opportunities future wealth may afford her to show herself off in the latest fashions:

> I began to plan what I'd buy when I was rich. We *would* be rich, I was sure – Sarah wouldn't have sent for me unless the shop was doing well. We weren't poor at home by any means [...] but it was impossible there to follow the fashions. And besides, even if I could buy the silk jackets and flowered tabby waistcoats I craved, who would see me wearing them in the country, apart from booby gamekeepers or woodcutters' sons?
>
> (10)

These thoughts are not obviously anachronistic, in the sense that no one of the period might reasonably have had them, but they do appear to be chosen so as to provide the greatest possible overlap and the strongest possible analogies with the supposed interests of twenty-first-century, consumer-minded teenage girls. Such selectivity may be said to be misleading in that it tends to elide the differences between modern and historical ways of being in the world, but may also be justified as a necessary compromise in the task of making the past both interesting and unintimidating to modern readers. (In this particular text it coexists with an abundance of historical detail and evidence of seventeenth-century *mentalité*.) The distinction between 'realistic' and 'anachronistic' may, in other words, be a matter of selection and of degree.

In seeking a more nuanced way to discuss anachronism we have found it useful to borrow the terminology of translation theory. The task of translating a text between languages has some illuminating parallels with that of representing one historical age to another. The most obvious of these lies in the area of language itself: the problem of finding appropriate modern words to convey what might have been said in a former time bears a clear analogy with that of matching source and target languages in the practice of translation. But language is merely the most visible manifestation of a far larger matrix of norms and knowledge that characterizes cultures. Translators are continually engaged in a negotiation that takes place at the level not just of words but also of the cultural differences that underlie words, which they can choose either to camouflage or else to emphasize. The American theorist Lawrence Venuti has dubbed these two approaches to translation 'domestication' and 'foreignization', distinguishing between:

> [...] a domesticating method, an ethnocentric reduction of the foreign text to target-language cultural values, bringing the author back home, and a foreignizing method, an ethnodeviant pressure on those values to register the linguistic and cultural difference of the foreign text, sending the reader abroad.
>
> (20)

A domesticating approach to translation tends to disguise and smooth out cultural differences, extending the translator's search for domestic *linguistic* equivalents for foreign words and phrases into one of finding domestic *cultural* equivalents for foreign beliefs and customs. It also aims to make the act of translation itself invisible, providing as unimpeded a view as possible of the source text's meaning. Advocates of domesticating translation, such as the Biblical translator Eugene Nida, see it as their goal to find a 'dynamic equivalence' between the way that a member of the source culture would understand a text, and the way that a member of the target culture would do so. Achieving that equivalence takes priority over both word-for-word accuracy and the preservation of cultural specificity, which are subordinated to the goal of communication. Thus, a metaphor that depends upon familiarity with a world that is past, such as being told not to hide one's light under a bushel, may be less effective as a means of communication than simply being told not to hide one's talents, and that would be reflected in a domesticating translation. Where readers are likely to be relatively lacking in background knowledge of the source culture, as will generally be the case with children's texts, even more latitude may be taken with the translation, so local references specific to a foreign country may be either omitted, or expanded to provide contextual information, or replaced by a domestic equivalent.

As Venuti points out, the belief that such an equivalence is to be found suggests a faith in the universality of fundamental human qualities: 'Nida's advocacy of domesticating translation is explicitly grounded on a transcendental concept of humanity as an essence that remains unchanged over time and space' (22). By contrast, advocates of foreignizing translation, such as Venuti himself, see this attempt to find equivalences and to flatten out differences between cultures as oppressive and dishonest, in effect if not in intent. A foreignizing translation is deliberately opaque, focusing the reader's attention on the recalcitrant differences between cultures, and making explicit the ways in which they may be founded on incommensurable beliefs and assumptions. In this sense it registers dissent both from the universalist brand of humanism underlying domesticating translation, and also from its ethnocentric bias towards the target culture: 'Foreignizing translation in English can be a form of resistance against ethnocentrism and racism, cultural narcissism and imperialism, in the interests of democratic geopolitical relations' (20).

It is hard not to hear in Venuti's discussion of foreignizing and domesticating approaches to translation an echo of John Stephens' account of the contradictory impulses lying behind much historical fiction:

> The forming impulse of historical fiction might thus be said to consist of two contrary impulses: on the one hand, in order to mediate between past and present it will seek strategies by which

> to render the strangeness of the past familiar; on the other, in order to construct the literary illusion of an older discourse, it will seek to make the encoding discourse seem in some ways strange or 'other'.
>
> (202–3)

We will return to Stephens' more general argument in the final chapter of this book. Here we will simply observe that the urge to render the strangeness of the past familiar is in effect a domesticating one; while historical foreignizers march under a banner proclaiming that 'The past is a foreign country'. However, these contraries coexist in different ways in every historical text, as in every translation. Neither domestication nor foreignization is realizable in a pure form. The *reductio ad absurdum* of the foreignizing approach would be an outright refusal to write about the past on the grounds that understanding was impossible; while an extreme domesticating text would insulate its readers from the knowledge of change to the point where historical texts no longer appeared to be set in the past at all. Inevitably, all actual texts employ both domesticating and foreignizing elements. The very fact of writing about the past implies a belief that its difference from the present is not so radical as to render it incomprehensible, and at the same time an acknowledgement that it is different *enough* to render an account of it interesting and useful to modern readers.

The analogy between translation and the representation of history is not a perfect one, and we may argue about whether the past can be regarded as a text in quite the same sense as the source text of a translated book. Nevertheless, the extent to which foreignization and domestication strategies are emphasized or de-emphasized, and the ways in which they are played off against each other, can tell us much about a text's implied audience and ideological structures. Considering anachronism from this point of view also foregrounds the ethical questions involved in representing history. If the past is a foreign country – or a continent of them – then in representing the past many of the same issues arise as in cases of translation between contemporary cultures. Given Venuti's hostile assessment of domesticating translation as oppressive and exploitative, we might ask whether analogous arguments could be applied to 'domesticating' historical fiction. Barnhouse's impatience with texts that import modern attitudes into historical settings could be rephrased in the language of such an exercise, and we might also enquire what impulses lie behind the decision to write and publish books about certain periods at all.

In practice, the tension between domestication and foreignization plays itself out in two broad areas in historical novels, those of language and of what we might call the 'mental world' of the book and its characters. By contrast, the material world, as manifested in such matters as clothes, food, transport and technology, is conventionally treated with far less flexibility. Except in fantasy contexts, we are unlikely to see a knight's battle axe replaced with a 'domesticating' (because more familiar) gun, or a medieval workman dressed in jeans. That such accommodations would be jarring may seem self-evident to us, but it is worth reflecting that this too is a matter of shifting cultural norms. In the Middle Ages themselves, as we may see from paintings and illuminated manuscripts, it was standard practice to depict Biblical and classical subjects in terms of contemporary (that is, medieval) costume, architecture and technology. It is much harder, however, to say with confidence what this practice implies. It may mean that medieval people had a fundamentally different sense of their relationship with the past from our own – or perhaps simply that they chose different domains of domestication, reflecting their different purposes. In an illustration of a parable, for example, a visual style that allowed viewers to identify themselves with the people and situations depicted might seem 'obviously' appropriate, however far removed in terms of material detail from first-century Palestine. Even as late as the time of Shakespeare, material artefacts were sometimes treated with (to modern eyes) startling indifference to anachronism. Famously *Julius Caesar* has its striking clock, while the sole contemporary sketch of the Shakespearian stage shows 'Roman' soldiers carrying halberds.[3] Were Shakespeare and his company unaware that halberds were not standard legionary issue in the period when *Titus Andronicus* is set? Were they reluctantly forced to use whatever props were to hand? Did they have a 'domesticating' eye to making the soldiers' function easily comprehensible to their audience? Or was the practice intended and received more in the spirit of a modern-dress production of today? As in the case of the Bible parable, there is also the consideration that history was to be seen not as an assemblage of facts, but rather as a demonstration of God's Providence – a view quite explicit in Tudor historiography and in literary texts such as *A Mirror for Magistrates* (1559). Compared with the importance of communicating that, the presence of some anachronistic material details might seem to be of secondary importance, just as for some modern authors anachronism is a price worth paying in order to avoid the appearance of endorsing racial or religious prejudice.

Anachronism and language

Whatever its significance, the fact that our tolerance of material anachronisms has since become so low is, as far as it goes, a victory for the foreignizing approach. In the area of language, however, matters are very different. English as it was spoken before about 1550 is likely to be formidably difficult for a modern child reader to understand. Prior to 1400, it will be more or less incomprehensible. For this reason, texts set in the Middle Ages have linguistic anachronism thrust on them.

The representation of older forms of speech, like that of material culture, has a history of its own. Until the late eighteenth century there is little evidence of writers attempting to use archaic forms of English for the speech of characters from former times. The pivotal figure, certainly in terms of popularizing if not originating the use of period speech, was Sir Walter Scott, whose novels (in the words of C. S. Lewis) 'almost created that historical sense which we now all take for granted' (*They Asked for a Paper* 103). This is something of an exaggeration, of course: historical techniques had long been applied to language, as Lewis well knew. For example, Lorenzo Valla's fifteenth-century proof of the forged nature of the Donation of Constantine depended largely on his knowledge of the differences between fourth- and eighth-century Latin. However, Scott was the first major writer in English to carry that historical understanding of language into the practice of historical fiction, and he was immensely influential on the work of the historical novelists who followed him in the nineteenth century, such as Harrison Ainsworth and (for children) Pierce Egan. Since their time writers have always had to make a choice, when describing eras sufficiently distant that authentically historical speech will not be easily understood, about how to represent that speech.

There are numerous possible approaches, each with its advantages and dangers. The simplest would seem to be to write speech (or, where applicable, first-person narrative) in modern English, using vocabulary and syntax familiar to contemporary readers. This may seem like the ultimate domesticating move, obliterating the fact of language change and camouflaging one aspect at least of the past's alienating difference from the present. It is also, as we have noted, the approach taken by almost all writers before Scott. However, in a context where readers have assimilated period speech as part of the generic repertoire of historical fiction, matters become more complicated, and the choice of modern language can seem paradoxically obtrusive. If a fourteenth-century character begins a novel by talking about her 'compulsions', as in K. M. Grant's *Belle's Song* (4), then a reader familiar with the conventions of the historical novel may be disconcerted. This could be a case of a writer modernizing language for the purposes of relevance or accessibility, but it could also be a postmodern device, or authorial ineptitude.

Historical writers who use modern English for their medieval characters' speech generally refrain from overt references to modern technology and concepts. Even the most determinedly 'modern' medieval protagonist is unlikely to allude to a person undergoing psychotherapy, for example. However, words may carry information in their etymology, history and connotations, as well as in their denotative meaning, that render the avoidance of such explicitly anachronistic language insufficient. When Belle talks of her 'compulsions', she is using a word dating from at least the fifteenth century, and describing a phenomenon that no doubt existed in the time of Chaucer, but she is doing so in a way that implies a familiarity with the discourse of psychoanalysis, for 'compulsion' was not used in this particular sense until 1913, in the English translation of Freud's *The Interpretation of Dreams*, and can be understood only as the product of a mind exposed to Freudian and post-Freudian concepts. The same is true to a still more marked degree in Eve Edwards's Elizabethan adventure *The Other Countess* (2010), where we find one character telling another that he needs his 'head examining' (55). People in Tudor England were of course familiar with the concept of madness. It is easy to imagine someone being told that they had lost their wits, and the reference to having one's head examined may seem like a simple domesticating equivalent; but ideas about the causes and nature of madness, let alone its treatment, have changed so dramatically in the intervening centuries that this is an area where equivalence is simply not to be found. There was no one in 1584 whose business was to 'examine heads' in this sense, and the effect is to rupture rather than maintain the fiction. In *The Other Countess* this use of idioms that evoke specifically modern ways of thought is something of a habit:

> Will knew this, of course: the sport was another display of the sovereign's power as her noblemen risked their necks in her honour, she the focus of their knightly love and duty. It was a rite of passage he had to pass through if he wanted to make an impression at court.
>
> 'I just hope I sustain the romantic illusion and don't end up flat on my back in front of the spectators.'
>
> 'Think positively, Will. You're not a bad horseman,' said James. (56–7)

Apart from 'focus' and 'romantic', all the words in this passage were current in 1584. However, the ways in which many of them are used indicate a speaker familiar with the thought of a much later date. Amidst the pageantry of the Accession Day tilt we find 'rite of passage' (an anthropological term coined by Arnold van Gennep in 1909 in his book of that name); 'romantic illusion' (a phrase implying familiarity with the Romantic movement of the late eighteenth and early nineteenth centuries, or at least with the Enlightenment); and 'think positively' (an admonition closely associated with Norman Peale's 1952 self-help book, *The Power of Positive Thinking*). These phrases are so firmly embedded within certain discourses of modernity as to defy easy transplantation, demonstrating that contexts of usage are as important as the dates of words themselves in signalling anachronism. Sometimes indeed the effect works the other way around: when Karen Cushman's Elizabethan protagonist Meggy Swann (in *Alchemy and Meggy Swann* [2010]) uses the word 'gobsmacked' (111) to indicate astonishment, she is employing a word first recorded by the *OED* as late as 1987. However, because 'gobsmacked' is a back-formation composed of older slang elements belonging to a register appropriate to Meggy's character and station, and because Meggy has been established as a fertile coiner of insults, her lexical anachronism is far less apparent. Although there is no record that anyone used the word 'gobsmacked' in Elizabethan times, it is easy to believe that, had they done so, they would have been understood.

The opposite approach to using an approximately modern form of English is to adopt a self-consciously period style, replete with 'thous' and 'varlets'. This historical register, which derives from medieval English largely by way of Victorian melodrama, is little used by writers today, and it is not difficult to see why: it would be impenetrable to most child readers, while affording insufficient compensation in terms of historical authenticity. (Even so, the characters in *The Other Countess*, when not exhibiting their knowledge of Freud and twentieth-century anthropology, are capable of exchanges that might have appeared in the pages of Harrison Ainsworth: '"Careful with that pauldron, young sir!" growled Turville. "Peace, ye fat guts! I've not harmed it"' [54].) The juxtaposition of archaic and notably modern language can also jar, as in the passage from Sally Gardner's *I, Coriander* (2005) that gives this chapter its title. In this scene, set in the 1650s, the protagonist's stepmother Maud is demanding to see her daughter:

> 'Please keep your voice down, mistress. Your daughter is still poorly.'
>
> 'I care naught for that. She be faking it so that she can get out of working.'
>
> (155)

Maud's use of 'care naught' and the auxiliary 'be' mark her speech as archaic, in contrast to the relatively unmarked speech of her interlocutor. However, the verb 'faking' did not come into use until the mid-twentieth century, and while it might pass unremarked in a context that was less ostentatiously 'period', its introduction here creates a discordant effect.

In practice, many writers have developed an historical style distinct from both modern and actual historical speech, steering (as Geoffrey Trease disarmingly put it) 'a middle course, avoiding both Gadzookery and modern colloquialism; a frankly "made-up" form that has the right sound to it' (qtd. in Collins and Graham, 19). Rosemary Sutcliff is a good representative example of this approach. The language of her historical characters (as John

Stephens has observed) is characterized by a fairly constant set of lexical and grammatical features, whether they be Roman officers, pre-Roman Celts or Vikings. Stephens' analysis, while it does not pretend to be exhaustive, effectively establishes some of the ways that Sutcliff's characters depart from modern standard English, including such grammatical and stylistic features as 'preservation of subjunctive forms', 'heroic metonymy' and 'formal left-branching syntax' (222). The overall effect is one in which colloquial and informal speech is interspersed with features indicative of a mind with a rather different architecture from that of most modern readers.

A more recent writer who establishes her own historical style is Karen Cushman. *Catherine, Called Birdy* differs from Sutcliff's Roman and Dark Age novels in that Cushman is dealing with characters who would historically have been speaking an older form of English rather than Latin or Brythonic. Nevertheless Birdy, writing her diary in 1291, would be incomprehensible to modern readers were Cushman to attempt to reproduce that form accurately. Instead, like Sutcliff, she uses a restricted selection of archaic features to indicate that Birdy's is indeed an older version of English, without making any very onerous demands on a modern reader's comprehension. Some of the archaic features relate to the vocabulary of the physical world: Birdy does not feel the need to explain what a 'solar' is, for example, and leaves her readers to deduce the word's meaning from context. Just as important, however, is Cushman's use of a select group of grammatical forms and formulaic phrases. The diary's opening entry establishes the book's register:

> 12TH DAY OF SEPTEMBER
>
> I am commanded to write an account of my days: I am bit by fleas and plagued by family. That is all there is to say.
>
> (1)

This short passage is fairly representative of Cushman's approach in *Catherine, Called Birdy* in terms of its deployment of familiar and unfamiliar forms. The diary format will be familiar to modern readers, but the wording of the date (with that superfluous 'day of') estranges it slightly. We may wonder why and by whom Birdy has been compelled to keep a diary, but her oddly formal choice of verb – 'commanded' rather than 'told' or even 'ordered' – hints at a world and a family structured with a more explicit sense of hierarchy than is the case for most twentieth-century teenagers. 'Bit' rather than 'bitten' is a noticeable archaism but an eminently comprehensible one, and the choice of 'plagued' takes advantage of readerly associations between the Middle Ages and the Black Death, especially occurring as it does in conjunction with mention of flea bites. (Neither of these associations need be conscious on Birdy's part: living in 1291, she predates the Black Death by almost 60 years, and the discovery of its transmission by fleas by several centuries.) Finally, the terse 'That is all there is to say' is reassuringly simple and utterly modern, but sufficiently unidiomatic not to call attention to its modernity.

In Birdy's speech medieval grammatical forms are selected with an eye to comprehensibility, and the nature of unusual items of vocabulary is normally made clear through context. Birdy's exclamations and oaths such as 'Corpus bones!' and 'God's thumbs!' are not those of a twentieth-century girl, but their function is immediately apparent – and in the case of 'God's thumbs!' Birdy even discusses her use of it as a means of making herself distinctive, a stereotypically 'teenage' preoccupation. Cushman handles the form of the book with similar flexibility. The intimate teenage diary is a standard setting for modern young-adult literature, and might seem anachronistic in a thirteenth-century context, an impression accentuated by the tag line 'She's not your average damsel in distress', blazoned on the jacket of some editions. Nevertheless, Birdy accounts plausibly for the fact that she is recording her daily deeds and thoughts: it is at the behest of her elder brother Edward, a monk, who has given her the book as an exercise in spiritual self-examination. Her custom of mentioning which saint's feast is celebrated on each day also gives her account an affinity with the books of saints and hours owned by noblewomen such as her mother.

Sutcliff in her Roman and Dark Age books, and Cushman in *Catherine, Called Birdy*, approach the problem of developing a suitable language for historical fiction by crafting a restricted but flexible dialect that draws on the linguistic features of both modern and older forms of English. A quite different way of tackling the issue is exemplified by Alan Garner in his 1973 novel *Red Shift*. This book interweaves three connected narratives set in the second, seventeenth and twentieth centuries, the earliest of which involves a small group of Roman soldiers stranded in rural Cheshire after the destruction of their legion, the famous Ninth. Garner, writing at the height of the Vietnam War, has his legionaries speak a pastiche of GI slang, giving them names such as Magoo, Buzzard and Logan:

> 'When we hit their perimeter, Macy should kill four, five just like that. We grab assets, then eliminate [...] As the Ninth, there will be no abort; but if we louse it up, survivors cut ass out on their own. Questions?'
>
> (32)

In adopting this form of speech, Garner establishes an analogy between the hostile Vietnamese jungle and the experience of the Romans in Britain, a highly effective device for shocking readers from the cosily distant view of the Romans as 'ancient history', and indeed of Cheshire as somewhere intrinsically unthreatening. However, there is a danger that the contemporary reality of Vietnam will overshadow the actual circumstances of the Ninth Legion and 'throw readers out' of the second-century fiction. In fact Garner largely avoids this fate through his authoritative recreation of the material lives and beliefs of early Roman Cheshire, but such trade-offs are in the nature of analogies, and in using them Garner takes a calculated risk.

Garner handles language very differently in the other historical thread of the book, which describes the events surrounding a massacre by Royalist troops at Barthomley church in Cheshire in 1643. While Garner's Romans would have been speaking Latin, and the medieval characters who have dominated this chapter so far would have used forms of English more or less incomprehensible to modern child readers, by the mid-seventeenth century English had attained a form sufficiently close to that of today to make a 'straight' presentation of it feasible. Garner takes advantage of this fact, in his use both of educated voices (those of the Vicar and his son and the Royalist officer attacking the village) and of the Cheshire peasantry. While the dialect of the latter may be selectively deployed with an eye and an ear to accessibility, nothing spoken by the peasants Dick Steele or Randal Hassall would be an impossible utterance for a person of their time, place and class. The contrast between Garner's treatment of speech in his two historical sections is indicative of a more general divide in the possibilities for historical fiction as we move into the Early Modern era.

Analogy versus mimesis

The late sixteenth and early seventeenth centuries mark, very approximately, the point at which a new approach becomes available for historical writers, who are no longer confined to finding a modern equivalent for historical speech (as Garner does with his Romans) or to producing a stylized and cut-down version of historical speech (as Cushman does in *Catherine, Called Birdy*), but have the option of giving their characters language that is more realistically historical. We can illustrate this by turning briefly from Cushman's *Catherine, Called Birdy* to her 2010 novel *Alchemy and Meggy Swann*. Despite its being set almost 300 years later, the language of *Alchemy and Meggy Swann* can actually be more opaque to a modern reader than that of the thirteenth-century Birdy. Meggy's opening sentences, 'Ye toads and vipers!' (1) and 'Well met, carter' (3) both signal her linguistic distance from the world of the reader at least as firmly as anything written by Birdy, as does her Shakespearian fecundity when it comes to insults: 'Cease your bibble-babble, you gleeking goat's bladder!' (45) Paradoxically, in moving closer to the present it seems that writers may create a world apparently more linguistically archaic than that of the deep past, an effect accentuated in the case of *Meggy Swann* by the fact that the Elizabethan speech of its characters is juxtaposed with a modern-English third-person narration.

The transition from a workable substitute for historical speech to historical speech itself, and hence to a more mimetic representation of the past, is one that we see mirrored in non-linguistic areas. We have already noted that the analogies between past and present implied by Garner's allusions to Vietnam invite readers to understand unfamiliar aspects of history by reference to their own experience, and not just in terms of linguistic expression. His narrative of a rich, well-equipped empire brought low in the 'jungles' of a distant theatre of war offers readers a mutually enlightening perspective on the politics of both the second and twentieth centuries. However, once we begin to deal with more recent periods of history, in which the world looks and sounds more like our own, such explanatory analogies may seem increasingly superfluous. As we approach the present day, not only do forms of English tend to converge, but so do technology, politics and culture generally. This has important implications for the practice of historical fiction. The disputes that lie behind the English Civil Wars, for example, are still to some extent current, in a way that those between Richard II and the Lords Appellant no longer are. Questions of religious freedom and the established Church, of rights to political expression, of the role (if any) of the monarchy within the state, of the location of sovereignty, and so on, were debated throughout the 1640s and 1650s in terms that sound very familiar. Moreover, we are to an extent still living with the dispensation that arose directly out of the Civil Wars and of the 1688 revolution that was in many ways their final act. In contemporary Britain, meritocracy still sits uneasily with the notion that some people are born to rule, and this ambivalence leaches more generally into what has proved a remarkably tenacious class system. In terms of land ownership, Britain remains feudal in a way that most European countries do not, with some two-thirds of the land owned by just 189,000 mostly aristocratic families (0.3 per cent of the population) (Cahill 6), largely because the social radicalism of the English Revolution was checked and to a great extent reversed.

The ways in which historical writers treat the Civil Wars and the events surrounding them therefore have direct political implications, as well as the potential for analogical reading. Indeed, it would be hard to read a story of the Civil Wars that did not offer some kind of perspective on the current political order in the UK. This is not of course to deny that the history of the 20 years between 1640 and 1660 also deserves to be understood in its own terms. The Civil Wars were an extremely complex series of events: they were not a conflict between King and Parliament only, but at various times between Protestants and Catholics; between Laudians and Covenanters; between England, Scotland and Ireland; between Parliament and the Army; between Presbyterians, 'Congregationalists' and Commonwealth men, and between pragmatists and idealists of every stripe. With its reversals of fortune and power, its compromises and alliances of convenience, its intermeshing of political, religious and military struggles, this is a challenging and fascinating period.

In terms of children's fiction, the Civil Wars have elicited two broad approaches. The first considers the conflict as part of the national story, which in its divisions illuminates the variety of human nature and of human sympathies, as well as the specific political situation. This approach may well focus also on the tragedy of families and communities divided against themselves. The alternative is a more partisan approach, in which one side is seen as essentially justified in its cause, and the issue becomes one of whether right will triumph. In terms of partisanship, the Royalist cause has long been in the ascendant within fiction generally, and children's fiction in particular. In 1976 the children's writer and critic Robert Leeson sampled 'some two dozen "recommended" books on the English Civil War period', and his findings from that time do not seem dated now:

> I find that fourteen lean towards the Royalist side, some horizontally, five are in the increasingly familiar area of 'conflict of loyalties', and the other four may be said to do justice to the Parliamentary side. In this area we are barely out of the prehistory of the genre. It is to be much regretted that the whole of the 'Puritan' movement with its Prynnes and Lilburnes, its Miltons and Bunyans, its Cromwells and Winstanleys with their spiritual forebears and successors, still rates lower than the Royal tree-hopper and his followers, though its contribution to our present is so much greater.
>
> (Leeson 176)

This imbalance is perhaps not surprising: a view of Charles I as a suffering and even saint-like figure had been given classic expression in *Eikon Basilike* within days of his death, and became a constituent of his official reputation at the Restoration, with the anniversary of his execution being observed in *The Book of Common Prayer* as late as 1859 as the Feast of King Charles the Martyr. This context could hardly fail to leave its mark on early children's books such as Frederick Marryat's *The Children of the New Forest* (1847), but even for those who took a less adulatory view the Interregnum might still seem an anomalous period in English history, as the word itself implies, to which the return of Charles II to England offered a natural resolution. Beyond this there was (and is) a persistent contrast between the popular image of the Royalists as flamboyant and romantic figures, and of the Parliamentarian cause (particularly in its Puritan aspect) as the preserve of dour and joyless fanatics.

Some Civil War books attempt a more nuanced approach, and there is a long tradition of acknowledgement that this was not a conflict that divided the country along neat ideological lines. *The Children of the New Forest* itself is certainly a story that favours the Royalist cause, following as it does the misfortunes of the children of a Royalist officer killed at the battle of Naseby; but it includes as one of its major characters a sympathetically portrayed Puritan – Heatherstone, the Intendant given the task of managing the Forest lands. This pattern, of a fundamentally royalist book allowing for the possibility of 'good' Parliamentarians is one we see repeated in later nineteenth-century books such as G. A. Henty's *Friends, Though Divided* (1883). As Thomas Kullman has observed:

> This fictional formula [...] allows for the integration or 'containment' of systems of value which differ from the dominant conservative discourse. The straightforward and self-denying honesty of Cromwell and his Puritan followers is also given its due; the Restoration period is seen as a paradigm for national reconciliation.
>
> (77)

A more politically balanced variation on this theme is offered by Rosemary Sutcliff's *Simon* (1953), which traces the fortunes of two close friends. Simon, the protagonist, is the son of a Devon farmer critical of King Charles's policies, and is raised believing that 'unless the King learns better – unless he's *taught* better – soon there'll be no more freedom in England, for he grows into more and more of a tyrant every year' (29). Simon's friend Amias, however, son of the local doctor, is a Royalist, and to Simon's horror the two find themselves on opposing sides in the war. Their fractured friendship is a synecdoche for the ruin of England itself. 'Son against father, brother against brother, friend against friend', as Simon's father puts it: 'Civil war is a hideous thing' (34). Many of the features we noted in the discussion of Roman and British perspectives in Sutcliff's 1954 novel, *The Eagle of the Ninth*, are anticipated in the depiction of civil war in *Simon*: neither the Royalist nor the Puritan side is portrayed as homogeneous or as wholly virtuous or villainous, and ultimately, personal ties will help heal the fractured nation. By the time the war is over Simon and Amias's friendship has been restored and they can debate the issues without bitterness. Simon agrees that, for all the Commonwealth's virtues (and it is made clear that there is more justice than under Charles), it will be a temporary institution, and that monarchy is the natural form of government for England. In conversation, he justifies what Amias calls the 'dreariness' of post-War England as a regimen appropriate to a sick patient:

> 'You're a surgeon, leastwise you will be soon. You know how to deal with a man who's sick; you knock off all the things he likes doing, and make him eat plain food, and bleed him and give him black draughts; and maybe he doesn't like you while the treatment lasts. But he's all the better for it afterwards.'
>
> 'Aye, but is there going to be an "afterwards"?' Amias countered.
>
> 'Surely. This isn't – natural, somehow, not for England. One day we shall have a King again.'
>
> (252)

The case of *I, Coriander*

Given these precedents it is striking that Sally Gardner's historical fantasy *I, Coriander* (2005), possibly the most prominent children's book to be set in this period during the last decade, takes such a radically Manicheistic view of the conflict, identifying virtually all the sympathetic characters with the Royalist cause, and making the Parliamentarians almost uniformly cruel and hypocritical. It is worth taking some time to examine why and how this is accomplished, for in *I, Coriander* many of the issues we have discussed in this chapter come together. The mixed genre of the text, along with its openness to both mimetic and analogical readings, allow its identification of royalism with the forces of good to appear narratively inevitable, but only by dint of a good deal of historical manipulation.

The story, told by Coriander at some point after the Restoration, begins about the time of the execution of Charles I, when she is six. Coriander's father, Master Hobie, is a wealthy London merchant, her mother Eleanor (secretly) a princess from Faerie, and the whole household is staunchly Royalist. When Eleanor dies, a friend warns Hobie that his wealth may be confiscated by Cromwell, and suggests he marry 'a good Puritan woman' (56) to prevent this. Hobie agrees and weds Maud, a Puritan hypocrite who uses her feigned religious devotion to justify her cruelty to her own daughter Hester. Soon Maud introduces a preacher into the household, Arise Fell – a man who is not only Maud's erstwhile partner in witch-finding and extortion, but has also acted as her pimp. Hobie flees the country after receiving warning of his imminent arrest for his Royalist sympathies, abandoning Coriander to the mercy of Maud and Arise, who abuse and starve her. Finally, Arise locks Coriander in a large wooden chest and leaves her to die.

To her surprise, Coriander awakes in Faerie, a land where the politics are curiously reminiscent of those in both her own household and England generally. Here, Nablus is the king, but real power lies with his second wife, Queen Rosmore, who is effectively a usurper. Having killed Nablus's first wife and his daughter, Rosmore is about to marry her own daughter, Unwin, to the reluctant Prince Tycho. Coriander, who learns that Nablus's daughter was her mother Eleanor, falls in love with Tycho and eventually manages to save him from Rosmore, but feels she must then return to this world to discover what has happened to her father. The couple fear they will never be reunited, since time moves differently in the two worlds. Back in London Coriander finds that her father has returned, now that Cromwell is dead and the monarchy restored. The family goes to watch Charles II process into London, and in an inexplicable (or at any rate unexplained) scene Coriander meets the King's eyes, then those of his horse, before experiencing an epiphany that sends her running to her father's garden. There she finds Tycho and they embrace, somehow knowing that they can now be together, and that the two worlds of Faerie and England have been made one.

It is possible to fault *I, Coriander* in terms of its historical accuracy concerning material culture and language. It is unlikely that Mr Hobie would have been drinking morning coffee in his own house in the early 1650s (61) or that his family would have toasted Charles II's return in 1660 with 'glasses of champagne' (290), for example, or indeed that Coriander would regard medicinal leeches as 'instruments of torture' (45); but in this respect the novel is not exceptional amongst recent children's historical texts. In terms of politics and ideology, however, its systematic omissions, elisions and distortions make *I, Coriander*'s conservative political stance unusually explicit. To begin with, for such a politically committed book there is a notable lack of historical context. The uninformed reader might imagine that religious and political persecution were recent Puritan inventions. The oppressions of the Stuart era (which led to such well-known events as the sailing of the Mayflower) are omitted from this account, as are the 11 years of Charles I's absolutist rule, his abuse of power through the notorious Star Chamber, his ingenious methods of taxation and his support for Archbishop Laud's attempt to impose religious conformity throughout England and Scotland. There seems to be no legitimate motive at all for dissent from Charles's rule, in fact, and those of the Parliamentarian persuasion are accordingly drawn very negatively, as fanatics or (more likely) hypocrites. The two apparent exceptions to this rule are Hester's father, described by her as 'a tall man without a grain of ill humour' (158), and her brother Ned. Hester explains her father's reason for fighting in the Parliamentary army in idealistic terms: 'In the eyes of the Lord all men were equal, he said, and so it should be on earth' (158). However, this gesture towards something like the dialogic nature of books such as Sutcliff's *Simon* is immediately undercut by the attribution of a far less noble motive, that of escaping a harridan: 'I think my father was glad when the war came and he could escape [...]. He said a thousand Royalists would be hard pushed to match my mother when the temper was upon her' (158–9). It seems that, while all the book's Royalists are Royalist on principle, Parliamentarians are driven by less exalted considerations, and may even become Parliamentarians by accident. Ned is said simply to have 'got caught up in the fighting and joined Cromwell's New Model Army' (278), which sounds a rather haphazard form of military commitment. Moreover, he is said to look 'pleased' at Charles II's return. Ned may be a nominal Puritan, but his good nature allows him to be happily reconciled to monarchy.

Gardner's narrative seems designed to channel reader sympathy towards the Royalist cause, and this leads it to make some very eccentric historical assumptions. For example, as a London merchant Coriander's father, Mr Hobie, belongs to the class historically most likely to hold Parliamentarian sympathies, yet Hobie is a passionate Royalist. This is not impossible but it is sufficiently anomalous to warrant some kind of justification or explanation, yet none is offered. It is taken for granted that Hobie, as a good man, will also be loyal to the King. Similarly, Coriander is brought up to love reading and writing by her Royalist parents, but her Puritan stepmother Maud disparages literacy. In reality Puritans, with their emphasis on the importance of reading and understanding the Bible, were far more likely to educate females than were other members of society. A book-hating Puritan is no more an impossibility than a Royalist London merchant, but both are such atypical creatures, and both tend to corral reader sympathy in so much the same direction, that this begins to look like more than a random oddity.

I, Coriander is not of course only a realist historical novel but also a fantasy, and its genre is important to its rhetorical presentation of the era's politics. This is evident in its personification of the Parliamentarian cause in the figure of Oliver Cromwell. Rather than being one increasingly prominent person in a complex alliance of army and Parliamentary forces, Cromwell in this novel is a usurper, placed in stark personal opposition to the true king. Thus Coriander refers to Ned's having joined 'Cromwell's New Model army' and fought 'for Cromwell' (278, 280). This perspective is established early in the book, in a passage that voices the text's ideology through the words of the trusted family servant, Danes:

> 'It was nothing short of murder', she said, wiping the tears from her eyes.
>
> 'Who has been murdered?' I asked with interest.
>
> 'It is the King', she replied. 'It is a wicked thing they have done, and no good will come of it.'
>
> 'Who has done what?'
>
> 'Oliver Cromwell and his axe man', said Danes. 'Terrible.
>
> Who would think that we would live to see our very own King have his head chopped off?'
>
> (10)

This reduction of the Parliamentary cause to an individual man amounts to a serious historical distortion, but its effect is to make Cromwell structurally equivalent to the story's other 'usurpers', Maud and Queen Rosmore, and to assimilate him to the fairy-tale morality within which the novel places them, where stepmothers and wicked queens may be labelled unproblematically as evil.

The fairy-tale discourse extends into other areas, such as physical appearance. *I, Coriander* makes use of the kind of moral shorthand offered by stories like 'Cinderella' in order to establish an easy correspondence between physical and moral beauty. Thus, while

Coriander's dead mother Eleanor was beautiful (like Coriander herself), both Maud and Queen Rosmore's daughter Unwin are fat and ugly, and Arise is 'crooked' in body as well as mind. Ironically, Coriander's attitude might be described as puritanical in its disgust for fatness and physical appetite. Maud is regularly likened to a pig: in one of many descriptions of her overeating, she 'stuff[s] another large piece of meat into the tiny slit of her mouth' (81), while Unwin has 'double chins that spilled down on to her chest' and 'flesh squeezing out like an over-filled meat pie' (114). While this way of using body-type to indicate moral status is typical of fairy-tales (Stephens 141) it sits less comfortably within an historical fiction dealing with such a complex and morally nuanced event as a civil war and its aftermath.

Nor are these the only ways in which *I, Coriander*'s fantasy and realist elements are combined to striking ideological effect. Early in the book we hear that, before Coriander was born, Master Hobie's only ship sank, leaving his business on the verge of ruin. However, his fortunes changed after he met Medlar (an intimate of King Nablus from the court of Faerie) on the road on Midsummer's Eve. Medlar told him he had been robbed, and Hobie generously gave him his cloak. Medlar promised that his kindness would be rewarded, and the next day Hobie met his future wife Eleanor for the first time. Not only did Medlar arrange this, but Hobie's ship also returned safely and from that time on his life was 'charmed with love and good fortune' (6). This encounter is later glossed by Medlar himself, who tells Coriander that he liked her father, because '[h]e did not wish, like other mortals, for things to be better. He accepted his fate with grace' (132).

This fairy-tale episode is narratively self-contained, but it finds a striking parallel later in the book. When Master Hobie escapes to France to avoid arrest, he 'put[s] his only remaining ship at the service of His Majesty' (261), and with the Restoration is again well rewarded for his generosity to the exiled king. The parallel with his charity to Medlar is clear: in both Faerie and the real world, generosity to one supposedly down on his luck is rewarded materially. Fairy-tale conventions are thus made both to trump economic reality (a merchant who did not wish 'for things to be better' would be unlikely to thrive in the fierce trading conditions of mid-seventeenth-century London), and also to legitimate a quietist political position (those who accepted their 'fate with grace' would presumably be disinclined to resist the injustice suffered under a would-be absolute monarch such as Charles I).

Towards the end of the book, Coriander enjoys a supper with her father, Ned, Hester, their friend Master Thankless and several others. The structural function of this harmonious episode is to foreshadow the final fusion of England and Faerie upon the return of the King himself. Coriander looks fondly around the room, and notes the variety of people there: 'a Roundhead who had fought for Cromwell and Royalists who had supported the King, each one willing to die for his beliefs, and yet here we all were with more to unite us than divide us' (280–1). The tone of reconciliation is clear; yet Coriander's words stand in contrast to the story she herself has told. Of those present, only Ned has in fact been willing to fight, let alone die, for his beliefs. The others have done their best to stay out of trouble. Her father, notably, not only married a woman whose beliefs were antithetical to his own in order to preserve his fortune, but subsequently fled the country and abandoned his daughter to a cruel stepmother so as to save his own neck. Yet such is Coriander's narrative anxiety to present this reconciliation and the king's return as the natural consummation of the book's events that this passes unnoticed both by her and (to judge by the reviews) by many readers as well. A comparison with similar scenes in Sutcliff's *Simon* or Rosemary Wells's American Civil War novel *Red Moon at Sharpsburg* (2007) makes clear the extent to which the rapprochement in *I, Coriander* pays lip service to multivocality and breadth of sympathy, while doing little or nothing to expand its partisan viewpoint.

The conclusion of *I, Coriander* makes the text's (and not just its narrator's) political orientation even more explicit. The restoration of Charles II not only stands in parallel to events in Faerie, it is also shown to be in some way identical with them, to the extent that the return of the English monarchy is sufficient to unite Faerie and the mundane world, although what this might mean for our understanding of Restoration England remains mysterious: 'in that moment I knew that this world and the world beneath the silvery mirror had become one, all was well and the future was ours for the taking' (293).

More perhaps than any other historical novel of recent times, *I, Coriander* depends on the wholesale adoption of a dualistic, fairy-tale reading of events, including fairy-tale's intolerance of non-beautiful bodies and political systems other than absolute monarchy. In Gardner's novel fairy-tale becomes not only a metaphor for real-life events but a political and social ideology, to be read directly in the politics of seventeenth-century England.

Its political crudity notwithstanding, *I, Coriander* has been an extremely successful book, both commercially and critically, winning positive reviews and the 2005 Nestlé Children's Book Award. In her review in *The Times*, the influential critic Amanda Craig singled out the modern relevance of the story for praise: 'Gardner's passionate loathing of the Puritans, backed up by considerable research, is particularly resonant at a time when London is under attack from another brand of fanatics' (Craig). Significantly, Craig identifies the story's value for her own time in the 'loathing' expressed through its othering rhetoric, and associates the government of Cromwell with the terrorist acts that had killed 56 people in London some three weeks before the publication of her review, enabling both to be dismissed as 'fanatics'.

The comparison between Gardner's hypocritical Puritans and the murderous but far-from-hypocritical London suicide bombers of July 2005 may seem quite tenuous, and that between the bombers and the historical English Commonwealth still more so; but both tell us something about the way in which Craig read the book, with Cromwell and the Puritans standing not only for themselves or their own political and religious principles but for 'fanatics' of every stripe. The bombers' suicides are a mark of their fanaticism, but for those whose cause the text approves, being 'willing to die for [one's] beliefs' (as Coriander puts it) is read as admirable. We have discussed analogical writing in connection with books such as *Red Shift*, but in this case the mechanism involved is rather different. *I, Coriander*'s Puritans do not invite specific comparison with Islamic jihadists in the way that *Red Shift*'s legionaries do with GIs. Rather, Craig sees Gardner's book as 'a rich fairytale for our times' – a far vaguer phrase.

I, Coriander is, in part, literally a fairy-tale, and its parallel stories – one set in seventeenth-century England, the other in Faerie – work rhetorically to reinforce and legitimate each other. In *I, Coriander* religious, political and even personal details are obliterated by the broad archetypal brush strokes of fairy-tale in a way that flattens out and systematically distorts history, turning human beings into creatures whose moral status is instantly recognizable from their body shape, half a suffering nation into fools or hypocrites, Cromwell into a usurping villain, and the Stuarts into a line of just and benevolent kings. It is at this point, perhaps, that we should cease thinking of *I, Coriander* as primarily an historical fantasy, and recognize it as a species of propaganda – and one made all the more potent because the historical period in which it is set is not widely taught, meaning that child readers may have relatively little contextual knowledge to set against its partisan portrayal.

In proposing a distinction between analogy and mimesis in the representation of the past, we suggested the decades around the turn of the seventeenth century as the period at which it becomes practicable for modern writers to attempt a mimetic representation of language, and recognized that – as in the case of the Civil Wars – the political issues of this period are still 'live' in a way that is not true to the same extent of earlier history. Gardner's dual narrative of Britain and Faerie in *I, Coriander* enables both a mimetic and an analogical approach. As a mimetic representation of the politics of the 1650s the text's allegiance is clearly royalist and anti-Puritan. However, as Craig's review demonstrates, the present-day applications of this political orientation are also available to an analogical reading, which is facilitated by the modern tradition of reading fairy-tale plots so as to highlight their archetypal significance.

Taking account of *I, Coriander*'s status as an historical fantasy allows us insight into the function of genre in historical representation, a subject to be explored more extensively in the next chapter. Rather than see the fairy-tale parts of the narrative as discrete from the book's representation of history, we believe them to contribute significantly to the rhetorical force of its more conventionally historical passages, enabling the text's distortions to pass unremarked, and allowing the generic conventions of fairy tale to 'bleed' into the realist and the political parts of the narrative. This is not to suggest that it would have been impossible to write and successfully publish a non-fantasy book that included many of the same tendentious historical claims and interpretations. As we have noted, the Puritans in particular have acquired a popular reputation that makes them vulnerable to a two-dimensional representation, of which Gardner's book is one amongst many. The image of Puritans in general, and of Cromwell in particular, as oppressive and humourless continues to fulfil a function within British political and cultural discourse quite independent of whatever historical truth it may or may not have.

In this chapter we have attempted to find a more adaptable methodology than Rebecca Barnhouse's with which to discuss texts that depart from historical fact, noting a number of circumstances that might justify anachronisms, and making a case for the inclusion of attitudes and beliefs beyond those that written history and literature have represented as 'typical'. We have adapted the terminology of foreignization and domestication, first developed within translation theory, in order to describe the compromises necessarily involved in representing a world in many respects alien to today's readers, and analysed the consequences of different textual choices in the areas of language and of ideology. Overall, we have argued that the question of authorial responsibility is far more complex than one of simply approving of historical accuracy and disapproving of anachronism. This does not mean that the question disappears, and there are texts – *I, Coriander* amongst them – where the consequence of a cavalier attitude (to coin a phrase) towards history has been pernicious, both to the representation of history itself and in its application to present-day politics. However, some types of historical book do not merely permit anachronisms and other departures from historical fact, but are fundamentally *dependent* upon such departures. How such texts operate, and what becomes of the concept of authenticity in such a context, will be the subject of Chapter 5.

5

Dreams of Things That Never Were: Authenticity and Genre

In Chapter 4, our discussion of authenticity in historical texts for children centred on the concept of anachronism. In considering a number of works set in the six centuries following the Norman Conquest, we found that defining writers' obligations simply in terms of fidelity to the material and mental realities of the past, as advocated by Rebecca Barnhouse, did not provide adequately for the complex demands inevitably made on texts, not least in terms of accessibility to modern readers. A further limitation of her model, to which we have so far alluded only briefly, is that it does not take account of the ways in which historical considerations intersect with those of genre. Although the subtitle of Barnhouse's book refers in a general way to 'young adult literature', in practice she confines her analysis to realist historical fiction, her preference being for texts featuring plausible and representative characters and events. Where she acknowledges the existence of other genres it is largely to set up a *cordon sanitaire* between them and realist history. For example, although Barnhouse devotes a chapter of her book to fiction set in medievalesque fantasy worlds, her emphasis is on distinguishing such texts from realist historical fiction and deprecating those critics who confuse the two, rather than on what fantasies may actually be doing with historical material; and she entirely ignores the more difficult case of historical fantasy set in our own world. As became clear in our discussion of *I, Coriander*, however, genre has a profound effect on the ways in which texts and their relationships to history are read.

When readers process a text, they provisionally assign it to a position on a generic map, a position that has important implications for the way in which anachronism (amongst other things) is likely to be understood. Anachronism in a text recognized as belonging to a playful or parodic comic genre, for example, will be read quite differently from anachronism in a realist historical novel. In Valerie Wilding's contribution to Scholastic's 'Dead Famous' series of comic histories, *Boudica and Her Barmy Army* (2005), it is stated several times that the Celtic Britons had no system of writing, yet the book includes an illustration of Boudica's birth announcement (15), pages from her secret diary, a recruitment advert for trainee druids (41–2) and the 'Spring Wedding Issue' of the British magazine *Greetings!* announcing the forthcoming marriage of Boudica and King Prasutagus (63–5). This inconsistency is unlikely to be criticized, however, and indeed the obtrusiveness of the anachronism is both one of the ways in which the text indicates its comic status and a source of humour in its own right. Conversely, if Cynthia Harnett were to introduce electric shears into her assiduous recreation of the fifteenth-century wool trade, *The Wool-Pack* (1951), then her text's effectiveness as a realistic historical novel would be greatly undermined.

This is a simple example, but it illustrates the more general point that readers' assumptions about the kind of text they are reading profoundly affect the way in which they interpret any anachronistic or otherwise unhistorical elements they may encounter. In this chapter we will explore further the ways in which genre conventions shape the reading of historical texts, and in doing so we will focus on alternative history, as a genre defined precisely by its divergence from historical consensus. Where such texts are published for children they face particular challenges, because children are in general unlikely to have as thorough a background knowledge of consensus accounts of history as adults, and the cues that might be expected to alert them to a text's allohistorical status (in the form of 'obviously' non-historical elements) may consequently be less visible. These issues are not the sole preserve of alternative histories, however, and we will also consider related questions in connection with books exhibiting intertextual, and what we call 'quasi-historical', qualities, as well as books depicting real historical individuals in fictional situations.

Alternative histories

By 'alternative histories', we refer to texts that show, not what happened in the past but what *might* have happened had circumstances differed in one or more respects. Most critical discussion of alternative history has been either by historians, who typically call alternative histories 'counterfactuals' and use them as the basis of thought experiments to model historical change, or by critics working on science fiction, who tend to view alternative history as belonging within that genre (William Collins; Hellekson, 'Toward a Taxonomy', *The Alternate History*). The latter group in particular has provided a number of helpful taxonomies. Karen Hellekson divides 'alternate histories' (the term commonly used in science fiction criticism) into nexus stories, 'true alternate histories', and parallel worlds stories. The first two of these assume the central importance of a 'break' or splitting-off point between our own world and that of the alternative history, with nexus stories being about the events that cause the break, and true alternate histories being set at some later date. The third type, the parallel worlds story, posits a multiplicity of worlds, each of which instantiates one of the many possible directions history might have taken – a model sometimes assimilated to Hugh Everett III's 'many worlds' quantum mechanical model (Hellekson, 'Toward a Taxonomy' 251).

Another taxonomy is offered by William Collins, who categorizes alternative histories primarily in terms of their relationship to the reader's point of view. Thus his 'plural uchronia' is a tale of (at least) two worlds, which sets the alternative history alongside that familiar to the reader, while the 'pure uchronia' covers texts that allude only to the world of alternative history without reference to any other. Collins's 'infinite presents' category corresponds roughly to Hellekson's 'parallel worlds'; while 'time-travel alteration', as its name implies, involves travellers moving through history and altering the course of events in consequence, as in Ray Bradbury's 'A Sound of Thunder' (1952).

These high-concept approaches to alternative history provide a useful vocabulary, and work well for the science fiction texts to which these critics tend to apply them, although some have questioned if either time-travel or multiverse stories belong with the genre of alternate history strictly defined (see James, 'The Limits of Alternate History'). Within children's literature the generic situation is frequently rather more mixed. For example, a well-known work that uses some alternative history tropes is Philip Pullman's 'His Dark Materials' trilogy (1995–2000). The first of these novels, *Northern*

Lights, includes an explicit description of the way in which history may branch in more than one direction at a given 'nexus event' (to use Hellekson's phrase, itself borrowed from Poul Anderson).[1] As Pullman's Lord Asriel explains:

> '[...] that world, and every other universe, came about as a result of possibility. Take the example of tossing a coin: it can come down heads or tails, and we don't know before it lands which way it's going to fall. If it comes down heads, that means that the possibility of its coming down tails has collapsed. Until that moment the two possibilities were equal. But on another world, it does come down tails. And when that happens, the two worlds split apart.'
> (376–7)

The world of *Northern Lights* is one in which the break from our own history appears to have occurred in the sixteenth century, although this is not explicitly stated. In this world's history the Reformation never happened and Calvin, although he existed, became Pope instead of founding his Genevan theocracy. Without the fatal weakening of its temporal power occasioned by the Reformation, the Church has established its hegemony over much of the world. Although many of the institutions in *Northern Lights* are familiar (there is still a University of Oxford), post-sixteenth-century inventions tend, where they exist, to be given unfamiliar names, with electrical devices, for example, being described as 'anbaric'. We might describe *Northern Lights* as a 'true alternate history' (in Hellekson's terms), in that it is set some considerable time after the point at which the history of its world diverges from ours, and in Collins's terms as a plural uchronia, in that some at least of its characters are aware of the existence of worlds beyond their own.

If we choose to consider Pullman's text in this way, however, it quickly becomes apparent that it is actually a rather problematic example of alternative history. The differences between the world of its heroine, Lyra Belacqua, and our own are far more fundamental than could be accounted for in terms of the non-occurrence of the Reformation. Lyra's world features witches, talking armoured bears, cliff-ghasts and other creatures unknown in our own history either before or after the sixteenth century. Still more fundamentally, not only is every human in that world accompanied by a daemon, a physical manifestation of their soul in animal form, but this appears always to have been the case, so that (for example) their Bible makes reference to the daemons of Adam and Eve. For this to be an alternative world in the sense that Lord Asriel describes, the nexus event must have occurred at a point far earlier in history, or more likely prehistory. In that case, however, the problem of explaining how Lyra's world and our own remain nevertheless so eerily similar in so many respects appears insurmountable.

Considered from the point of view of the theories of alternative history current within science fiction criticism, *Northern Lights* is guilty of gross inconsistencies: its metaphysics crumble at a touch. Nevertheless, judging from its huge popular and critical success, this has not been experienced as a major problem by most readers. Even those who are critical of Pullman's work tend to site their disagreements elsewhere, in his hostile attitude towards the Church, for example, and in his didacticism, rather than on the question of his multiverse's errant nexus event. We may therefore ask whether an approach to alternative history that relies exclusively on the perspectives provided by science fiction criticism may be in danger of missing much of what is going on in the book's approach to history. The orientation of such theories towards discussion of the mechanism by which alternate histories come into being, and the physical and metaphysical relations between various worlds, may be of limited value for discussing texts in which such matters are not always foregrounded, even if (as in Lord Asriel's speech quoted above) they are explicitly set out.

'His Dark Materials' is usually discussed as fantasy rather than science fiction, and in his entry for 'Alternate Worlds' in *The Encyclopedia of Fantasy* John Clute makes a distinction between alternative worlds in these two genres that may be helpful in Pullman's case:

> If a story presents the alteration of some specific event as a premise from which to argue a new version of history – favourite 'branch points' include the victory of the Spanish Armada in 1588, the victory of the South in the American Civil War, and Hitler Wins scenarios – then that story is likely to be sf. If, however, a story presents a different version of the history of Earth *without arguing the difference* – favourite differences include the significant, history-changing presence of magic, or of actively participating

> gods, or of Atlantis or other lost lands, or of crosshatches with Otherworlds – then that story is likely to be fantasy.
>
> (21: emphasis in original)

This is a sensible distinction, and might plausibly be applied to some aspects of *Northern Lights*. We might, for example, want to argue that Pullman's novel represents 'our world but with talking bears and witches', just as we could say that Patricia Wrede and Caroline Stevermer's *Sorcery and Cecelia* (1988) is 'the Regency but with magic', or Naomi Novik's adult 'Temeraire' series (2006–present) is 'the Napoleonic wars but with dragons' – and simply accept these premises as axiomatic. Again, we could place the steampunk elements of Pullman's text in the same tradition as such fantasies as Philip Reeve's Victorian *Larklight* (2006) and Scott Westerfeld's Great War *Leviathan* (2009) (both the opening books of trilogies). Westerfeld has described steampunk as 'an art of collaging technologies and history' ('Teatime with Scott Westerfeld'): although it is possible to look at the genetically engineered creatures used as engines of war in *Leviathan* and question how his 'Darwinists' managed in a few decades not only to understand evolution but also to master gene theory, DNA, and genetic engineering of a sophistication far exceeding current real-world capabilities, we are more likely to accept this as a premise of his book's world and genre (which commonly features such retro-futuristic elements) than as a puzzle requiring an alternative-history solution.

In the case of *Northern Lights* this latitude is not as easily available, in that Pullman's novel *does* have at least an implied 'branch point' and does 'argue the difference' between worlds (an argument continued at considerable length in the succeeding books of the trilogy), even as it also exhibits many of the features Clute identifies as distinctive topoi of fantasy. Part of the difficulty in reading Pullman's trilogy, then, is that his books' generic cues are mixed. On the one hand, we have Lord Asriel's explicit description of the nexus point principle, and a resolution of the trilogy that depends on a science-fictional understanding of its various worlds and the ways in which travel between them can be possible. Moreover, the world of the Mulefa, described in the third book in the series, *The Amber Spyglass*, presents us with an extended portrait of how evolution might have taken a different course from that followed on earth, a theme closely allied with the concept of nexus events and the various histories that may branch from them. On the other hand, these features coexist with fantasy elements, such as daemons and talking armoured bears, that seem insusceptible to evolutionary explanation; while the nexus event of Lyra's world is either too recent to account for the differences between it and our own, or else too far in the past to account for the similarities.

In effect, Pullman's text seems to require that we run the reading techniques of fantasy in tandem with those of science-fictional alternative history. Lyra's world is framed not just as a 'might have been' but also as a dark satire, a distorted version of our own world as it actually is. Pullman's Church is a vessel into which everything that Pullman finds objectionable about organized religion has been poured: its intolerance of dissent, its bureaucratic lack of feeling, its misogyny, hypocrisy and horror of human sexuality. Conversely, those aspects of Christianity Pullman finds more appealing, notably the figure of Jesus, are absent. This schematic simplification may serve a purpose in making Pullman's satirical point clearer than would have been the case had it been diffused through the complex filter of a more realistically represented world. However, from an alternative-history perspective it, along with the effective absence of any world religion other than Christianity, is a weakness. The extent to which the generically heterogeneous and, at times, contradictory nature of Pullman's creation detracts from the overall success of his achievement in 'His Dark Materials' depends in part no doubt on the personal tastes and priorities of his readers. Pullman's inventiveness, storytelling power and accomplishment as a stylist provide rich compensation for the inconsistencies in his worldbuilding, but inconsistencies they remain. To the extent that 'His Dark Materials' offers an historical counterfactual critique of organized religion and ecclesiastical power, his work is weakened by them.

A very different example of an apparent alternative history that turns out to be unexpectedly problematic is Jenny Davidson's *The Explosionist* (2008). As her 'Author's Note' explains, Davidson's book is set in a world with a specific nexus event, having 'split off from our own when Napoleon beat Wellington at the Battle of Waterloo on June 18, 1815' (450). One might expect, then, that part of the book's interest would lie in tracing the consequential chain of events stretching from that moment to the time the novel is set, in 1938, and at first this appears to be the case. The story is told by 15-year-old Sophie, a schoolgirl living in Scotland. At this point Scotland (but not England) is part of a new Hanseatic League, while England has fallen to Europe at the end of a conflict somewhat resembling the Great War of our history.

At this geopolitical level Davidson's alternative history works well, and her supposition that the Hanseatic League of Baltic cities might have been revived in response to Napoleonic dominance of continental Europe is an original and plausible one. However, from the point of view of alternative history there are two serious problems. First, although this is a 'pure uchronia' in which no character is aware of other possible histories than their own, Sophie still appears to recognize the presence of a nexus event: 'Modern European history was a subject one couldn't *not* be interested in, at least in Sophie's opinion. Every one of the abuses and atrocities that filled the daily papers could be traced back in one way or another to the fatal day in 1815 when Napoleon defeated Wellington and slaughtered the British forces at Waterloo' (57–8). Significant as a Napoleonic victory at Waterloo would undoubtedly have been, from the perspective of a girl living in an independent Scotland in 1938, that battle would surely be but one event amongst many, with other events leading to and from it, rather than being recognized as the *fons et origo* of all the world's woes. Stripped of our extra-narrative awareness that this is when Sophie's history split from our own, it is highly unlikely that Waterloo would be seen as the historical reset button it is portrayed as here.

Still more problematic is the facetious way in which Davidson plays with the histories of some historical individuals. In Sophie's world the telephone was invented by Aleksandr Tolstoy Bell, 'son of an eminent Scottish educator of the deaf and his glamorous Russian wife' (183). In reality, however, the deafness of Bell's mother, Eliza Symonds, was one of the main factors that spurred him to research the nature of sound transmission, and it is not obvious that his career would have taken quite the same turn had his father married a glamorous Russian. The achievement of Marconi as the inventor of radio (or 'Marconi waves' [219]) remains, but elsewhere there are arbitrary changes. Thus Sophie claims to like talking about 'the theology of Count Tolstoy, the novels of Richard Wagner, the verse of Albert Einstein, or the operas of James Joyce' (62). Perhaps the prize for the strangest reimagining must go to Davidson's version of Oscar Wilde, here pictured in his new career as an obstetrician and inventor of the baby incubator (282).

A world in which none of these people is famous for the things that gave them renown in our reality is making an obvious point about the unexpected outcomes that might follow from a single change to the historical record, but it undermines that point by assuming that all these men would have retained their eminence, even if in different fields – as if greatness were a quality independent of historical circumstance. This kind of switch may raise a smile, and it may be that Davidson felt the need to include some eye-catching details in order to alert her (primarily North American) teenage readers to the alternative-historical nature of her story, but the price paid in terms of the novel's coherence as an alternative history is high. In a note at the end of the sequel to *The Explosionist* (2008), *Invisible Things* (2010), Davidson admits that many of her assumptions are 'monumentally unlikely', given her world's premises, adding (with reference to her treatment of Neils Bohr as an example) that she has taken 'a very great liberty, given the rules of alternate history, and [...] taken it ruthlessly and without remorse' (263–4). But to acknowledge the issue is not to remedy it.

Alternatives to alternative history

Pullman's and Davidson's texts both signal their commitment to the principle of the nexus point and the alternative history consequences that flow from it, and it is for this reason that we have been somewhat critical of their inconsistencies in this regard. However, some texts appear committed neither to science-fictional alternative history (as epitomized by the nexus point) nor to fantasy alternative history on the lines suggested by Clute. Rather, they sit between fantasy and realist historical fiction, and can be seen as deriving primarily from either tradition. All fantasy writing borrows elements from the mundane world, even if only such generic items as clothing, food, roads and weapons, or social and political institutions such as family and kingship. Considered from the fantasy perspective, alternative history can be seen as a type of fantasy that happens to borrow additional items: physical geography, names, borders, languages and some historical events. Conversely, all realist historical fiction diverges from known history inasmuch as it introduces fictional characters and events. Viewed from the realist historical perspective, alternative history is simply a form of historical writing that goes further than most in this divergence. While historical fiction typically operates in the interstices of the historical record, refraining from offering outright contradictions of consensus accounts of history, alternative history goes further and offers precisely such a contradiction. This may seem like a sharply drawn line to overstep, but references to the seemingly solid body of 'the historical record' should not blind us to the extent to which history is an interpretative enterprise through and through rather than a set of palpable facts, and as such has fiction-making at its heart. As the historian Richard Lebow has argued, 'the difference between so-called factual and counter-factual arguments is greatly exaggerated; it is one of degree, not of kind' (551).[2]

A rich example that will illustrate the case is Joan Aiken's series of novels beginning with *The Wolves of Willoughby Chase* (1962), and continuing with *Black Hearts in Battersea* (1964), *Night Birds on Nantucket* (1966) and *The Cuckoo Tree* (1971) amongst others. Collectively these novels relate a series of adventures (primarily those of the sharp-witted Dido Twite) in a nineteenth century where the Stuarts are still on the throne, wolves have entered England through the recently constructed Channel Tunnel, and there is a constant threat from Hanoverian plotters wishing to install the Pretender, Bonnie Prince Georgie, as king.

How can we characterize these books, in terms of their handling of alternative history? They make no mention at all of other worlds, but it is certainly possible to use the science-fictional approach discussed above and seek out a nexus event that splits the history of Aiken's world from our own. The novels could then be considered as a 'true alternate history', or 'pure uchronia'. Until the time of Charles II, at any rate, the history of Aiken's England appears identical to ours, with Wren building St Paul's Cathedral to the same plan after the Great Fire of London, for example. Perhaps the most obvious nexus event would be the series of machinations that in our world led to the Elector of Hanover being invited to assume the title of George I in 1714, but in Aiken's presumably did not. Alternatively the event might be the Old Pretender's 1708 attempted landing in Scotland, in reality repulsed by Admiral Byng but in fiction perhaps the start of a successful attempt to wrest the throne from Queen Anne. However, both these dates are rendered problematic by the fact that the king in Aiken's 1832 England is James III – a regnal number that had already been claimed by James II's son, who would no doubt have used it had he succeeded in establishing himself. Again, Aiken may have had in mind an England in which Anne's young son, William, Duke of Gloucester, did not die in 1700 from a chill caught through excessive dancing at his 11th birthday party (thus extinguishing the Stuarts' Protestant branch) but lived to continue the dynasty (Waller 352). That scenario has the appeal of poignantly illustrating how precarious the great events of history can be (for want of an early bedtime the kingdom was lost), and Aiken did indeed suggest in a 1996 essay that her world supposed 'that all Queen Anne's children had not died' ('Interpreting the Past' 72). However, in that case the Hanoverians would not have been even distant contenders for the crown. It was only once the 1701 Act of Settlement, passed in the wake of William's death, had disbarred several dozen Catholics with closer blood claims than the Elector that George became a likely heir. The same objection applies to an England in which James II saw off the Glorious Revolution of 1688.

A nexus event for Aiken's series thus proves strangely elusive. Not only that, Aiken also presents us with a England that, while differing wildly from the historical nineteenth century in some respects, in others resembles it far more closely than one might expect in a world that had branched from our own in about 1700. Richard Lebow terms this the 'interconnectedness' problem, that is, the tendency to 'assume that one aspect of the past can be changed and everything else kept constant', whereas 'even minimal rewrites of history may alter the context in such a way as to render the consequent moot or to undercut the chain of events or logic leading to it' (575). *The Cuckoo Tree* refers to Trafalgar and to Prime Minister Pitt (246), yet it seems most unlikely that either the Napoleonic Wars (had they taken place at all) or British domestic politics would have proceeded along quite such familiar lines had the House of Stuart reigned throughout the eighteenth century. And such examples of implausible continuity can easily be multiplied.

Nevertheless, even to write the above paragraphs is to become aware that this kind of analysis misses the most distinctive qualities of Aiken's books, which are decidedly not a serious counterfactual enquiry into the processes that drive historical change, still less a philosophical one into the nature of time and contingency. It is not simply the absence of a nexus event, or the fact that it is easy to 'catch out' the novels in their inclusion of details that should not exist in a non-Hanoverian England (the presence of Christmas trees in *The Cuckoo Tree*, for example, without any Prince Albert to introduce them to England [58]). It is also that Aiken's books are manifestly engaged in something other than the kind of alternative history practised by science fiction writers and historians. At no point, for example, is the rivalry between the Stuarts and the Hanoverians ever put in denominational terms: the England of James III seems (as far as one can see) to have the Church of England firmly in place, and the Hanoverians themselves are generally motivated not by political or religious ideals, or even by personal devotion to the Pretender, but by the venal expectation of financial reward should their cause triumph. In effect the Hanoverians are convenient villains rather than the product of a serious historical hypothesis.

Once we acknowledge that alternative history as defined by nexus events is not the most productive model through which to understand the structure of Aiken's world, or at any rate is not a sufficient one, we can recognize that Aiken also organizes her books according to a number of other principles. For example, as well as being a 'branching' world that derives in a linear fashion from the given date at which it splits from our own, hers is also a 'mirror' world, reflecting an inverted version of historical reality. Thus, in *Black Hearts in Battersea* we find Mr Twite (a Hanoverian sympathizer) singing the following ditty:

> 'My Bonnie lies over the North Sea,
> My Bonnie lies over in Hanover,
> My Bonnie lies over the North Sea,
> Oh, why won't they bring that young man over?
> Bring back, bring back,
> Oh, bring back my Georgie to me, to me...'
>
> (22)

This is of course not a realistic construction of what a Hanoverian song might have looked like, but simply a mirror image of a famous Jacobite air, superficially adapted to Hanoverian purposes (though revealing its Jacobite origins through its retention of the Scots 'Bonnie'). Throughout the series we see Aiken having fun with these kinds of inversions, which serve not so much to make a point about how things 'might have been' as to establish a carnivalesque reversal of orthodox and heterodox, establishment and dissident. Indeed, this is the emphasis that she herself put on her creation:

> I think what happened was that my subconscious, called on to produce ideas for a children's book, let out a shout of joy, and instantly came up with this plan for a historical tale set in a period of history that never was, that anybody could claim for their own, a nineteenth century – not too long ago, still within reach, but turned upside down with the Stuarts on the throne instead of Queen Victoria, and Hanoverians plotting to bring back Bonnie Prince Georgie from over the water.
>
> ('Thread of Mystery' 39)

As well as an inverted image of our own world and a kind of alternative history, Aiken's books provide a deliberately exaggerated and fanciful version of the nineteenth century. It presents us with an England overrun by wolves; a gun that can fire a missile 3000 miles across the Atlantic with fearful accuracy; an unconscious girl kept alive for months on molasses and whale oil; a plot to mount St Paul's Cathedral on rollers and slide it into the Thames. Aiken has written that she intended such 'exaggeration and nonsense' to act as a generic indicator, encouraging 'readers to understand that this is fantasy – not serious history' ('Interpreting the Past' 72). However, there are many jokes that appear to be included for the author's own amusement as much as for that of her child readers. The aristocracy of Aiken's England tend to be named after rather unglamorous (at the time of composition) areas of London such as Bayswater and Notting Hill, while the Duke of Battersea has an elaborate palace more or less on the site of Battersea Power Station. There is even a Viscount Bakerloo, whose title derives from a 1906 nickname, later officially adopted, for a London Underground line running between Baker Street and Waterloo stations. So far from being unfortunate errors, these 'bad fits' between Aiken's England and ours form part of the novels' exuberant playfulness, which communicates itself even to those readers not in a position to pick up on every reference or deliberate inaccuracy. (As a variation on this theme, Aiken is quite capable of inserting a solemnly pedantic footnote, as when she records in *Night Birds on Nantucket* that the Sankaty Light, which features in that book, did not become operational until three decades after the date of novel's action [58].) According to Aiken, the opportunity for freedom from historical accuracy was a catalyst in freeing her imagination generally:

> Have you ever noticed how peculiarly liberating it is to follow a conventional pattern in nearly all respects, but to include one odd factor? [...] At a sticky children's party, if you simply paint a blue nose on every guest the effect is very uninhibiting. One step aside from the normal and you're away. This was what I found with [*The Wolves of Willoughby Chase*] – having a Stuart king and a few wolves in the middle of the nineteenth century somehow set me free to enjoy myself. I wrote a straightforward rags-to-riches-to-rags-to-riches nineteenth century tale, and had tremendous fun filling in my own details.
>
> ('Thread of Mystery' 39)

Aiken's approach gives her world a flexible and even improvisational quality, which is not easily compatible with the science-fictional or historical conceptions of alternative history, preoccupied as they are with following chains of cause and effect. In one book, *The Stolen Lake* (1981), we even meet an ancient British tribe who have founded a civilization in South America, which adds another branch of alternative history to Aiken's primary invention of a Stuart nineteenth century – an elaboration tossed off, four books into the series, with the following insouciant explanation in an 'Author's Note': 'Everybody knows that the Ancient British *didn't* migrate to South America when the Saxons invaded their country; this is just my idea of what it would have been like if they had' (5). For such texts our suggested model, under which alternative history is understood as a flexible hybrid drawing on both fantasy and historical writing, seems to provide a more responsive and accurate account of what Aiken's books actually do.

Quasi-historical fiction

It is clear that many features of Aiken's books could be viewed as weaknesses if she were read as attempting either realist history or science-fictional alternative history. However, her anachronisms and the vagueness about her world's nexus event (or events) work to advantage in her series as ways of manipulating our generic expectations and concentrating our attention on the immediate events of her story. Aiken's books clearly have historical *settings*, and to this extent the judgement of Humphrey Carpenter and Mari Prichard that 'In no sense at all are Joan Aiken's books historical novels' (10) is far too absolute; but those settings are to a large extent dislocated from any wider historical *context*. They provide a picturesque stage set for her narrative, and take much of their power from their ability to evoke her readers' own ideas of nineteenth-century life, both in reality and in literature; but they do not invite us seriously to imagine their historical landscape continuing far beyond the wings.

It is this combination of qualities that we have in mind when we describe Aiken's books as 'quasi-historical' – a term we have coined in order to designate, not a discrete genre (quasi-historical characteristics can be found in various genres), but a distinctive set of textual relationships to history. In short, quasi-historical texts are distinguished by their emphasis on the past primarily as a setting for narrative, rather than on history *per se*. They may feature famous people, places and events; however, these function not to provide insights into crucial historical moments, but rather to serve as props and backdrop for the plot.

Quasi-historical texts may be light-hearted, and may pay homage to canonical works of literature or allude humorously to their own dependence on literary convention and historical cliché. They are often selective in their commitment to accuracy, paying careful attention to one or two aspects of the past, such as clothing, but being far less strict about others, such as language, attitudes, manners and the actions of historical figures. Where this is done consciously the result can be a kind of camp knowingness, of the sort seen in films such as *Shakespeare in Love* (1998) and *Pirates of the Caribbean* (2003), or television costume dramas such as *The Tudors* (2007 on). None of this implies that the relationship between a quasi-historical text and its historical context need be slapdash. Quasi-historical books may exhibit a good deal of historical and cultural knowledge, as in Patricia Wrede and Caroline Stevermer's *Sorcery and Cecelia* (1988), an historical fantasy set in Regency England that consists of letters between two young ladies, one living in rural Essex and the other visiting London for the Season. The writers' use of Regency slang, their descriptions of fashions, the set-piece social occasions (tea parties, balls, walks through Vauxhall Gardens) are all scrupulously observed. The political situation of this version of England too is recognizable, barring a distracting implication that the American colonies are still under British rule. However, this is a world where magic and wizardry are widely practised, and accepted to the extent that there is a Royal College of Wizards. Wrede and Stevermer's skill and much of the novel's pleasure lie not so much in the authors' ability to write a changed history, fully reimagined in all its political and social ramifications, as in their plausibly maintaining the manners and lifestyle of their characters as recognizably Regency, given this fundamental difference.

Quasi-historical texts for children and young adults tend to fall into well-defined generic categories, notably mystery/adventure and romantic/erotic fiction. Andrew Lane's 'Young Sherlock Holmes' series, for example, belongs to the adventure genre, and features a 14-year-old Sherlock whom Mycroft takes out of school and sends to stay with elderly relatives, where he receives tutoring from the brilliant and idiosyncratic American Amyus Crowe.[3] In the course of the first two books in the series Sherlock gains experience which informs the canonical Sherlock's expertise in boxing and his interest in the violin, bees and tattoos, and there is a hint as to how he may later have come to develop a drug addiction. In the second book, Mycroft provides a useful summary of Sherlock's first months under his care, which draws overt attention to the extent to which they have diverged from plausibility, however exciting and however neatly dovetailed into the later events of the detective's life:

> 'During the past few months you have spent more time looking death in the eye than most men experience during the course of a lifetime. You have been knocked out, kidnapped, whipped, drugged, chased, shot at, burned and nearly stabbed, not to mention forced to survive unsupervised in the dangerous London metropolis, in a foreign country and in rough Channel waves at night.'
>
> (*Red Leech* 111–12)

Mycroft is criticizing his own record as a guardian, but the effect is inevitably to highlight the book's generic status as high adventure rather than historical realism. The Victorian setting of the books is important precisely because of its fecundity in providing opportunities for these types of peril.

For a quasi-historical romance we can turn to Emily Whitman's time-travel fantasy, *Wildwing* (2010). The story of Addy, an illegitimate 15-year-old living in 1913, begins with her being withdrawn from school and put to work as a maid. Addy's life changes when she comes across a time machine at her employer's home and accidentally travels to the thirteenth century. There, Addy finds herself mistaken for a noblewoman and is able to live a life of luxury and respect that she could previously only dream of. What makes this text quasi-historical is the narrative's tight focus on the state of Addy's mind and heart (for it is not long before she meets Will, the handsome falconer) rather than on the past itself. That past, as seen through Addy's narration, is conceived in a strikingly naïve way. When she first sees a group of thirteenth-century people walking towards her, for example, the experience is distinguished by its picture-book quality:

> [...] I see there are more people coming up the dusty road. And it's the most wonderful thing: they look like they've stepped from the pages of *Robin Hood*. There are men and a boy in earth-colored tunics, belted at the waist, with leggings snugged to their calves and funny little night-cap hats. A handful of women chatter along in browns and greens, their headdresses strapped like bandages across their foreheads and under their chins, hiding all their hair, so their faces shine out like the centers of daisies. A straggle of children brings up the rear.
>
> (52–3)

It is a similar story when Addy arrives at a town. Not for her a Middle Ages characterized by poor sanitation and dirt. Her town is a mud-free vision that might have appeared in one of the watercolours in *Our Island Story*. Far from being noisome with unwashed humanity and animals, it features nothing more offensive than the fragrance of good home cooking:

> [...] I gasp at what's before me: a perfect little walled town, its gate open wide, colorful pennants flapping in the breeze. [...]

> Half-timbered houses crowd the narrow street, their upper stories jutting out overhead. I'm in a river of people, surging past shop fronts and whitewashed walls, past shutters thrown open to display bread or cloth or meat inside. The street spills out into a marketplace crowded with carts and stalls, laughter and music, people in homespun and others in silk. [...]
>
> Oh, the air sings to my senses, with the scent of meat pies wafting from laden trays, a rainbow of fabrics spilling out across tables, the lilting strains of a flute!
>
> (54)

This childlike description of an historical scene is more than a reflection of Addy's own enthusiasm: it is also underwritten by the events of the narrative. When she is initially mistaken for a noblewoman, for example, it is because she has the presence of mind to fashion the tablecloth she happens to be holding into a cloak:

> I give the tablecloth a good shake, sending a last flurry of dust flying, turn the smudged side inward, and toss it around my shoulders. The sun blazes the cloth into a beautiful field of red roses. I pull off my cap and shove it in my pocket, only to be pricked by a pin. That will be the brooch for my crimson cloak. Finally, I pull off my apron and wrap it around my head, looping the ties under my chin. Now I look as if I belong.
>
> (53)

An early twentieth-century girl with a maid's apron round her head and a tablecloth over her shoulders might 'look as if she belongs' in the context of a school production of *Ivanhoe*, but it is most unlikely that people born and raised in the thirteenth century would mistake her for one of them – yet in *Wildwing* the disguise is entirely effective. When Addy returns to the Middle Ages for a second time, she even raids the local theatrical company's dressing up box for a robe, with similarly successful results. This is fantasy projected onto the past-as-backdrop, rather than an attempt to imagine what the past might have been like for those formed by the experience of living there.

Libba Bray's *A Great and Terrible Beauty* (2003) (the first in her Gemma Doyle trilogy), qualifies as quasi-historical for another reason. In writing this book, set in an English girls' boarding school in the 1890s, Bray utilizes commonly held assumptions about the sexual repression of the Victorian era to evoke a heightened Gothic eroticism that has little to do with the knowledge and experience that a respectably brought up 16-year-old in the heroine's situation would be likely to possess. After Gemma (whose narrative it is) is attacked by a man, for example, she is tentatively questioned by her brother: 'Tom clears his throat. "What I mean to say is, did something happen to you? Did he... are you quite all right?" ' This is vague, but Gemma understands instantly that Tom's question is about rape: 'You want to know if I'm still chaste' (29). Once in the boarding school, Gemma finds and reads a diary written by a pupil a generation before. She shares it with some friends who have formed a secret society, complete with a blood-binding ritual and middle-of-the-night meetings in a cave in the school grounds. When they come across a 'drawing of a woman with grapes in her hair coupling with a man in animal skins' they all 'gasp and call it disgusting while trying to get a better look'. Only one of the four girls is ignorant of what the picture depicts, and asks what the couple is doing:

> 'She's lying back and thinking of England!' Pippa shrieks, invoking the phrase that every English mother tells her daughter about carnal acts. We're not supposed to enjoy it. We're just supposed to put our mind on making babies for the future of the Empire and to please our husbands.
>
> (149–50)

It is unlikely that girls of Gemma's age and station would have been told anything about sex at all, let alone instructed to lie back and think of England – a cliché of Victorian attitudes to female sexuality for which there is no evidence until well into the twentieth century. Equally implausible is Gemma's reaction to being asked in class for her response to Tennyson's poem, 'The Lady of Shalott': '*What do you feel?* I've never been asked that question once. None of us has. We aren't supposed to feel. We're British' (100). This reads like a parody of Victorian Britishness rather than an attempt to develop a convincing historical voice.

Quasi-historical novels are not, we should emphasize, simply inept historical novels (although they may be that too, as in the cases of Whitman and Bray). Some are highly accomplished, but they are distinguished by the *use* they make of the past. In a quasi-historical text the past is a resource that may be drawn on for local colour, for texture, for technology or for other features, but there is no serious attempt to recreate it for its own sake. Some texts hint at an awareness of this instrumental approach to the past, as in Mycroft Holmes's speech quoted above, but with others, such as *Wildwing* and *A Great and Terrible Beauty*, readers must draw their own conclusions. Either way, in a quasi-historical text history is primarily (in the words of Elfrida Arden, in E. Nesbit's *The House of Arden* [1908]) 'a place [...] for adventures to happen in' (172).

Intertexts and history

In one sense all historical literature is intertextual, because history itself is a fundamentally textual discipline. What we know of the past, and certainly of the periods with which this book has so far been primarily concerned, derives largely from written sources, whether primary sources such as wills and church records, or secondary sources, including the work of historians. In this section, however, we will be considering intertextuality in a rather narrower sense, addressing the ways in which modern books that represent history to children do so by drawing on previous *literary* representations of the past.

Some such debts, which take the form of specific allusions to individual works, appear quite circumscribed in effect. In Aiken's *Night Birds on Nantucket*, for example, we meet Jabez Casket, a whaling captain obsessed with chasing a legendary pink whale. The tribute to *Moby Dick* (1851) is obvious, and any reader who is aware of Melville's novel will no doubt appreciate this nod to its mid-century, Nantucket setting, but such awareness is far from necessary to the understanding and enjoyment of Aiken's book. The relationship between man and whale (in her story ultimately an affectionate one) is integrated into the plot, and the central character of Melville's dark meditation on mortality and the human condition becomes, in her hands, a fallible eccentric who takes his place quite comfortably within the fictional landscape already established by her series.

Isolated as such allusions may appear to be, one consequence of a novel's participation in other texts is to emphasize its fictive nature, and (more relevantly for our purpose) the fictive nature of its historical world. The opening of C. S. Lewis's *The Magician's Nephew* (1955) is a classic example of intertextual reference being used in this way. 'In those days Mr Sherlock Holmes was still living in Baker Street', we are informed on the first page of Lewis's book, 'and the Bastables were looking for treasure in the Lewisham Road' (9). With these two literary points of reference Lewis fixes his story not only historically and geographically in Edwardian London but also emphasizes its status as fiction, just as the Wife of Bath did in setting her tale in the days of King Arthur.

More significant than the Melville references in *Night Birds on Nantucket* is the debt Aiken owes to Charles Dickens, which presents us with a more pervasive intertextual relationship. Dickens's influence extends far beyond such specific references as, for example, the inclusion in *Black Hearts in Battersea* of a character called Fitzpickwick. The popular conception of the sights, sounds and smells of the mid-nineteenth century, and especially of London, is informed as much by the stories and novels of Dickens (and their innumerable adaptations) as by more formal sources of historical information, and Aiken draws freely on this Dickensian inheritance in order to give her world much of its texture. For all their many points of originality, her novels are Dickensian in terms of their concern for poverty and injustice, their wildly eccentric characters, their use of distinctive idiolects and speech patterns, and the dependence of their plots on unlikely coincidences and revelations. The net result is that the nineteenth century depicted in her books has, in addition to the other characteristics already discussed, a distinctively Dickensian overlay, which interposes itself as one more filter between the reader and whatever the reality of nineteenth-century England may have been.

Dickens's influence on Aiken (and on some other historical writers for children, notably Leon Garfield) is widespread and diffusive (Lathey), but in some respects this makes it difficult to isolate for analysis. For our purpose it is more convenient to investigate the phenomenon of intertextuality in a set of texts that occupies a middle ground between the ubiquity of Dickens's influence and the specificity of individual references to Captain Ahab or Mr Pickwick. These are modern novels that have been written specifically as sequels to, or spin-offs from, older canonical texts. The dependence of Hilary McKay's *Wishing for Tomorrow* (2009) on Frances Hodgson Burnett's

A Little Princess (1905), or of Nancy Springer's Enola Holmes novels (2006–10) on the Sherlock Holmes novels and stories of Arthur Conan Doyle (1887–1927) is in one sense obvious: in both cases the modern texts take their settings and some of their characters from their late nineteenth- and early twentieth-century predecessors. Such a close intertextual relationship raises the question of what it means to class either Springer's or McKay's work as an historical novel. Certainly they are novels set in the past; but can their depiction of that past stand independently of their homage to (or critique of) their source texts, or must it be subordinated to their relationships with those texts? Are they set in 'the' past, or in Burnett's and Doyle's *versions* of the past, and what does this mean for the ways that we read them? Given the admission with which we started, that history is a textual discipline through and through, this distinction may turn out to be one of degree rather than kind: after all, there is no non-textual past to which Springer and McKay could even in principle refer. But questions of degree are well worth asking.

We can start by considering what factors an author such as Springer or McKay might take into account in creating this kind of text. Clearly there will be considerations of 'fidelity' (whether of letter or of spirit) to the canonical setting. There is also the question, explored at length in Chapter 4, of how far the world of the original text should be recast so as to allow for the sensibilities, values and tastes of contemporary readers. In making these judgements, modern writers may find that some of the materials necessary for adapting the texts to modern taste are available in the period of the older text itself. As well as extrapolating a sense of the historical period *out of* their source texts, in other words, they are likely to introduce *into* their intertextual revisions of those texts a wider knowledge of that period, drawn from other sources.

Nancy Springer's stories about Enola Holmes (the younger sister of Sherlock and Mycroft) are a case in point. Enola, whose father died when she was four, is raised by her mother, her adult elder brothers being largely absent from her life. Like Sherlock and Mycroft, Enola is intelligent, a good observer and takes naturally to detective work. These qualities are duly called upon in the six books of the series, beginning with *The Case of the Missing Marquess* (2006), during the course of which she shows herself the equal, and in some respects the superior, of her better-known siblings.

Springer is able to establish new ground for her heroine by taking advantage of the fact that Enola Holmes is both young and female. To write stories that bring her out from the shadow of her illustrious brothers is a move with obvious feminist potential (Sherlock's sister being the detective equivalent of Shakespeare's sister, as imagined by Virginia Woolf in *A Room of One's Own* [1929]), but it is also a practical one with regard to finding original material for her sleuthing. Sherlock (and, *a fortiori*, Mycroft) are bachelors to their bones: there are aspects of female life within Victorian society that Doyle's stories leave untouched and that Enola is far better positioned to investigate. 'Enola's advantage over Sherlock is her knowledge of feminine arts which he has chosen to ignore', Springer has suggested ('Interview with Author Nancy Springer'). Accordingly, in the first book in the series, Enola subversively uses symbols of feminine restriction as the very means by which to achieve her own unorthodox freedom after her mother disappears. Enola discovers the money that her mother has hidden for her by deciphering a series of messages concealed within *The Language of Flowers*, a conspicuously feminine book. She is then able to avoid the prospect of boarding school and a life of dangerously tight-laced corsetry by hiding the money necessary for her escape within her bustle – an otherwise impractical item of female fashion – before setting out for an independent life on that trusty conveyance of the late Victorian New Woman, a bicycle. Here Springer has adapted her material to the concerns of modern readers, not by introducing anachronisms but by looking beyond the world of her source text to the wider historical context of nineteenth-century Britain.

The intertextual relationship between Hilary McKay's *Wishing for Tomorrow* and Frances Hodgson Burnett's *A Little Princess* is in one sense more conventional than that of Springer's stories to Doyle's: it is conceived as a sequel. However, this does not make the task of negotiating the historical terrain any less challenging. In fact, *A Little Princess* has some historical complications on its own account: it was first published in 1905, but its origins lie 17 years earlier, in a serialized magazine story entitled 'Sara Crewe'. This doubleness makes the relationship of Hodgson's novel to its historical setting immediately ambiguous. Is the published novel set in 1888, when 'Sara Crewe' appeared, or in 1905? Is it simply an expansion of the earlier story, or an updating as well? The difficulty is exacerbated by

Burnett's clear debt to an ahistorical fairy-tale tradition, and particularly to the story of Cinderella. Sara Crewe, a privileged girl who falls on hard times through no fault of her own and endures a period of cruelty and hardship before an equally unexpected exaltation to her former position, is a character the logic of whose story follows the rules of Grimm rather than of Marx, and is not easy to locate within a specific historical 'moment'.

When we first meet Sara she is indulged beyond measure by her loving but imprudent father: she is bought the finest clothes and the most luxurious toys; her room in the boarding school where she is lodged is palatial; and she is given all kinds of privileges by the headmistress, Miss Minchin. On the news of her father's death and loss of fortune Miss Minchin regards her as a charity child and turns her into a servant, and Sara endures penury for a while before in due course she is discovered by her father's old partner, and (her father's fortune turning out not to have been lost after all) restored to her previous status. Psychologically, we may wonder why Sara seems so entirely unaffected by the indulgence and favouritism lavished by her father and (initially) Miss Minchin. Despite a lifetime of this treatment she remains unspoilt, unaffected, thoughtful and generous, a princess by nature as well as by fortune. Still more remarkably she retains that nobility of mind even when abruptly orphaned and reduced to a life of poverty in an attic. Not only does she continue to be kind to others, but she retains the devotion of her fellow maid Becky, who is clearly born to serve every bit as much as Sara is born to be a 'princess'. Within this fairy-tale milieu the novel's blurriness over whether its setting is Victorian or Edwardian seems in the end to be of no great consequence. Its status as a Cinderella fantasy outweighs any commitment to social realism.

In this context we may note how completely the novel glosses over the source of Captain Crewe's, and hence of Sara's, wealth – which is derived from the Captain's ownership of an Indian diamond mine. Rather than being explained in terms of his career within the Raj, or of Britain's colonial relationship with India, the mine exists only as a romantic image, a fabulous and inexhaustible source of riches. On the one occasion on which it is described, it is in heavily idealized terms:

> 'Diamond mines' sounded so like the 'Arabian Nights' that no one could be indifferent. Sara thought them enchanting, and painted

> pictures, for Ermengarde and Lottie, of labyrinthine passages in the bowels of the earth, where sparkling stones studded the walls and roofs and ceilings, and strange, dark men dug them out with heavy picks.
>
> (49–50)

Burnett's text, although it has much to say about the privations of life as a servant at Miss Minchin's school, gives us no account to set against Sara's Arabian Nights vision, nor any hint as to what the reality of manual labour in such a mine might actually be like. Instead, India is preserved as a place of magic and romance throughout the book, notably in the person of Ram Dass, the Indian manservant who spirits mysterious and exotic feasts to Sara's garret across the rooftop from a neighbouring house.

A Little Princess was not, of course, written as an historical novel, unless the gap between 1888 and 1905 is sufficient to make it so. If it presents an historical period to modern readers, it does so accidentally, by virtue of its longevity. We will search in vain for the kinds of historical place markers that a modern historical writer might be tempted to include, such as references to national events that could 'fix' the action in time. Neither is Burnett in a position to mediate the Victorian/Edwardian attitudes of her characters and world for modern audiences. We have noted the text's unselfconscious orientalism with regard to India and its obliviousness to the exploitation that keeps Sara Crewe in luxury. Western consumers continue to exploit Third World labour, but in an age when critics hotly debate the role of Sir Thomas Bertram's Antiguan plantations in *Mansfield Park* (e.g. Said 112, White *passim*) and *A Little Princess* itself has been analysed in similar terms (McGillis), such complacency may seem rather conspicuous. Nor are postcolonial critiques the only kind that might be applied to the world of *A Little Princess*. When Captain Crewe first delivers his daughter into the care of Miss Minchin, he instructs the headmistress to 'Drag her away from books when she reads too much [...] She ought to play more with dolls' (13–14). This regime, presumably designed to turn Sara into a suitably maternal girl in whom any symptoms of incipient intellectualism are kept firmly in check, is clearly open to objection from a feminist viewpoint. There is no indication that Sara's love of reading has in any way held back her socialization, nor even that she is indifferent to dolls, which makes Captain Crewe's admonition seem still less apposite. Yet, while he is not portrayed as the wisest of men, he is shown as a loving father who wants the best for his daughter, and at no point does the text offer any alternative perspective to his apparent belief that diverting a girl from books to dolls is a worthy objective.

We have considered in previous chapters the problem faced by all writers of historical fiction, of steering a middle ground between appearing to endorse outdated ideological views and too-obvious anachronism. In producing a sequel to a book like *A Little Princess*, that problem is made even greater by readers' attachment to the historical world of the novel, which is a complex mix of 'the' past and Burnett's *version* of the past, in which the claims of social justice do not make themselves felt beyond the streets and attics of London. The tools Hilary McKay brings to this formidable task in *Wishing for Tomorrow* include her own sense of the historical period, which extends well beyond the confines of Miss Minchin's school; a mastery of ensemble and family stories (honed in her 'Exiles' [1993–6] and 'Casson Family' [from 2001] series); and the concomitant arts of affectionate irony – whether directed at her characters or (occasionally) at her authorial predecessor. She also displays a sensitivity to the ways in which changes in ideology affect generic tastes, which occasions a subtle modulation from Burnett's somewhat heightened parable of virtue rewarded to a more universally humane account of fallible people finding and developing the potential for goodness and happiness in themselves.

A major element of this generic modulation is McKay's movement of her narrative's centre of gravity away from Sara Crewe herself, to the larger community living at Miss Minchin's. As written by Burnett, Sara is a paragon, a type that does not sit comfortably within McKay's more realistic style of ensemble fiction. Rather than attempt to maintain this perspective on Sara, or else debunk it, McKay keeps Sara off-stage for the majority of the book, as the absent addressee of her more plodding friend Ermengarde's letters about life at the school, Sara herself having moved to live with her rich new guardian with Becky in tow. (Meanwhile at Miss Minchin's, the naturally servile Becky is replaced by Alice, who is cheerfully aware that working as a servant is a job rather than a vocation, and that there are other potential employers than the Misses Minchin.) By the time Sara does re-enter the narrative, it is into a fictional world that is both well established and flexible enough to accommodate her.

In an efficient use of exposition-as-character-development, the concluding weeks of the story of *A Little Princess* are recounted near the beginning of *Wishing for Tomorrow*, but from the point of view of Ermengarde rather than of Sara herself. At this period Sara and Becky are the recipients of baffling gifts of food and exotic furnishings from the rich gentleman in the house next door, but are wisely keeping their good fortune a secret. Loyal Ermengarde, who knows nothing of this, has been feeling sorry for her friend's fall into poverty, but noticing Sara's sudden cheerfulness realizes that something has changed. Torn between being pleased at Sara's happiness and hurt at her own exclusion from the secret, Ermengarde offers a very different perspective on the events of *A Little Princess*, one that – without in any way denigrating Sara's actions – begins to broaden our sympathy beyond the tight circle of manifest oppression on which it had been focused in Burnett's original.

This more inclusive perspective reframes the narrative's view of many of the characters in Burnett's book, including the unpleasant ones such as the snobbish pupil Lavinia and even Miss Minchin herself. *A Little Princess* had shown Lavinia's mean-spirited competitiveness, but McKay's book reveals Lavinia's attitude as born not of motiveless malice but rather of frustration at her absent mother's indifference, and at her limited prospects for independence and intellectual fulfilment, either at Miss Minchin's or in the world beyond. Once she learns from a chance encounter that it is possible for women to attend university her attitude changes, and she devotes her considerable energies to procuring the necessary tuition. Her tongue is still sharp, but humour and pointed observation take the place of the unkindness that had been her trademark in *A Little Princess*. In the case of Miss Minchin we are given an insight, through her sister's memories, of her own frustration at seeing her younger brothers educated to a far higher standard than herself:

> Maria [Minchin] had been a difficult child. Large-boned, intelligent, always tormenting her parents with questions. 'Why must

> only the boys learn Latin? Ride in the park? Visit the museums? Why must the boys have new suits *again*?' And, most of all, '*Why* are things so unfair? *Why* was I born a girl?'
>
> (14–15)

Miss Minchin's consciousness of having been thwarted by life's skewed opportunities, combined with her partial disgrace after Sara's departure, lead her (or so an adult reader may deduce) to a dependence on gin. She becomes a pitiable figure, but also an indictment of a patriarchal system that fails to value women's talents and stifles their energies. In depicting these two women McKay takes the opportunity to reflect, in a way that Burnett did not, on the restrictions placed on intellectually ambitious women at this period: it is hard to imagine this narrative allowing an admonition to replace books with dolls pass unremarked. However, she also depicts with sympathy the plight of people such as Ermengarde, expected by her intellectual family to shine academically and despised when she falls short, whatever her other qualities. If Lavinia and Miss Minchin illustrate the possible fates of intellectual women at this time, Ermengarde and her Aunt Eliza (who featured in *A Little Princess* only as the subject of a slighting remark from Ermengarde's father [25]) form another diptych, of women who are able to forge an independent life for themselves through persistence, courage and emotional wisdom. *Wishing for Tomorrow* is never in danger of becoming a tract – its humour alone would prevent that – but its more expansive social framing does move Burnett's tale of individual endurance and nobility into an area that acknowledges the wider role of social institutions in shaping the lives of individuals, and especially of women. Different as McKay's text is from Springer's, it also shares with that other intertext a general strategy: that of reflecting modern liberal values, but doing so without resort to anachronism. In both cases this is achieved by looking beyond the source text at the wider historical context of the period, and co-opting those discourses and events (notably the rise of early feminism and the movement for women's higher education) that seem amenable to modern values. The 'worlds' of Sherlock Holmes or *A Little Princess*, the affective and ideological contours of which are shaped by the demands of genre and narrative as much as by a commitment to the mimetic reproduction of reality, are clearly very different from the world of the nineteenth and early twentieth centuries as understood by modern historians (which is shaped by that discipline's own generic demands). The task undertaken by Springer, and especially by McKay, is that of marrying these two worlds in order to create a new historical setting.

'Did you once see Shelley plain?': Depicting real people in fiction

Discussion of sequels and other forms of intertext can be dogged by moral questions, anchored in the concept of fidelity to a literary source, as well as to historical fact in general. This is true *a fortiori* of our last category of texts, those that depict real historical individuals in a fictional context. Many of the books we have discussed in this chapter test or contradict consensus versions of history; and in texts featuring public figures, the events of whose lives are well known and plentifully available, this kind of departure may be especially conspicuous. In the nineteenth century the latitude some novelists allowed themselves in such matters was great, as we may see by the example of Mark Twain's *The Prince and the Pauper* (1881). In this novel, Henry VIII's son Edward exchanges identities with his impoverished lookalike, Tom Canty, only to reveal the deception in the very public setting of his own coronation. The coronation of Edward VI was well chronicled at the time, and contemporary accounts of the occasion make no mention of any such revelation, but this appears to have concerned Twain not at all. Similarly relaxed attitudes are evident in other popular historical novels, such as Alexandre Dumas's *The Three Musketeers* (1844) and Harrison Ainsworth's *Windsor Castle* (1841), which take comparable liberties with such luminaries as the Duke of Buckingham and Cardinal Wolsey.

In works of the last hundred years it is rare for a realist historical novel to be so casual with the public lives of well-known people. In the case of children's historical fiction, this may be partly because its subjects tend to be fictional figures (usually children or young adults), occupying what we earlier called the interstices of the historical record and doing things that, however interesting or significant in themselves, are unlikely to attract the attention of the chroniclers. While these protagonists may be caught up in, or stand at the fringes of, great historical events, it is rare for them to be public figures of the kind who largely populate the history books. Even when well-known people do figure in historical fiction they may be shown at a relatively obscure period in their lives. Scholastic's 'The Royal Diaries' and 'My Royal Story' series, for example, which comprise the fictionalized first-person accounts of royal women, portray most of their subjects at an age before they were in a position to have any significant impact on history, as with Kathryn Lasky's 11-year-old Mary Queen of Scots.[4]

Nevertheless, famous people do feature in modern children's historical novels, especially in non-protagonist roles. In books set in Elizabethan London, for example, it is common for Shakespeare or Queen Elizabeth (or both) to make at least a cameo appearance. However, these texts tend to steer well away from outright conflicts with consensus history of the kind exemplified by Twain. Susan Cooper's time-slip fantasy, *King of Shadows* (1999), for example, uses William Shakespeare as a major character, but Cooper is careful not to show him behaving in a way incompatible with the known circumstances of his life: he is still the resident playwright of the Lord Chamberlain's men and the colleague of Burbage, and she presents us with a man whose intelligence and sympathy are easy to associate with the plays and sonnets that bear his name.

Shakespeare's life and personality are notoriously underdocumented, but when Queen Elizabeth arrives for a brief backstage visit after a performance of *A Midsummer Night's Dream* she too behaves in accordance with her popular historical image, evincing the charismatic combination of imperiousness and wry wit generally associated with that monarch (133–6). She is recognizably the same Elizabeth, in fact, who appears in the final scenes of Geoffrey Trease's *Cue for Treason* (1940), where a meeting with the Queen constitutes the narrative 'reward' for the young protagonists, Peter and Kit, who have spent much of the book foiling an attempt on her life. Trease's Elizabeth, like Cooper's, is given lines and a personality that sit comfortably within the conventional contours of her image: politically shrewd, with a dry sense of humour and well aware of the value of money ('I think we might grant this boon, eh? After all, it won't cost us anything' [239].)

An even safer (and arguably more realistic) option is to show the Queen as a figure in the distance. In Karen Cushman's *Alchemy and Meggy Swann*, which is set in London in the 1570s, the protagonist

Meggy and her friends crowd to the bank of the Thames at one point in order to see the Queen's barge float by:

> The queen! Such a day, Meggy thought, that offered sugared almonds and the queen! Her hair flamed red and gold, and her dress was ivory satin covered with pearls and emeralds. She looked, Meggy thought – how best might she state it? – she looked in sooth like a queen.
>
> (100)

Elizabeth takes no further part in the story, which may be part of Cushman's reason for depicting her in this way: not *every* child in Elizabethan England had a telling encounter with the Queen, and Meggy's inability to fill out her impressions of Elizabeth with anything more specific than that she 'looked [...] like a queen' is indicative of the extent to which public figures function as a screen onto which our expectations are projected.

These portrayals of Elizabeth may be of a human being rather than of a rigid profile on a coin, but they are not likely to surprise any reader's expectations. The actual character of Elizabeth is not available to any of us directly, but only as an amalgam of inferences, drawn from accounts both fictional and historical, which we interpret in the light of our own experience and assumptions about human nature. Overall, it is striking that, while different writers of children's historical fiction may present Elizabeth more or less sympathetically, few make substantial alterations to the consensus account of her, or indeed of other well-known historical figures.

Even though modern historical texts tend to shun outright contradictions of consensus history, some undertake historical revisionism by other means. Changes to the public facts of history in the style of Twain or Dumas have become rare, but it is not uncommon to alter the circumstances that gave rise to those facts in such a way as to transform their significance. An early example of this device appears in E. Nesbit's *The Story of the Amulet* (1906), in which a group of time-travelling Edwardian children find themselves being interrogated by Julius Caesar as he sits on the coast of Gaul in 55 BC. Caesar is fascinated to hear their tales of 'railways, electric lights, balloons, men-of-war, cannons, and dynamite' (172), not realizing that they belong to a future period, and concludes: 'I had just decided that Britain was not worth the bother of invading. But what you tell me decides me that it is very much worth while' (172). (Caesar later comes to think of his conversation with the children as a dream, which explains its absence from his *Gallic Wars*.)

The Story of the Amulet is clearly written in a comic mode and the episode is not offered as a serious thesis about Caesar's motives for invasion, but this 'secret history' device (Schmunk) has been deployed in several more recent books, and not always to comic effect. Recently it has appeared with particular frequency in the depiction of famous authors, in which case the modern text typically offers a new account of how some canonical work came to be written. For example, Cora Harrison's *I Was Jane Austen's Best Friend* (2010) is a story of Austen's teenage years told from the point of view of her relative Jenny (Jane) Cooper. The novel exposes the young Austen to situations and characters resembling ones that later appear in her novels. '[Jenny's brother's] wife is rather modelled on Mrs Elton in *Emma*', Harrison explains in an 'Author's Note', and an example of that character's dialogue will illustrate the point:

> 'I said to my *cara sposo* – that's what I call my dear Edward-John. It's Italian for *dear husband*,' she said kindly, glancing across at Jane, who nodded gravely. 'I said to him, just this very morning – Jenny will confirm, won't you, Jenny – "Tell me, dear," I said to him, "is my gown over-trimmed?" '
>
> (31–2)

Although Harrison's character is based on Mrs Elton, her position as a character from Jane Austen's youth implicitly reverses this dependence, suggesting that the wife of Edward-John was Austen's *inspiration* for her later character. However, while anyone can be cornered by a self-aggrandizing bore, there is no attempt to suggest that creating great art from such experience is a simple matter. Harrison's Jane Austen, like the historical one, is an acute observer potentially capable of turning everyday tedium into literature rather than simply recording what she has heard with dogged fidelity.

A rather more problematic example of a classic author playing a central role in a modern children's historical occurs in Lewis Buzbee's *The Haunting of Charles Dickens* (2010). This story is set in 1862, not long after the publication of *Great Expectations*, and involves the eponymous author in an adventure with 12-year-old Meg. One oddity is that the pair encounters many names and locations familiar from novels written by Dickens *before* that time, including Mr Micawber, Bill Sikes, Sam Weller and Mr Bumble, as well as a model for Jenny Wren, from his yet-to-be-written *Our Mutual Friend* (1864–5). They even enter a building called Satis House, to find an ancient wedding cake on the dinner table, as described in Dickens's most recent work – yet at no point does Dickens remark on the uncanny resemblance between these features and his own books. These references give an impression of what an inspiring milieu London is for Dickens (something to which he attests [77]) but are confusing in alluding both to already-published and to still-unwritten works. *The Haunting of Charles Dickens* also takes the opportunity to criticize Dickens's portrayal of at least one young female character. At one point he reads Meg a passage from *Little Dorrit,* only to receive the following critique:

> 'It's not that I don't like Little Dorrit, Mr. Dickens. I like her in all the ways I am meant to like her. She is dutiful, and even-tempered, and thoughtful, and possesses a kind heart.'
>
> 'But?'
>
> 'She is nothing but all those very good things. I like her well enough, but I would never want to be her. She does not suspect she could be her own hero. She waits for others to be that for her.'
>
> [...]
>
> 'Thank you, Meg,' he said. 'No one is ever that candid with me, at least not face-to-face. Bold of you, and necessary. And correct. If I had known you before I wrote that book, if I had known how brave a girl could be, which you have proven to me, well, *Little Dorrit* might have been – a much better book.'
>
> (229)

Buzbee is an enthusiast for Dickens and his work, and *The Haunting of Charles Dickens* celebrates the writer as a creator of worlds and characters, as well as adeptly creating a Dickensian atmosphere. The book largely succeeds as pastiche; however, having a character instruct Dickens in how to create an admirable and heroic female protagonist cannot but look like hubris, especially when Buzbee offers his own character as, in effect, a model of how it ought to be done. The clumsiness of this as an attempt to update Dickens' portrayal of female agency may be contrasted with Hilary McKay's subtlety in *Wishing for Tomorrow*.

Another perspective on the responsibility of modern authors to the predecessors whose lives they represent is provided by K. M. Grant, author of the novel *Belle's Song* (2010). As explained in the last chapter, *Belle's Song* is set on a pilgrimage from London to Canterbury, one of the travellers being Geoffrey Chaucer himself. It is implied that many of the pilgrims in *The Canterbury Tales* are based on the characters encountered by Chaucer in the course of events in *Belle's Song*, which again gives the inadvertent impression of putting the earlier author in the later one's debt, besides implausibly framing Chaucer's own poem as an exercise in mimetic realism. Interestingly, Grant has addressed the issue of her use of Chaucer's characters in an online discussion of her book:

> One day, I asked Chaucer right out loud whether he really didn't mind my giving some of his characters new and rather different lives. His answer came back loud and clear: 'Don't be so silly! Who am I to mind! I'm the Father of English Literature and you're a mere scribbler! Get on with it!' 'I'll take that as a "no", then,' I replied, and happily carried on writing.
>
> ('*Belle's Song* and Help from Chaucer')

For all her scruples about using Chaucer's fictional characters, however, Grant appears to have had none about depicting Chaucer himself – and not in flattering terms either, but as a weak, vacillating 'trimmer' in the disputes between Richard II and the Lords Appellant. As Grant's Chaucer puts it:

> 'A trimmer, Belle, is the worst kind of person. A trimmer's somebody who doesn't want to end up on the wrong side.' He gave me a very frank look. 'In my public life, that's what I've always been, and very successfully so.'
>
> (81–2)

It is hard not to wonder whether the Father of English Literature would have been quite so breezy about having this self-description put into his mouth, and why it appears not to have occurred to Grant that this might represent at least as much of an ethical problem as her co-option of his characters.

This example raises in a rather stark way a dilemma that potentially applies to all uses of real people in historical fiction. By putting words into people's mouths, and attributing to them actions that they never performed, it is possible for a narrative to edge – if not into libel, which is the legal prerogative of the living – then at least into misrepresentation, not just of history in general but of individual human beings. This is by no means a problem confined to children's literature (Shakespeare's depiction of Richard III has done much to shape the public perception of that monarch for centuries, to the irritation of historians), but it is arguably a more serious issue in books marketed to children, who are more likely than other readers to be encountering such individuals for the first time, and to lack the background knowledge against which any depiction could be assessed. The injury, if such it be, is thus perpetrated not only on the person being misrepresented but also on readers.

The fantasy writer Guy Gavriel Kay is one of several authors and academics who have in recent years expressed misgivings about representing real people in fiction, partly on these grounds.[5] In 'The Fantasy of Privacy: Fantasy and the Past' he acknowledges (citing Shakespeare and Tolstoy) that fictional versions of real people have existed for a long time, but contends that the modern era has witnessed a new sense of what he calls 'entitlement' – specifically the assumption that no one's private life should be free from the attention of writers of fiction, accompanied by an unjustified confidence that fiction can offer a powerful form of 'truth' about the people and their interior world not otherwise available. As an example of this entitlement he quotes Bruce Duffy, author of a novel featuring Wittgenstein, who declared himself 'disgusted – no, *outraged* is the word – that, to some, Wittgenstein's life was clearly considered off-limits' (qtd. Kay 244). Kay, for his part, finds such expressions of entitlement reprehensible and appropriative. (It is unclear whether he believes that earlier texts that traduce historical figures, such as *Richard III*, are reprehensible – or, if not, why not.)

Kay recommends the fantasy genre as one way of talking about the past without these moral difficulties, and cites two advantages of fantasy over historical fiction for this purpose. First, Kay argues that putting someone's story in a fantasy context universalizes the situation being depicted, making it easier for readers to see analogies and applications, perhaps to their own times and lives. Second, and more relevantly for the present discussion, fantasy allows writers to consider historical characters (under different names) at one remove, without implying that they have privileged access to their thoughts and motives. The genre thus acts as a kind of *caveat lector* in and of itself. Kay's argument that fantasy removes historical fiction from the realm of truth claims, and therefore of entitlement and the appropriation of real people, recalls some venerable defences of poetry against the charge of lying, such as Sir Philip Sidney's answer to Plato: 'Now for the poet, he nothing affirmeth, and therefore never lieth [. . .] the poet never maketh any circles about your imagination, to conjure you to believe for true what he writeth' (Sidney 123–4). However, in the context of Sidney's 1580s discussion 'poet' is roughly equivalent to 'imaginative writer' in general, which makes his defence a far more inclusive one than Kay's. The status Kay reserves for fantasy, that of not making truth claims, is for Sidney a feature of fiction as a whole, even when the subject of that fiction is or was a real person. When Tasso writes about Godfrey of Boulogne and the siege of Jerusalem during the First Crusade, he uses an historical event and (some) real names – but he does so in such a way as to make a moral as much as an historical point. The same is true when the writer of *A Mirror for Magistrates* (or William Shakespeare) puts words into the mouth of Richard II or another figure from history – and even when Tacitus has the Caledonian chieftain Calgacus deliver a classical oration before his battle with the Romans.

This might remind us that historical fiction is a hybrid genre, and a slippery one at that. For this reason, the generic firewall Kay seeks to erect between it and fantasy is probably inadequate to the task. If one writes a fantasy based on the life of El Cid but gives the central character a different name (as Kay did in *The Lions of Al-Rassan* [1995]), how much defence from charges of appropriation does that move really offer, especially if one expects readers to recognize the historical base underlying the fantasy superstructure? In effect, fantasy becomes a form of *roman à clef*, offering only nominal protection; and we might reflect (in Fielding's words) that 'this artful and refined distinction between communicating a lie, and telling one, is hardly worth the pains it costs' (318). Conversely, when Geoffrey Trease, or Susan Cooper, or Karen Cushman write fictions about Elizabeth I, their creations may share a name with an historical person, but these versions are not offered as definitive of some extra-textual truth. To assign texts discrete moral positions and responsibilities along generic lines, in the absolute way Kay appears to recommend, seems both impractical and insufficiently responsive to the variety and generic hybridity of historical fiction, and is in this respect comparable to Rebecca Barnhouse's attempt to bracket fantasy in her discussion of historical literature.

'Fantasy' and 'historical fiction' are both broad terms, and not every text that falls under the aegis of either bears the same kind of relationship to the past. Some keep very close to a version of the historical record, but some, as we have seen, slide through the gaps in that record; some use counterfactuals, some heightened versions of reality, deliberate anachronisms or metatextual commentaries on the process of fiction-making itself. No generic label is sufficient to inoculate a text against charges of misrepresentation, nor is there any simple solution to the problem identified by Kay and others, except to say that the writing of historical fiction, like other human activities, should be characterized by the respect due to people and to truth. And that is not simple at all.

This does not mean that writing fiction involving historical figures must be given up as a pernicious activity. We might remember that historians too spend much of their time assigning motives, intentions, points of view and actions (and not always creditable ones) to the dead without feeling that they are bringing their profession into disrepute. As Jane Austen's Catherine Morland observes of history, 'I often think it odd that it should be so dull, for a great deal of it must be invention. The speeches that are put into the heroes' mouths, their thoughts and designs – the chief of all this must be invention, and invention is what delights me in other books' (84). Although one can attempt to draw a line between the fiction writer, 'making it up', and the historian, building plausible hypotheses consistent with the available evidence, that too is a naïvely absolute distinction, which gives credit neither to the ways in which fiction writers are constrained by the historical record nor to the imaginative element involved in historical writing. As with many of the difficulties encountered in the current and previous chapters this is an area where top-down analysis falters, where differences of kind almost always turn out to be differences of degree, and where there is ultimately no effective substitute for close engagement with individual texts and the contexts of their reading. And this, we feel, is not to be regretted.

6
Ancestral Voices, Prophesying War

So far in this book we have steered a chronological course, from the Roman invasion of AD 43 through to the age of Victoria. One tendency that has remained relatively consistent in this journey is that, the later the period being discussed, the more historical sources tend to be available to those who might wish to write about it. With the age of Arthur we were dealing with a period for which there is relatively little archaeological evidence, and very few written sources – so few, indeed, that we were able to discuss most of them individually. From the medieval period on, we see a rapid growth in the volume of available material, in terms both of documents and of surviving buildings and artefacts. Whether historical writers consider this proliferation as helpful scaffolding or prefer the scope for imaginative construction offered by less well-documented eras, such a blooming of evidence changes the nature of their task, in whatever genre they may be working.

Nor is the change merely one of volume. It is no coincidence that the earliest substantial document in British history, Caesar's *Gallic Wars*, is principally a self-promoting description of the author's own actions – a textbook case of history being written by the winners. Increasingly, in later periods the historical account no longer consists exclusively of events selected by those in power and told from their point of view. Especially once printing becomes widespread and relatively cheap, we begin to hear from those whose voices have traditionally been left unrecorded: from the poor, from women and from those whose views challenge the orthodoxies of their day. Although such voices are of course subject to censorship and other forms of suppression, and the documents that record them are far less likely to be preserved than those written by (or reproducing the discourse of) people in positions of authority and power, the range of sources available for recent centuries means that history is far more polyphonic than in earlier periods, and this trend becomes still more pronounced once near-universal literacy is achieved in the nineteenth century.

These observations are far from original, of course, and are largely implied in Louis Montrose's classic dictum about 'the textuality of history':

> [...] we can have no access to a full and authentic past, a lived material existence unmediated by the surviving textual traces of the society in question – traces whose survival we cannot assume to be contingent but must rather presume to be at least partially consequent upon complex and subtle social processes of preservation and effacement.
>
> (20)

Such remarks bear repetition as we begin to consider children's books written about the more recent past, for here the 'democratization' of history undergoes yet another series of transformative developments, on two broad fronts. The first is in terms of media and the nature of the physical evidence of the past. Not only are all the long-term movements sketched above still operative, but the advent of sound recording, moving film and portable cameras with sufficiently short exposure times to capture an unposed image, mean that the aural and visual aspects of the twentieth century are available as no other period of the past has been. In addition, more recent developments in the technology of reproduction, communication and information retrieval, most notably in the form of the Internet, have rendered this material accessible as never before.

The second important difference between the twentieth century and earlier periods, from the point of view of current historical writers for children, is that much of it is still within living memory. This means that there is yet another potential source of information about its history available, in the form of stories and memories passed down through family and friends. More, there is a sense of personal, family and community investment in that past. The battle of Waterloo is an historical battle, but the Blitz is something that a child's grandparents may have experienced for themselves. Souvenirs of twentieth-century history are familiar household artefacts: not just museum pieces kept behind glass but family possessions with personal stories attached. Young men and women looking out from black-and-white photographs can be recognized in still-living faces, able to be questioned – and indeed such questioning was long a staple part of the homework undertaken by children studying the Second World War in particular. In short, the distance implied by the word 'history' is foreshortened not just in terms of the smaller number of years between those events and our own time, but by the greater variety of ways in which the events are made available to us and by the affective relationships we may have with those who lived through them.

In this chapter we will consider this more intimate understanding of the past, paying particular attention to its relationship with history conceived more conventionally as a public discourse dealing in verifiable facts and aspiring in principle to objectivity. To what extent does this personal form of witness constitute an alternative or rival source of authority about the reality of the past? Initially our discussion will centre on books set in the Second World War, and especially on those written by authors who were themselves children at that time. In such texts, children's historical fiction may intersect to a significant degree with genres such as autobiography and memoir, which are sometimes defined in opposition to history. We will go on to argue for the continued potency of the Second World War as an affective symbol, one that may be invoked in texts set well outside the period of the War itself. In particular, many of those who write near-future dystopian fiction have drawn on the War as a recognized touchstone of communal privation, danger and resilience. Finally, we will examine some of the ways in which the significance and even the generic status of texts may be affected by a changed context of reception. This holds for all texts, but those that centre on periods of crisis and that are understood by reference to a vocabulary of communal memory have an especially dynamic relationship with the passage of time, their survival depending on that vocabulary's capacity to be renewed and reapplied in diverse circumstances.

Looking back

When writers of historical fiction address a period within their own memory, not only are their usual sources of information (written records, history and archaeology) supplemented by others, such as oral history and personal recall, but the nature of their relationship with that material changes. They are no longer passing on facts only, but also experience, and whatever wisdom may come with experience. In the case of the Second World War, this responsibility is felt most clearly and urgently in the literature of the Holocaust, which for younger schoolchildren is often focalized through the figure of Anne Frank, who has become the personal witness *par excellence* to Hitler's persecution of the Jews. That history lies beyond the scope of this book, but the impulse to bear witness is evident too in books written about the Home Front. Many authors who were children in the Second World War have used that experience in their own writing, and the decade from 1970 on saw a particular flourishing of such literature. By this date the generation of wartime children was rising to prominence, not just as writers but as publishers, reviewers and members of prize committees – all of which helps to account for the proliferation and critical success of titles about children's wartime experience at this time, including Susan Cooper's *Dawn of Fear* (1970), Jane Gardam's *A Long Way from Verona* (1971), Nina Bawden's *Carrie's War* (1973), Robert Westall's *The Machine-Gunners* (1975) and Alan Garner's *Tom Fobble's Day* (1977). Notable more recent additions to the genre from this generation are Michael Foreman's *War Boy* (1989), Dennis Hamley's *The War and Freddy* (1991) and Victor Watson's *Paradise Barn* (2009). All these books are still in print (Garner's as part of *The Stone Book Quartet*), and *Carrie's War* has long featured in the National Curriculum in English schools.

It is not surprising, of course, that these children's writers should make fictional use of the dramatic circumstances that loomed so large in their own childhoods. Bawden has written of the war and her evacuation: 'It's the most important thing I can remember from being young' (Rustin), and it is easy to find similar attestations from her contemporaries (Butler 9–10). However, the books listed above are far more than fictions informed by a general first-hand knowledge of the period. Robert Westall, in advising readers to 'Think of *The Machine-Gunners* as a historical novel, written by somebody who was there at the time', adds: 'the book is based on my own wartime experiences as a boy of nine to fifteen' ('About *The Machine-Gunners*'). Similarly, Susan Cooper has commented that *Dawn of Fear* is 'an autobiographical story' in which 'every word [...] is a recording of events that actually happened' ('Swords and Ploughshares' 139). William in *Tom*

Fobble's Day is the same age as Alan Garner, living in exactly the same part of Cheshire, in identical family circumstances. Dennis Hamley, like the fictional Freddy, was a three-year-old boy at the outbreak of war, and several of Freddy's adventures are seeded in Hamley's own memories of wartime Kent.[1] Nina Bawden has denied that Carrie in *Carrie's War* is a self-portrait, even though Bawden, like Carrie, was evacuated to a Welsh mining town; but she notes too that when the BBC was searching for a location in which to film the television serial, the book's descriptions led them to exactly the same town (Blaengarw, unnamed in the book) and even the same street, where she herself had been housed (*In My Own Time* 41–2).[2]

Unsurprisingly, the ways in which these narratives are orientated with regard to the past vary. Jane Gardam's protagonist, Jessica Vye, resembles her creator in being a would-be writer living in a Redcar-like town on the North Yorkshire coast in the early part of the war. However, *A Long Way from Verona* differs from the other books we have mentioned in that Jessica, the book's first-person narrator, is still 13 at the time of writing. Gardam's novel contains many of the staple features of Home Front fiction, such as ration books, ARP wardens, blast tape on the windows, Churchillian speeches, an encounter with a prisoner of war and descriptions of bombing. However, these elements are largely incidental to the intense emotional life of Jessica herself, none of whose family or friends is serving in the forces, and who seems to experience the war as an inconvenient backdrop rather than as the determining fact of her life. The perspective provided by distance, which is an integral feature of many of the books listed above, must here be supplied by the reader.

By contrast, Michael Foreman's *War Boy* is written explicitly as a memoir of his childhood in wartime East Anglia. His narrative about his own experiences as a young boy near Lowestoft is accompanied by illustrations of the scenes described and even diagrams (such as one depicting the trajectory of an incendiary bomb that fell through the ceiling of his bedroom and bounced into the fireplace); but we are also shown literature produced at the time: government propaganda posters, cigarette cards, advertisements and other material to which the young Foreman might have been exposed. Like the other books we have mentioned, *War Boy* is about personal memory as much as public history, but its format suggests that it is also an attempt to place personal experience within the wider experience of the nation and world. In some respects these two elements act in tension. We are aware that there are at least two 'versions' of the war on offer here: the war as experienced by a small boy, with a small boy's priorities, and the war that is shaping history all around him. History and memory, even where they do not contradict each other, approach the past with different priorities, aims and methodologies. Some historians, such as Pierre Nora, have characterized this difference as antagonism:

> Memory and history, far from being synonymous, appear now to be in fundamental opposition. Memory is life, borne by living societies founded in its name. [...] History, on the other hand, is the reconstruction, always problematic and incomplete, of what is no longer. Memory is a perpetually actual phenomenon, a bond tying us to the eternal present; history is a representation of the past. Memory, insofar as it is affective and magical, only accommodates those facts that suit it; it nourishes recollections that may be out of focus or telescopic, global or detached, particular or symbolic – responsive to each avenue of conveyance or phenomenal screen, to every censorship or projection. History, because it is an intellectual and secular production, calls for analysis and criticism. Memory installs remembrance within the sacred; history, always prosaic, releases it again. Memory is blind to all but the group it binds [...] History, on the other hand, belongs to everyone and to no one, whence its claim to universal authority. [...] At the heart of history is a critical discourse that is antithetical to spontaneous memory. History is perpetually suspicious of memory, and its true mission is to suppress and destroy it.
>
> (8–9)

Nora's conception of history as exclusively a public, intellectual and rational practice is an excessively narrow one, and we do not follow him in placing it in outright opposition to memory; but his statement is useful in characterizing one end of a spectrum of discourses about the past, in which history is defined partly in terms of its excision of the personal and subjective. A book like *War Boy* (and this is true to a greater or lesser extent of most of those listed above) may be viewed as a *lieu de mémoire*, to use Nora's phrase: that is to say as a monument in which the discourses of history and memory can be brought into a temporary accommodation, in this case by means of Foreman's *bricolage* technique.[3] We suggest that this aspect of Foreman's book, its yoking of memory and history, constitutes a significant part of its appeal, and more generally the appeal of those Second World War texts that incorporate their authors' personal memory within a fiction that acknowledges the wider concerns of history.

One factor in the decision of these authors to turn to the subject of wartime childhood may have been that, by the time these books were written, many were themselves parents, with children of an age similar to their own during the War. Westall is emphatic on this point, recalling that he wrote the book initially for his son Christopher:

> He had shown me how life was for him at twelve and I suddenly felt the need to show him how life had been for me at twelve. I wanted to invite him back into my world and let the two generations, just for a moment, stand side by side in time.
>
> (*North Shields 173*)

The Machine-Gunners, though a literary artefact, thus acts in the same way as oral history, using narrative and memory as a way of achieving a continuity of identity between generations, whether at the level of family or of community. For Westall, the desire to pass on his experiences to his son acted as a key that gave him access to memories of his own childhood:

> And then, suddenly, the whole time that I was twelve came back to me in one great surge of memory. The smells, the fears, what we ate – total recall. And I began to write [...] only it wasn't a literary activity, it was a social activity.
>
> (*North Shields 173*)

The act of remembering is personal, but is triggered by the social desire to communicate personal experience to others. While we may question the extent to which the writing of *The Machine-Gunners* was not 'a literary activity', there was clearly more to its composition than the desire to produce a well-crafted piece of fiction, or even a well-researched historical novel. As with other stories of wartime childhood by Westall's generation, its derivation from memory rather than (or in addition to) the combination of research and imagination that conventionally supplies the material of historical novels, alters both the nature of the book and its relationship to its readers. One function of these texts seems to be to elicit this kind of personal and immediate evocation of experience. 'Why does the smell of burning kerosene make me feel safe?', Westall recalls a friend asking, adding that the question 'carried me back to the air-raid shelters of my youth' (*North Shields 173*). Foreman writes of his gas mask training: 'We were taught to spit on the inside of the mica window to prevent it misting up. Gas masks were good for rude noises and fogged up anyway' (23). In Victor Watson's *Paradise Barn* (of which its author has said that it draws 'very strongly on my memories of the War'),[4] one of the children notes that wartime restrictions have reduced *The Daily Express*'s Rupert Bear cartoon strip from two panels per day to just one (23). Such a detail might be accessible by other means – a study of the newspaper's archive, for example – but its effectiveness here comes from the recognition of memory manifesting itself in fiction.

Michelle Magorian, whose *Goodnight, Mr Tom* (1981) has become a classic novel of evacuation, is certainly the best-known writer about children's experience in the Second World War not to have been a child at the time herself (she was born in 1947), but she too has repeatedly stressed the importance of talking to those who were there, and hearing their stories:

> I love researching. [...] I spend hours in the Newspaper Library soaking up period detail [...] Speaking to people, hearing their reminiscences.
>
> (Agnew)

> As soon as I started researching that period at the beginning of the war, I found myself wanting to know the answers to so many questions, so much so, that I lost all my shyness and would ask complete strangers in queues about their memories.
>
> (Dines)

> [My mother] was a nurse in London on a children's ward and also on a burns unit during the Blitz. [...] She told me lots of stories about the children she nursed. One boy, like William is in the book, had been sewn into his winter underwear – some children even had their underwear lined with newspaper to keep the warmth in.
>
> (Edwards)

Historical research here does not lie in opposition to memory: memory is its raw material. And memory begets memory: Westall reports that, after the publication of *The Machine-Gunners*, he received many letters, 'more than half [...] from forty-year-olds, wanting to share their war with me' (*Children of the Blitz* 11). The result was a volume, *Children of the Blitz*, compiled by Westall and composed of such memories, which constituted the record of what he called a ' "secret war" [...] a whole Children's War, never recorded' (11). Westall is aware that these decades-old versions of childhood experiences (many no doubt honed by years of retelling) are not the stuff of '*pukka* history', but defends his collection as 'a hurried, scattered rescue-dig' (12). His language suggests a sense of urgency, an awareness that the material of memory is ephemeral and that even in the 1980s those who were children in the war were beginning to die off. 'If a history of the Children's War was not going to be lost for ever, it was now or never' (11).

The process of converting memory into narrative is modelled in some novels, with Bawden's *Carrie's War* particularly explicit in using story as a means of passing on personal memory between generations. *Carrie's War* begins with the return of the adult Carrie to the scene of her wartime childhood. Recently widowed, Carrie has come back to Wales in the company of her children, to whom she tells the story of her evacuation. The title of the book makes it clear whose story this is, but to emphasize the point Carrie's children are left pointedly unnamed. Instead, they are referred to simply as 'the oldest boy', or 'Carrie's daughter', their own experiences being subordinated to those of their mother. At the end of the novel, however, when Carrie has finished her story, it is they who make their way through the wood to Druid's Bottom, the house where Carrie and her brother spent their happiest times, while Carrie herself hangs back fearfully. For 30 years Carrie has mistakenly blamed herself for the house's destruction by fire and the presumed deaths of all inside. However, on arriving there her children meet Hepzibah Green and Mister Johnny, two of the adults who had befriended Carrie during the war, still alive and living in the house's remaining outbuildings, and from Hepzibah they learn that Carrie's fears are unfounded. Where Carrie has tried to separate her memories of that time from her later life, the novel's conclusion re-establishes the continuity of time and individual lives, and in the book's final lines the children return to fetch her, only to meet her already 'coming through the Druid's Grove' (159).

In this book a narrative of the past is not born only of the desire to share experience: like Westall's 'total recall' of previously neglected facts as an involuntary 'surge of memory', Carrie's is a cathartic, and perhaps therapeutic, act. A similar example is that of Penelope Lively's *Going Back,* first published in 1975 as a children's book (although later republished for adults). Like *Carrie's War, Going Back* begins with the return of an adult, the book's narrator Jane, to the scene of her wartime childhood at Medleycott, a large house in north Somerset. There she recalls her experiences with her brother Edward during the war, and recounts them to her husband, who has accompanied her on the trip and is (like Carrie's children) unnamed. In both *Carrie's War* and *Going Back* it appears that the protagonists are driven to re-establish some broken link with their own childhoods; and in both cases a recent death in their own generation (Carrie's husband, Jane's brother Edward) is implicated in their decision – or rather, need – to revisit and communicate their experiences.

Books written about the Second World War by those who were children at the time are in some ways no more than particularly striking examples of a more general truth – that authors of historical fiction, as of other books, write with a degree of personal investment in their subject. Michelle Magorian, writing about the 1940s at one remove, may lack the direct memories available to her seniors, but she has strong emotive ties to many of the people (such as her mother) who have acted as sources of story and information for her novels, and feels that 'The period chose me really' (Agnew). Probably very few people commit the energy and time necessary for the writing of an historical book without a measure of identification with the people and events involved. Where novels about events within living memory are concerned, however, this engagement may include a need, both psychological and moral, to tell a story not only as an artist or even (in a narrow sense) as a teacher, but as an 'elder' within a community in which each generation is driven to bequeath something of itself to its successors, and to let 'generations [...] stand side by side in time'.

Looking forward

There is an obvious asymmetry between the positions of an historical novelist looking back along the track of time and a futurologist looking forward. As Judith Wright wrote of her future self, 'She will remember being me,/But what she is I cannot see' ('Counting in Sevens'). However, this should not blind us to the equally important symmetry of historical *curiosity*. We reconstruct the past, but we also construct possible futures, inevitably using some of the same materials. To suggest that the backward-facing activity of representing the past could be seen as illuminating the preoccupations of books set in the future may be counterintuitive, but we believe that it does so, partly through modelling ways to think about the nature of historical change itself (a subject to which we shall return in Chapter 7), but also because such representations are informed by the symbolic and ideological structures the past has assumed for writers and readers in the present, which in turn shape the kinds of future that can be imagined and accepted as both plausible and meaningful. In this section we consider a number of near-future books from this point of view, focusing specifically on their use of topoi associated with the Second World War.

For our purposes 'near-future books' means those set within the likely lifespan of their readers. Such books are often focused on the processes of history, in that they tend to chart quite carefully the course by which the world might move from actual present to imagined future. This need not imply that such books are simply predictive, however. Rather, they may utilize a number of rhetorical modes, ranging from Dreadful Warning to Optimistic Blueprint, with many working by way of the selective extrapolation of current tendencies in society, technology or nature. Books such as John Rowe Townsend's *Noah's Castle* (1975), or more recently Meg Rosoff's *How I Live Now* (2004) and Saci Lloyd's *The Carbon Diaries 2015* (2008) all imagine a near-future Britain, taking as their starting point a world much like their readers' own. In each case, they identify features prominent at the time of writing (inflation, the 'war on terror' and climate change, respectively), and by extrapolating from them demonstrate how quickly and fundamentally the world with which their readers are familiar might be cast into another mould.

When Townsend's *Noah's Castle* was first published in 1975, rising prices were much on the minds of most British adults. A combination of the 1973 oil crisis and bad industrial relations meant that inflation, which had stood at 9.2 per cent in 1973, was by 1975 running at 24.2 per cent, and it did not seem too wild a speculation that the country might succumb to the kind of hyperinflation experienced by Germany in the early 1920s or Hungary after the Second World War. This is the premise of Townsend's novel, in which Norman Mortimer, a man who prides himself on his organization and foresight, buys a large detached house and secretly stocks it with sufficient supplies to look after his family for the duration. The book is told from the point of view of Barry, one of Norman's children, who is torn between loyalty to his father and the knowledge that the world beyond his house is increasingly hungry, desperate and violent. Townsend charts the loss of amenities in the world outside: power cuts and food shortages, the rise of barter and the division of society into those in work (whose pay packets more or less keep pace with rising prices) and those on fixed incomes, such as pensioners, who are rapidly reduced to penury. In the context of 1975 nothing here is inherently implausible, and Townsend's 'Author's Note' acknowledges (while deprecating) the possibility that his book might be read as simple prediction:

> This story is set in a future which you can suppose to be two or three years after the time at which you are reading it. But I am not predicting that the conditions it describes will actually come about. It is a work of fiction, not of forecasting.
>
> (5)

Meg Rosoff's *How I Live Now* is rather more vague about the threat facing Britain, and indeed this vagueness is an important component of her text. Rosoff's narrator, Daisy, is a New York teenager who has come to live with her English cousins in a large, dilapidated house in the countryside, and she is more interested in her cousin Edmond than in the political situation; but this is in any case a world in which information is both scarce and unreliable. The events of *How I Live Now* are largely obscured by the fog of war, and the text does not place them within a specific political context. For large parts of the book Britain appears to be under occupation by an enemy that is certainly foreign but not identified with a particular nationality or ideology, although some of the ways in which they are described seem designed to align their methods with those of terrorism: 'Major McEvoy said Think about it as a Hostage Situation with Sixty Million Hostages so I did' (93). As with *Noah's Castle*, the book starts from a kind of normality, or at least from a situation containing many regular features of young adult fiction, including family friction, an eating disorder, love and sexual desire, and then walks us step by step into chaos before achieving a partial and slightly more hopeful resolution.

Finally, Saci Lloyd's *The Carbon Diaries 2015* begins just after the 'Great Storm' of December 2010, and recounts the travails of one family in London as they try to survive the strict carbon rationing introduced in response, and the subsequent extreme climate events, which include both a drought and a flood that overwhelms the Thames Barrier. As with Townsend's and Rosoff's books, the trajectory of *The Carbon Diaries 2015* runs from a situation of comparative familiarity into one of disaster, with most of the book detailing the stitch-by-stitch unpicking of the social fabric. The 'Great Storm', it is clear from the map at the front of the book, largely spared the eastern side of the country, and the book's narrator Laura, like Daisy in *How I Live Now*, is at first able to pursue her life with little more than a sense of mounting inconvenience, keeping up her school work, her crush on the boy next door and her ambitions for her band, the *dirty angels* – although she is far more aware than Daisy of the political and environmental issues that underlie the crisis. By the end of the book, however, although the London flood has receded and there is some indication that other countries will follow the UK's lead in rationing carbon, the fragility of what Laura and her family have regarded as normality has been starkly exposed.

As the brief summaries above suggest, these three books model the future according to a common pattern, in which reality of a kind familiar to contemporary readers is degraded over the course of the novel to the point where society gives way to near chaos (although all three books end with an indication of hope, or at least of respite). To concentrate exclusively on this common narrative shape is however to neglect the fact that, as well as working forward from the present, these books also intensively rework the *past*, drawing significantly on historical references for their material and their symbolism. This relationship with the past operates in more than one way. First, there is the extent to which near-future narratives inevitably refer to recent events simply as part of the process of embedding themselves into history. Thus, Townsend assumes the actual recent history of rising inflation in *Noah's Castle*, while Lloyd cites events such as the 2005 Hurricane Katrina (170) in establishing her novel's context of increasingly frequent extreme weather events. All three books make this kind of move, which has the effect of presenting contemporary readers with a vision of their own present, and even of their near future, as potentially historical – an example of the latter being the case of the 2012 Olympics, which is repeatedly referred to by Lloyd's narrator as an event from the recent past, although lying in the future for her original readers.

In addition, these novels claim a relationship with a deeper past, framing the deprivation and social threat by reference to events that have continuing emotional and historical resonance. Here the Home Front during the Second World War is both a potent example and a rich source of imagery. In *Noah's Castle*, we are told early on that Norman Mortimer 'served all through the Hitler war' (8), and was commissioned just before its end despite having left school without qualifications. The war remains the one time in his life when he found a theatre for his talents, and the subsequent decades of running a shoe shop have left him a disappointed man. Norman seizes the financial crisis as a chance to revive his more glorious days, and also to replay (though with a happier outcome) the Depression of the 1930s, when his own family suffered with an alcoholic father who 'had a small business and drank the profits' (35). He even disinters his army service revolver, and generally he treats the crisis as a military operation. But the book's parallels with the Second World War go much further, as rationing is reintroduced and a black market flourishes, butchers being (as in the War itself) figures of particular power and patronage. The narrator, Barry, becomes involved in a scheme to provide meals to pensioners, and finds that they too understand their situation by reference to a wartime past: 'The old people we fed were aware of their good fortune. They had been bred in hard old times. "I lived through two world wars," was a typical remark, "and I can live through this"' (97).

Saci Lloyd has stressed the importance of the First and Second World Wars to her research for *The Carbon Diaries 2015*, and emphasized the book's 'parallels with the Second World War and rationing. Everyone's in it together' (Jansen-Gruber). *The Carbon Diaries* too has an old person on hand to make these parallels explicit within the text, in the form of Laura's octogenarian neighbour Arthur, whom Lloyd based on her own grandfather (Jansen-Gruber). Laura adopts Arthur after being instructed by her teacher to find a needy person to look after, but finds that, thanks to his wartime experience, he is more resilient and resourceful than any of her other neighbours:

> 'Of course, I remember rationing in the war. We were out in the country, before I enlisted, so things weren't so bad. You could always bag a rabbit or a rook for the pot.'
>
> (314)

> 'The thing I remember about rationing most clearly was that everyone did their damnedest to carry on as if it were normal. And soon it *was*. I know it's a dreadfully dull thing to say, but in a way they were very happy times – all pulling together, knowing we were doing something good for the country.'
>
> (315)

The introduction of rationing makes such comparisons almost inevitable, but *The Carbon Diaries 2015* emphasizes the point by occasionally reproducing documents using much the same montage technique as Foreman's *War Boy*: these include a ration card, a map of Britain replete with ominous arrows (but showing advancing weather fronts rather than Axis armies), newspaper headlines and official notices, as well as more specifically modern items such as emails and computer printouts. In addition, the conversion of the garden into a smallholding, with livestock and vegetables replacing flowers, recalls the Dig for Victory campaign, as does (once again) the existence of a thriving black market.

In *How I Live Now* the wartime resonance is even stronger, in that Rosoff's book actually imagines the nightmare of a Britain under military occupation. As in the Second World War there is rationing and a renewed emphasis on working on the land, and large houses (such as that occupied by Daisy's cousins) are requisitioned by the military. Just as Arthur in *The Carbon Diaries 2015* and the recipients of free meals in *Noah's Castle* provide a direct personal link with the privations of previous wars, so here too there is an elderly Greek chorus ready with the appropriate comparisons:

> One crazy old man kept whispering to anyone who would listen that the BBC had been taken over by Malign Forces and that we shouldn't believe anything we heard on The Wireless but his wife

> rolled her eyes and said he was still worried about the Germans from last time around.
>
> (44)

> [...] it was pretty surprising to me how many of the older folks seemed to be right at home strangling a chicken. Piper said it was because of the Last War and rationing and everyone keeping chickens.
>
> (107)

There is much more to Townsend's, Rosoff's and Lloyd's books than the revival of wartime conditions, and no doubt hunger and scarcity have common features wherever and whenever they appear. Nevertheless, all three texts make considerable use of the symbolic potency of the Second World War in order to evoke their future worlds, and eloquently demonstrate the ways in which our understanding of the past is encoded into the ways that we are able to imagine the future.

Readers in time

In discussing books set in the past and in the future, we have until now been using those terms relative to date of publication. We have looked back to the Second World War, and forward to the near future, encompassing what is, at the time of writing, a span of time within living memory and living anticipation, and have suggested that fictions set within this period are likely to have relationships with each other and with their readers rather different from those set in more remote periods. However, as the phrase 'at the time of writing' indicates, the present is a moving target. In a few decades' time the Second World War will no longer be a living memory, and what was once the future will have been overshot by the movement of time. Some of the qualities we have identified as belonging to books set in, or inspired by, the Second World War may become invisible once the shared cultural context in which they were first read no longer exists. More generally, deictic categories such as 'living memory' and 'living anticipation' do not refer to stable sets either of events or of readers. We should thus acknowledge the literary implications of the reader's own changing position within history, and its effect on the ways in which texts can be experienced.

The readings offered by texts alter over time, frequently in ways that appear to open up or close down the possibilities of viewing them through the prism of particular genre conventions. E. Nesbit's *The Railway Children*, for example, was first read as a contemporary family story, something that is clearly no longer a possibility; and although it would be simplistic to claim that the passage of time has transformed it into an historical novel, the century that has elapsed since its first appearance in *The London Magazine* in 1905 means that its interest now lies partly in its portrayal of a period recognized as historical. Rosemary Sutcliff's *The Eagle of the Ninth* was rightly read as an historical novel in 1954, but the premise on which it is based, that the Hispana Legion disappeared under mysterious circumstances in AD 117, no longer represents the consensus belief amongst historians. Again, this does not mean that Sutcliff's novel has metamorphosed into an alternative history, but it does modify the experience of those readers aware of this change in historical orthodoxy.

Tom's Midnight Garden, by Philippa Pearce, presents a more intricate example of this principle. In Pearce's story, Tom Long finds himself transported nightly into the late-Victorian garden that once belonged to the house (now converted into flats) where he is staying for the summer. For children reading the book on its first publication in 1958, Tom's world was easy to identify as their own, and Tom himself was clearly their contemporary, while the Victorian garden and the girl Hatty whom he meets there just as clearly belonged to a previous generation. However, it is now over 50 years since *Tom's Midnight Garden* was published. Tom Long is almost as much an historical figure to children reading the book today as Hatty would have been to Tom himself. Tom's is a world where children are banished from their own houses for weeks on end for measles quarantine, where there are no home computers or mobile phones, where communication takes place by handwritten letter and where the readiest source of general information is a printed encyclopedia. Arguably this estrangement has made Pearce's an even more interesting text: however, it does mean that reading it has become a more complex experience for children today, who must appreciate not only the historical distance between Tom and Hatty on which the book turns, but also that between Tom and themselves. Such a reading calls for far greater historical knowledge, and also a sophistication about the nature of historical change, which must be recognized as a continuous process rather than a binary contrast between two discrete periods labelled the Present and the Past.

Books dealing with the near future are especially vulnerable to this kind of quasi-generic alteration. When a setting understood by a text's first readers as belonging to the future has become part of contemporary readers' past, the ways in which it may be read are necessarily modified. For example, although John Rowe Townsend insisted that *Noah's Castle* was 'a work of fiction, not of forecasting', its picture of hyperinflation in late 1970s Britain was certainly amongst the range of possible futures that might reasonably have been contemplated when it was published in 1975. From the perspective of the twenty-first century, the events it describes have moved from possible futurity into the category of 'might have been'. One effect is that of dislodging the story somewhat from its historical setting in the 1970s, and pushing it in the direction of more abstract readings in terms of parable and cautionary tale, with the specific economic circumstances described by Townsend coming to stand metonymically for any crisis in which choices have to be made between family and society at large. In a similar way (to take a far better-known example) Orwell's *Nineteen Eighty-Four* (1949), once its eponymous year had passed, arguably began to be regarded less in terms of political prophecy and more as a free-floating archetype of dystopian totalitarianism, the nominal historical placing of which was of only vestigial significance. In both cases, these more abstract interpretations were always theoretically available, but were more likely to be emphasized once events had made more historically specific readings harder to sustain.

This migration in the direction of abstraction is more easily undertaken with some texts than with others. *Noah's Castle* does not dwell to any great extent on the historical causes of the financial crisis: its focus is on the *response* to that crisis, and the moral and social questions it raises. Where does one's first duty lie? Should protest always be peaceful or is violence sometimes justified? Such questions are easily applicable beyond the immediate situation that gives rise to them in Townsend's book. They are present too in *The Carbon Diaries 2015*, but that is a text much more engaged in the politics of climate change than in simply responding to the crises caused by it, and where Townsend was at pains to point out that his was not a work of prediction, Saci Lloyd has stated that her characters 'are truly facing up to what I believe will be a near-future reality' (Jansen-Gruber). When one of Laura's neighbours describes the limitations of the Thames Barrier, for example, he is anticipating a future disaster, but he is also addressing (and alerting readers to) a situation that exists at the time of the book's writing: 'the Barrier has given London a false sense of security. Councils don't even have maps any more that show where in their borough is likely to flood and where's safe' (328). *The Carbon Diaries 2015* is not only a fiction about the near future but also an intervention in the politics of 2008. Indeed, these two aspects cannot be separated: in areas such as contingency planning and disaster prevention, present policy already implicates the future and shapes its possibilities. It remains to be seen how these aspects of Lloyd's text will affect the kinds of reading that it can accommodate in the future.

In this chapter we have considered the interaction of history and memory, both in representing the past and in anticipating the future. We have argued that books set within the period of the author's own recall, especially where they involve elements of autobiography, raise particular issues of personal legacy not present to the same degree when the setting is a more distant past. In A. L. Berridge's tongue-in-cheek formulation, 'A father may "belong" emotionally to his family, but an "ancestor" is public property' (Berridge). This difference in affect has implications for the writing and reading of books set in the recent past, but also for those set in other periods where the symbolic weight of such seminal events as the Second World War may be drawn on, for example to establish a sense of community and continuity from one generation to the next in near-future texts. The counterpoint between continuity and change is crucial to such texts: contemplating the paucity of the wartime butter ration inevitably evokes a contrast with the plenty enjoyed by most children in the West today, but may also lead them to question just how secure their environment of effortless amenity actually is. In the final chapter of this volume we will examine further the ways in which change is represented in books for children, as part of a wider enquiry into competing theories regarding the overall 'shape' of history.

7
Patterns of History

> I am merely considering how we should arrange or schematize those facts – ludicrously few in comparison with the totality – which survive to us (often by accident) from the past. I am less like a botanist in a forest than a woman arranging a few cut flowers for the drawing-room.
>
> C. S. Lewis, *De Descriptione Temporum* (1954)

Aspects of history: Sequence, causation and emplotment

Most children's books about the past, be they fiction or non-fiction, tend to concern themselves with particular periods of history rather than with providing a larger perspective on history in general, and our discussion so far has followed them in this. In this chapter we consider in a more sustained way those aspects of books about the past that relate not just to the periods being represented but to the conception of history as a whole. As our approach in this volume is literary-critical rather than pedagogic, our primary focus will be on the ways that such texts model history as part of the experience of reading, but we will give due weight to the close two-way relationship between that experience and the educational encounters of children striving to make sense of the nature and significance of the past. For our purposes we will distinguish three interrelated features of 'history as a whole': sequence, causation and finally that sense of history's having a shape, a pattern or a direction which can be summed up (to borrow Hayden White's term) as emplotment. We may consider these three as constituting a logical sequence, in that some grasp of each is a necessary precondition for the understanding of the next, and for this reason will discuss them in order.

The most fundamental of our three features is chronological sequence, a feature not much stressed in most historical children's books. Historical novels, concentrating as they typically do on the experiences of a limited number of individuals, are unlikely to extend their scope beyond a human lifespan, and children's books typically confine themselves to a far shorter period, such as the childhood of the protagonist. In the case of non-fiction, while a tradition of general histories does exist, from H. E. Marshall's *Our Island Story* (1905) to Ruth Brocklehurst's *The Usborne History of Britain* (2008), it is more common for books to deal with delimited periods, whether in the case of popular series such as 'Horrible Histories' (the individual titles of which include *The Measly Middle Ages* [1996], *The Slimy Stuarts* [1996] and *The Gorgeous Georgians* [1998]) or of books published with classroom use in mind. In England, the latter frequently reflect those topics mandated by the National Curriculum, which as far as British history is concerned are defined in period terms. For pupils aged 7–11, for example, they include the Tudors, the Victorians and the Second World War, all of which have had numerous books devoted to them, published in accordance with teachers' requirements.[1]

In educational terms, this concentration on individual periods has two unfortunate consequences. First, those periods that happen not to feature on the National Curriculum may be largely neglected. The 30 years following James II's accession in 1685, for example, which saw the Glorious Revolution, the Acts of Union and of Settlement, the Treaty of Utrecht and the Hanoverian succession, were arguably as important for the subsequent history of Britain as any other comparable span of time since the Norman Conquest, but little of this material is taught to children in English primary schools – who are, on the other hand, quite likely to be able to recite the names and fates of each of Henry VIII's six wives. In addition, the National Curriculum places relatively little emphasis on setting particular periods within a wider historical context. Even a general history such as Brocklehurst's, mentioned above, has been repackaged into smaller constituents such as *The Victorians (Usborne British History)* (2008), and while this makes good commercial sense for the publisher, designing the book to accommodate such time-slicing perpetuates the impression of history as essentially the sedimentary accretion of relatively discrete periods, with larger-scale processes rendered far less visible.

The lack of an overall chronology within which to set children's knowledge of particular historical periods has been repeatedly recognized as a problem in reports on school history by UK Government inspection bodies:

> Too great a focus on a relatively small number of issues means that pupils are not good at establishing a chronology, do not make connections between the areas they have studied and so do not gain an overview, and are not able to answer the 'big questions'.
>
> (Ofsted, *History in the Balance* 4)

> [... S]ome pupils found it difficult to place the historical episodes they had studied within any coherent, long-term narrative. They knew about particular events, characters and periods but did not have an overview. Their chronological understanding was often underdeveloped and so they found it difficult to link developments together. [...] In addition the curriculum structure for primary schools was itself episodic and militated against pupils grasping such an overview.
>
> (Ofsted, *History for All* 4)[2]

Traditionally, attempts to teach this aspect of history took the form of the memorization of regnal dates or of other significant events such as battles and Acts of Parliament. Such rote learning has long been unfashionable, partly on the grounds that it fails to engage children actively, partly because the kinds of event that can most easily be isolated in this way tend to reflect elite priorities less central to the social history now in vogue, and partly because it is ill-suited to recording more fuzzily defined events such as 'the Industrial Revolution' or 'the Enlightenment', which cannot be pinned down to particular dates except by arbitrary fiat. Nevertheless, such exercises provided a skeletal framework that allowed for the mental 'placing' of people and events, and for a sense of their order and their temporal distance from each other that seem a necessary precondition for more sophisticated forms of analysis and understanding.

In modern classrooms and textbooks some of these functions have devolved to the graphic device of the 'timeline', in which history is represented two-dimensionally, with words and pictures attached. Such devices are however not immune to the kinds of distortion identified earlier. To take *The Usborne History of Britain* as our example one more time (although it is far from a unique one), the timeline provided in the 'Factfile' at the end of that book does not use a consistent scale, with two-and-a-half pages being devoted to the twentieth century, while the two centuries from 1249 to 1453 are squeezed into a single page. The reasons for such an arrangement are entirely understandable, but an unsophisticated reader might well come away with the impression that years in the Middle Ages were considerably shorter or less significant than more recent ones.

As the quotations from Government reports above indicate, the perceived inadequacies of children's historical understanding lie not only in their ignorance of chronology but also in their inability to 'make connections' and 'link developments together'. Here the second of our three features, the principle of causation, is being invoked – the idea that actions have consequences, and that the events of one age set up the conditions for later events. This is easy to accept as a general principle, although the identification of historical causes is seldom simple. The analysis of causation depends in any case upon an ability to make comparisons between different times and to note that, for example, the material circumstances and the mental concepts denoted by the phrase 'the poor' are very different in 1300, 1600 and 1950. As we have noted, it is relatively rare for children's fiction dealing with the past to treat more than one period explicitly, the obvious exceptions being books depicting time travel and series that deal with a specific place or family over a number of generations, such as Rosemary Sutcliff's books about Roman and post-Roman Britain, Lucy M. Boston's Green Knowe novels (1954–76), Ronald Welch's books about the Carey family (1954–72) and Barbara Willard's 'Mantlemass' series (1970–81). Nevertheless, all historical fiction makes implicit comparisons between the past and the present, since what makes the past visible *as* the past is precisely its difference from the writer's and reader's own time.

That difference is seldom, if ever, registered simply and only as difference, however, but is rather invested with some kind of affective or ideological content. As John Stephens puts it: 'there are no "facts" without interpretations, and interpretations are morally grounded' (205). To make the point crudely for the sake of clarity, when people talk about the past as either 'a benighted age' or 'the good old days', they are making a value-laden comparison with the present. They are also assigning a direction of travel, at least to the span of time that lies between that period and our own, a trajectory that describes progress or decline, respectively. It is here that we might be tempted to look beyond the proximate causes of individual events, towards some larger-scale pattern within history as a whole – for, having drawn a line between that particular Then and our own Now we are free to extend it beyond those two points, further into the past or the future, and to conclude that history *in general* describes a process of decline or of ascent. In this sense, any book that represents the past has at least the potential to imply a 'theory of history', a general idea that events are disposed across time in a regular or at least non-random form. This is 'emplotment', the third of our three features.

Plotting history

The philosopher of history, Hayden White, uses the term 'emplotment' to refer to the use made by historians (and others) of existing narrative and symbolic structures familiar from literary genres in order to understand and articulate their perception of a 'shape' within history. According to White, historical narratives:

> [...] succeed in endowing sets of past events with meanings over and above whatever comprehension they provide by appeal to putative causal laws, by exploiting the metaphorical similarities between sets of real events and the conventional structures of our fictions. By the very constitution of a set of events in such a way as to make a comprehensible story out of them, the historian charges those events with the symbolic significance of a comprehensible plot-structure.
>
> (53)

White draws heavily on the Canadian literary critic Northrop Frye and his classic *Anatomy of Criticism* (1957) in discussing the various ways in which history can be viewed as conforming to the basic plot types: tragic, comic, romantic or ironic. In a previous chapter, for example, we discussed a number of texts dealing with the

Claudian invasion of Britain. Some of them presented that event as a fundamentally positive development, which brought civilization, luxury goods and order to a barbaric island; others as a cruel, imperialist assault aimed at wiping out the existing culture and reducing the Britons to servitude. Rather than feel obliged to judge between these views, which are both, after all, underpinned by the same data, White would identify them as the products of different generic conventions. In Frye's terms, the first is a comic emplotment (which does not necessarily imply humour in this usage), the second a tragic. Part of the historian's (or the novelist's) persuasive power lies in the efficacy with which he or she can assimilate the available data to the conventions, topoi and overall trajectory of these pre-existing plot types. This task involves decisions both of selection and of emphasis, as well as such literary techniques as 'characterization, motific repetition, variation of tone and point of view, alternative descriptive strategies and the like' (47). For White, such choices can radically change the nature of the historical plot, for example from tragedy to comedy or farce: 'How a given historical situation is to be configured depends on the historian's subtlety in matching up a specific plot-structure with the set of historical events that he wishes to endow with a meaning of a particular kind' (48).

We believe there are limits to how far subtlety will take an historian in matching a set of events to a preferred generic reading. Nevertheless, White's observations on the role of the teller in placing historical events within a particular generic context will be helpful in informing our discussion, not only of history proper but also of historical fiction, and of history as a whole as well as of particular historical episodes. We might note too that the fact that such genre choices are rhetorically effective suggests that the perception of pattern and direction in historical events meets a human desire for significance within history, as within personal experience. As Aaron Jackson notes, discussing the work of Hans Blumenberg: 'Dividing the past into epochs and eras structured around designated key events (wars, revolutions, natural disasters) gives it a structure and implies that it has meaning as it anticipates the present and explains our position in the world' (53).

We have already mentioned two of the basic 'plots' that underlie narratives about history: first, that it is a story of progress (even if punctuated with temporary setbacks); second, that it is a story of inexorable decline (perhaps with occasional remissions). Both of these are teleological theories, in that they posit a destination for history, and both come in a number of variants. Progressive versions of history include Marxism as well as so-called Whig history (Butterfield), which sees history as tending towards ever greater liberty, wealth and civilization; while the pessimistic view has found advocates in such disparate quarters as the *contemptus mundi* tradition of Christianity and the ecological movement, a classical example being the Greek division of history into a Golden Age, followed by the ages of Silver, Bronze and Iron, a succession indicative of steady deterioration. Teleological models of both types are discernible within children's books about the past, but they coexist with a number of others, including the humanist model (the principle of which is that the human condition remains essentially unchanging, despite variations in material conditions) and what we may call the formative model, in which history is understood and valued precisely as an identity-conferring narrative.

Before discussing these in more detail we should acknowledge that most books do not confine themselves to just one or other of these models. An illustrative example is Cynthia Harnett's *The Load of Unicorn* (1959), an historical novel set during the period when William Caxton set up his press in London in the 1470s. Much of the plot turns upon the fear of some professional scriveners that the newfangled printing press will make them obsolete, and on their attempts to sabotage Caxton's enterprise. Here we have a well-known example of a pattern repeated through much of subsequent history, most famously in the case of the Luddites, in which developments in technology threaten the livelihoods of traditional craftsmen. We might expect the presentation of this conflict to indicate the text's allegiance to one or other historical model: is new technology to be welcomed or deplored? In the case of *The Load of Unicorn* the sympathy is all with Caxton, who is presented as a kindly and enlightened capitalist. Although he is threatening the scriveners' livelihood, and the book's protagonist, Bendy, is himself the son of a scrivener, this is not held against him. On the contrary, it is Bendy's grown-up brothers, Matthew and Cornelius, who are presented as unsympathetic and also dishonest in their attempts to undermine their rival, so that their fate comes to seem deserved. Caxton, by contrast, is a man of culture who clearly loves not only his new technology and the profit it can make him but literature itself. The text's stance is thus clear, even without the explicit judgement of Bendy's wise father, who chooses to befriend Caxton and apprentice his son to him, with the somewhat anachronistic declaration: 'It is always fruitless to stand up against progress' (32–3).

As far as technology is concerned, the orientation of Harnett's book is clearly progressive and optimistic. The social implications of printing, with its ability to make books cheaper and to promote widespread literacy, are also profound. Yet these attitudes coexist with a deep cultural conservatism on Caxton's part. Harnett notes in her own postscript to the book that the prologues and epilogues the historical Caxton appended to his publications 'are vivid and full of his horror about the new world that was fast replacing the world of chivalry of his youth. To restore the old noble ideals was the object of almost every book that he printed' (233). This is reflected in his choice of texts to publish, which include Malory's chivalric *Morte D'Arthur* (featured in *The Load of Unicorn*), while at one point in Harnett's novel her fictional Caxton breaks from being the urbane and friendly printer to launch into an impassioned speech about the need for another crusade to the Holy Land (74). These paradoxical aspects of Caxton's own character reflect a wider tension within the world the book depicts, and an ambivalence about social change that cannot be divorced from the technology that enables it.

Books involving peripatetic time travel offer a convenient platform for the comparison of different ages, and two of the earliest, E. Nesbit's *The Story of the Amulet* (1906) and *The House of Arden* (1908), reveal a similar ambivalence about the direction of history. As a Fabian, Nesbit was committed to a belief in the progressive establishment of civilization and liberty on socialist lines, and this belief is given expression in *The Story of the Amulet* when her four young protagonists visit a future in which 'London is clean and beautiful, and the Thames runs clear and bright, and the green trees grow, and no one is afraid, or anxious, or in a hurry' (213). Nevertheless, Nesbit spends much of the book puncturing any complacent ideas her readers may have about the present's superiority to the past. A visit to pre-dynastic Egypt finds the children encountering a number of villagers, and impressing them with a cheap bangle they happen to have with them. But they also notice the careful craftsmanship of the villagers' own jewellery.

'I say,' said Robert, 'what a lot we could teach them if we stayed here!'

'I expect they could teach us something too,' said Cyril.

(59)

Back in their own time, the children come across a destitute girl who seems destined for the workhouse, but when they take her to pre-Roman Britain she is quickly adopted by the British tribe whom they encounter there: 'You would have thought, to see them, that a child was something to make a fuss about, not a bit of rubbish to be hustled about the streets and hidden away in the workhouse' (169). The implication is clear: Nesbit's 1906 present is morally inferior to the community values of its ancient British predecessors, and Anthea's 'sevenpenny-halfpenny trumpery brass' bangle from the Lowther Arcade (55), though it may impress through its novelty, pales next to the handmade flint bracelet of the ancient Egyptian woman to whom she gives it. This is an effective satire on presentist (and imperialist) pomposity, but it complicates Nesbit's sense of history as leading towards a utopian future of equality, happiness and comfort.

The House of Arden, unlike *The Story of the Amulet*, confines its action to England, but it too takes its young protagonists back in time – indeed, brother Edred and sister Elfrida are alerted to the possibility of historical adventures by reading the recently published *The Story of the Amulet*. Their journeys take them back in leaps of approximately a century at a time, seeking the treasure that will restore their ancestral home, an errand that tends to underscore the present diminished status of the Arden family in comparison with its former landed and titled glory. On seeing the family castle in its pristine state in Jacobean times, Edred can conceive of nothing more desirable than to restore it in the twentieth century: '"We'll bring it back," said Edred firmly – "when we find the treasure"' (172). Given that the siblings' adventures in the past take them from the relative poverty and obscurity of their present into the company of such luminaries as Sir Walter Raleigh and Henry VIII, and that the past is understood to be the location of the family's lost riches, there is little in the book's overall structure to suggest an understanding of history as progressive, at least as far as the protagonists are concerned. For society at large the picture is rather more complex. Linda Hall has commented that Nesbit 'tends to see history in the light of unreconstructed social practice that needs to be reformed and even transformed according to the Fabian heart's desire. The past is always inferior, therefore, to a more liberal present or a putative socialist future' ('Aristocratic Houses' 55). While *The House of Arden* certainly provides examples of this progressive movement – Hall cites a narratorial digression on the evils of persecuting so-called witches – it is far from unchallenged. Nesbit is always alert to possible complacency, and even in describing the treatment of witches she twice reminds her readers that 'those long-ago days [...] aren't so very long ago' (55), with the implication that any advance made since then is fragile and liable to be reversed.

On two occasions a specific comparison is made between the past and the 1907 present. In 1807, a local wise woman has an ecstatic vision of a future that appears to her almost magical:

> I see great globes of light like the sun in the streets of the city, where now are only little oil-lamps and guttering lanterns. I see iron roads, with fiery dragons drawing the coaches, and rich and poor riding up and down on them. Men shall speak in England and their voice be heard in France – more, the voices of men dead shall be kept alive in boxes and speak at the will of those who still live. The handlooms shall cease in the cottages, and the weavers shall work in palaces with a thousand windows lighted as bright as day.
>
> (59)

This sunny picture, in which industrial cotton mills are envisioned as brightly lit palaces, contrasts sharply with the account given by Richard Arden, a boy living in 1605 who has also spent time in the twentieth century:

> They make people work fourteen hours a day for nine shillings a week, so that they never have enough to eat or wear, and no time to sleep or to be happy in. They won't give people food or clothes, or let them work to get them; and then they put the people in prison if they take enough to keep them alive. They let people get horrid diseases, till their jaws drop off, so as to have a particular kind of china. Women have to go out to work instead of looking

> after their babies, and the little girl that's left in charge drops the baby and it's crippled for life.
>
> (222)

As descriptions of the lives of working people in the early twentieth century these could scarcely be less compatible, but the text does not arbitrate between them. The wise woman is generally presented as reliable, and Richard, although he speaks in bitterness, is giving voice to social concerns that echo Nesbit's own. It is of course possible to admire the ingenuity and energy of technological innovation while also acknowledging its human cost, and to see progress in one area as accompanied by (if not dependent on) deterioration in another, but such nuanced attempts at reconciliation are left to the reader rather than being performed by the text.

Time-slips – A pessimistic genre?

These two books by Nesbit (along with *The House of Arden*'s sequel, *Harding's Luck* [1909]) are relatively unusual in providing their protagonists with a tour of several different historical eras. In the decades either side of the Second World War, especially, time-slip novels have typically involved a movement between just two historical points, one being the text's own present. From Alison Uttley's *A Traveller in Time* (1939) through to Philippa Pearce's *Tom's Midnight Garden* (1958) and the work of Penelope Lively in the 1970s, amongst others, mid-century time-slips recount the experiences of a present-day child who gains temporary access to the past. In a series of articles on time-slip fiction, Linda Hall has argued that such books present the movement from past to present as a history of decline, in which morality, social order and the built and natural environments all suffer degradation under the onslaught of 'an epidemic of modernity and apparent hatred of the past', particularly in the form of planners and politicians who wish to sweep away the trappings of the past in favour of an angular new world built of steel and concrete. Against this movement such books offer a conservative protest, or at least record 'a sense of loss' at the passing of an older world ('House and Garden' 154).[3] In general we believe that such a univocal reading does insufficient justice to the multitude of competing discourses at work in such books, and in many cases (such as that of Lively) to the text's ability to undercut any unthinking identification of the past with better times (Butler 78–84). Nevertheless, such an identification is certainly a very visible element in several prominent time-slip novels of that era.

Probably the most celebrated book of this type is Philippa Pearce's *Tom's Midnight Garden*. As mentioned in Chapter 7, this novel concerns Tom Long, a modern boy who is staying with his childless aunt and uncle, while his brother is in quarantine for measles. The couple occupies a gardenless flat in what had been a large Victorian house; however Tom discovers that late at night, when the grandfather clock in the hallway strikes 13, he can gain access to the garden of that house as it was some 70 years before. In *Tom's Midnight Garden* the intervening conversion of the house into flats and of its garden into plots for more modest dwellings is presented unambiguously as a negative development, rather than as (for example) a welcome move in the direction of egalitarianism. Tom's forays into the garden by night are accompanied by luscious descriptions of its many flowers and walks. By day, however, the door leads to a very different scene:

> At the back of the house was a narrow, paved space enclosed by a wooden fence, with a gateway on to the sideroad at one end. There were five dustbins, and near the dustbins was parked an old car from beneath which stuck a pair of legs in trousers. A piece of newspaper bowled about, blown in from outside and imprisoned here; and the place smelt of sun on stone and metal and the creosote of the fencing.
>
> (34–5)

What had been beautiful and verdant has been destroyed, reduced to ugly sterility. Significantly, neither Tom nor the reader sees more of the Victorian era than is visible in the garden and house, one idyllic skating trip along the river excepted. There is no hint that this age could be home to poverty or ugliness of its own, and in so far as the garden functions metonymically for the Victorian past (which it inevitably comes to do), *Tom's Midnight Garden* offers what is a very selective impression. Conversely, we venture beyond the modern confines of the flat only to find the town in which it sits a lifeless and ugly wasteland:

> 'Here's your river, Tom!' said Aunt Gwen, triumphantly.
>
> It *must* be the same river, although it looked neither like the stretch Tom had glimpsed from Hatty's window nor like the one he and Hatty had reached through the meadow by the garden hedge. This river no longer flowed beside meadows: it had back-garden strips on one side and an asphalt path on the other.
>
> There was a man fishing by the bridge, and Aunt Gwen called to him: 'Have you caught any fish?'
>
> 'There aren't any fish,' the man replied sourly. He stood by a notice that said: 'WARNING. The Council takes no responsibility for persons bathing, wading or paddling. These waters have been certified as unsuitable for such purposes, owing to pollution.'
>
> (152)

Pearce's book is a psychologically subtle one, which has much to say at the level of individual persons about the inevitability of change and the possibilities of persistence; but in terms of presenting two historical visions of England, the picture it paints is stark: the past is preferable to the present in almost every way.

Hall is probably right that the tenor of British time-slips in the post-War decades was generally conservative, but this is by no means intrinsic to the time-slip form, as we can see by comparing one of her examples, Lucy M. Boston's *The Stones of Green Knowe* (1976), with Hilda Lewis's *The Ship that Flew* (1939). *The Stones of Green Knowe* is the last of Boston's six books set around the ancient manor house of Green Knowe, which was based on Boston's own home in Hemingford Grey in Cambridgeshire. Previous volumes provided access to a number of different ages, including the Regency and Restoration periods, but *The Stones of Green Knowe* takes us right back to young Roger D'Aulneaux and the house's foundation by his Norman father. When Roger travels forward to the modern era he is, as Hall notes, 'utterly stricken by the litter-strewn, malodorous, tar-macadamised desolation he encounters almost everywhere he looks' ('Time no longer' 47):

> The wide watermeadows were untouched on both sides of the river, but beyond them were houses again, not as in a city huddled together in narrow busy streets, smoky from a thousand wood fires, like Cambridge, but wastefully scattered everywhere,

> each house separate, and most of them without either roof-vent or chimney. Roger was staggered. Where did all these people come from, and what did they live on? How could the land provide food for them? No wonder they had no chimneys, for without a forest what would they burn?
>
> (100)

Within a different form of emplotment Roger's astonishment might be read as approval: after all, heating technology has moved on from open hearths and agriculture has grown more efficient at feeding people. Here, however, our attention is drawn rather to the 'wasteful' use of resources, and the breaking of the symbiotic bond between people and land. We can contrast Roger's reaction to the twentieth century with that of another Norman child, from Hilda Lewis's pre-war *The Ship that Flew*. In this book, a group of children from 1939 travel through time and space in a magic ship, landing at one point in their own village, a few decades after the Conquest. There they make the acquaintance of Matilda, whose father (like Roger's) is the local lord. During this initial encounter both parties find something to admire in the other's accomplishments: Matilda sees the modern children's ability to read as little short of wondrous, and they are equally impressed by her skill at embroidery. Honours are thus shared between the two periods. Later in the book, Matilda (like Roger) travels into the modern era, where she stays with the children in 1939 for a week. Unlike Roger, however, she finds her holiday in modernity an almost wholly positive experience:

> [. . .] as they approached the road, where the half-dozen houses stood, Matilda gave a cry of pleasure. 'Oh, it is pretty, pretty!' she exclaimed.
>
> 'What is it?' asked Sheila, pleased at Matilda's pleasure.
>
> The little girl waved her hand. She would have liked to explain how cosy the red-roofed house looked, with its gay curtains flying, and its red roofs and its red chimney-pots. After the great, gaunt, grey stone castle it seemed so little and friendly and warm.
>
> (180)

Where Roger is alienated by modern architecture, Matilda finds its human scale a welcome change from her grim castle home. She is equally entranced by the convenience of indoor running water, and enjoys such exotic foods as oranges and chocolate cake. At the village bazaar she takes part in a race (how liberating not to have to wear heavy clothes!) and donates some embroidery to raise money for the local church, originally built by her own father. Only at one point does the modernity of 1939 seriously grate, when the youngest of the modern children, Sandy, suggests that the church (which is in constant need of repair) may have outlived its usefulness: 'Cheaper to pull the old thing down and put a nice new one up instead!' (187). But Sandy's view is dismissed by her elder brother, who reassures Matilda that the modern villagers are 'proud [...] of their old Norman church and [...] people [come] for miles to see it' (187). The preference for modernity is thus tempered by a sense that the past too has value. This minor disagreement is indicative of a continual negotiation between the claims of past and present rather than a fundamental rejection of either, nor is there here the sense implicit in Roger D'Aulneaux's reaction to the twentieth century that something irretrievable and precious has been lost in the movement from the Norman to the modern era.

The humanist model

We have concentrated so far on teleological emplotments of history, partly because these are relatively visible, and in their optimistic and pessimistic incarnations offer a clear contrast with each other. However, these are not the only models available. Another is the humanist model, which is founded on the assumption that human nature and the human condition are essentially unchanging. Under this model history is the story of people like ourselves, facing problems which, though superficially different, are perennially familiar. Part of history's interest and importance then becomes its ability to teach: specifically, we can learn about our present by looking at similar situations that have arisen in the past. As John Stephens puts it in his account of the humanist position: 'History imparts "lessons" because events, in a substantial sense, are repeatable and repeated' (203). Thus Susan Cooper, talking about wartime books such as her own *Dawn of Fear* (1970), has suggested:

> Books about war can be valuable for children, pointing the way from swords to ploughshares. But they can do it only by saying to them, 'This doesn't *have* to happen again. It's up to you.'
>
> ('Swords and Ploughshares' 151)

In his classic discussion in *Language and Ideology in Children's Fiction* (1992), Stephens sees humanist assumptions as dominant within children's historical fiction, which has developed as an ideologically conservative genre as a result, although he notes that humanism is always in tension with the necessity of 'making strange' which is intrinsic to historical writing and which can be the agent of what Stephens identifies as 'cultural relativism' (203), or more specifically an historicist vision in which people's minds are the products of their unique historical circumstances. In its most radical form such a vision would render the past incomprehensible and the motivations of its people opaque, but in practice, as we have seen over the course of this book, historical texts execute a counterpoint between change and sameness, strangeness and familiarity, which attempts to do justice to the reality of both.

Stephens' discussion has been rightly influential in the two decades since it was published. It was groundbreaking in its direct examination of the ideological basis of children's historical fiction, and is exemplary as an account of this tension between humanist and historicist models of viewing history. However, his concentration on these modes, which in his argument become the binary poles to which all representations of the past can be reduced, means that he tends to ignore ways of thinking about the past not easily accommodated by them. For Stephens, the humanist position that 'humans behave and feel in ways that remain constant in different periods' constitutes one of the major criteria by which children's novels are evaluated (205), and he concludes from these criteria that such texts act as a powerful tool for 'inculcating social conservatism and for implicitly conveying the impression or, better, illusion that a reader's present time, place and subjectivity constitute a normative position against which alterities are to be measured' (205). However, the identification of these beliefs as part of the same ideological matrix seems to us to do insufficient justice to the variety and heterogeneity of historical fiction. For example, the elevation of the present to a normative position may in fact form the basis of a dismissive view of the past and its people as backward and definitively outgrown ('Cheaper to pull the old thing down and put a nice new one up instead!'), quite at odds with social conservatism of the kind mentioned above, which treasures the past as the original source of meaning and value and as the touchstone against which later developments must be judged.

This opposition between conservative and progressive models of history is largely orthogonal to that between humanism and historicism as Stephens defines them, and as such is not easily susceptible to analysis within his terms. Moreover, as we note above with respect to *The Load of Unicorn*, individual texts may accommodate contradictory views of history without ceasing to be effective as historical fiction.

Another feature of the humanist model is that history as a whole may be valued not only for its transhistorical continuity but also in terms of its *extent*, which allows us to see human action and ambition in proportion. The present, far from being the place to which history has been eagerly leading up, is recognized as just one point in a far larger landscape. The realization of this fact may act as a humbling corrective to presentism in general, and encourage the process of maturation in young readers, who are introduced by way of historical writing to a community of human beings that extends through time as well as space: 'Children need to sense that we live in a permanent world that reaches away behind and ahead of us and that the span of a lifetime is something to be wondered at, and thought about' (Lively, 'Children and Memory' 233). History under the humanist model is a source of consolation as well as of community. It draws us gently out of solipsism by showing that others have suffered before us (Butler 56–7), while its very scale affords a larger perspective within which to place the pain and conflict that oppress individual lives. Here, for example, is Rosemary Sutcliff's description of the aftermath of the Battle of Naseby in her Civil War book, *Simon*:

> Behind them, in the wide upland valley that had so lately been a battle-field, the prisoners were being rounded up, and the Royalist baggage-wagons brought in to serve the wounded, and the camp-followers were busy. It was not yet noon of a day that was still lovely, and the June sun shone warmly, gently, on the dead of two English armies, who lay tumbled uncouthly among the thyme and the little white honey-clover of the downland turf, here at the heart of England. High overhead, the buzzard still wheeled, mewing, on motionless wings and on every side the coloured counties fell away in shallow vales and hazy woodland, and little fields where the hay harvest was in full swing.
>
> (80)

In cinematic terms this passage pans out from the scene of conflict, a withdrawal from the intensity of battle not into indifference but into a longer view that understands war as one aspect of human existence, and contrasts it with the permanence of the land. The opposition of the two armies is irrelevant to those who lie together in death, 'tumbled uncouthly among the thyme and the little white honey-clover'. The reference to the hay harvest turns the deadly scything of sword and musket into a natural image, and invokes time as well as space, for such tasks are reminders of the seasonal cycles that continue irrespective of human strife, like the ploughman in Breughel's 'Fall of Icarus' who 'may/Have heard the splash, the forsaken cry, /But for [whom] it was not an important failure' (W. H. Auden, 'Musée des Beaux Arts', ll.15–17). The humanist model typically prizes history for its ability to teach humane values, a task to which the assumed universality of human experience is central; but it may also hypostatize history as something larger than any individual human life.

Writing in 1992, Stephens argued that the assumptions of humanism's 'intellectual and ideological bases are no longer dominant within Western society', and that this 'weakening of humanism's intellectual hegemony' (203) threatens to deprive historical fiction (which he sees as intrinsically committed to humanism) of its readership. From the vantage point of the present day this conclusion appears hasty. At any rate, the humanist model of history visible in older historical books such as Sutcliff's is scarcely less so in more recent texts, even if it coexists with historicist perspectives. As one recent example amongst many we may cite M. J. Putney's young adult historical fantasy *Dark Mirror* (2011), which tells of Victoria (Tory) Mansfield, an aristocrat living in the early 1800s. When Tory manifests magical abilities in saving her young nephew's life, she is banished to Lakeland Abbey near Dover. In Tory's society magic is not unusual in 'common people', but is utterly shameful in the well born, and at Lakeland the magically talented offspring of high society are trained to suppress their magic before being allowed to re-enter society. There she joins a group calling themselves the Irregulars, who are secretly learning to wield their talents in order to help the country in the event of a Napoleonic invasion. While trying to evade capture by the authorities, Tory inadvertently travels to 1940, where she meets descendents of some of the Irregulars. The text emphasizes the similarities between the two times (as Hester Burton put it in words quoted in Chapter 1 of this volume: 'Both seasons were a time of danger, stress, and joy; in both we were threatened by invasion and were fighting for our lives'), and Tory and the family she meets in 1940 establish an immediate rapport.

In its recognition of the 'repeatability' of history and its assumption that people born 150 years apart will establish an easy understanding, this text conforms to the humanist model as we have described it. However, it also features elements of historicism. Tory is a 1803 aristocrat, with social attitudes to match: when she is comforted by a servant she finds herself thinking, in terms that are unattractive from a modern point of view, although plausible for the daughter of an earl: 'What did it say about [her] life that she was grateful for a housemaid's approval?' (33). In 1940 she finds a radically changed society, and not merely in terms of new technologies and comforts such as hot running water and electricity. She discusses modern England with Allarde, a fellow Irregular and aristocrat, who has joined her and some others in coming to 1940 in order to help the war effort:

> 'It's fascinating,' Allarde replied. 'Forever England and in many ways unmistakable, but so very different in other ways.'
>
> 'I have mixed feelings about all the inventions people now take for granted,' she said. 'Many are very convenient. Others are just alarming. [...]'
>
> [...]
>
> 'I think England benefits from a more democratic society. There is greater fairness and talented men have many more opportunities.' Allarde hesitated. 'But it's not my England. I don't believe this era would ever feel quite like home.'
>
> (225)

Dark Mirror does not put the comparison between 1803 and 1940 to the service of an implicit theory of progress or decline: Tory and Allarde are aware that their reactions and opinions derive from their own backgrounds and personalities rather than from some transcendent truth about history. Their simultaneous experience of recognition and alienation is characteristic of the tension between humanist and historicist models, here experienced simply *as* a tension and a conflict of affective response rather than as a philosophical paradox.

The formative model

Its insistence on the universality of human experience distinguishes the humanist from the historicist model of history, but also from what we have called the formative model. By formative we refer to a view of history as a repository of identity-forming narratives. Under this model, part of what enables one to be fully English (for example) is an understanding of English history, and a recognition and acceptance of that history as part of one's own heritage and cultural identity. On a more intimate scale, family stories and anecdotes fulfil a similar purpose, renewing the bonds and the boundaries of communities, a function to which we alluded in the previous chapter's discussion of Second World War fiction. The formative model envisages the practice of history as an act of collective memory.

The formative model may have a teleological inflection, as it does in Kipling, whose *Puck of Pook's Hill* (1906) presents the history of England as essentially preparatory to the assumption of the responsibilities of empire. History in *Puck of Pook's Hill* is also formative, however, because the historical characters with whom the child protagonists Dan and Una are presented act as identity-forming exemplars, teaching them lessons that will be internalized so completely that the children will not even consciously remember them, but that will nevertheless contribute profoundly to their (and Kipling's readers') sense of themselves as English. In gaining access to these figures they are 'seized and possessed of all Old England' (48), and the English past with its triumphs and vicissitudes is established as an essential component of their identities. A year earlier, in a different genre, H. E. Marshall too insisted that the value of *Our Island Story* lay in its status as an accumulation of identity-forming stories rather than of facts. The presence of the first-person pronoun in her title defines both her readership and her purpose in writing:

> There are many facts in school histories that seem to children to belong to lessons only. Some of these you will not find here. But you will find some stories that are not to be found in your school books – stories which wise people say are only fairy-tales and not history. But it seems to me that they are part of Our Island Story,

> and ought not to be forgotten, any more than those stories about which there is no doubt.
>
> (xvii–xviii)

Just as personal memories (whether accurate or not) contribute to a person's character and identity, so stories about the past inform the character and identity of a nation, and their veracity may be less important for this purpose than the emotional significance and symbolic weight they have attained within cultural memory. Almost a century after Marshall, Geraldine McCaughrean was making very similar points in the 'Introduction' to her own collection of stories from British history, *Britannia* (1999):

> Certain stories are no longer told, because there may be only a grain of truth in them.
>
> But, wouldn't it be a terrible pity if, as a result, those stories were to wither and die? These grand adventures have forged our identity as a race of heroes, saints and underdogs destined for greatness. In my book, that makes them history.
>
> So watch out, as you read, for myth, propaganda, embroidery, and downright lies, but remember: these stories are, in themselves, a part of British history... as well as our national heritage.
>
> (7)

Some of McCaughrean's phrasing ('a race [...] destined for greatness') reads like a plea for British exceptionalism, but a formative model of history need involve no more than an acknowledgement of the role the past plays in forming a community's sense of itself, and a view of history's value and meaning as residing in that role.

The models of history we have considered here do not of course constitute an exhaustive list. We might add, for example, the dramatic model, in which history is conceived as the playing out of a divinely ordained narrative. This is a conception that has at times been dominant in Christian thought, and although it does not have a major presence in children's books about British history it may find a secular echo, as for example in Rosemary Sutcliff's stories set after the departure of the Romans from Britain, in which characters frequently evince a sense that civilization is about to enter a dark age, but an equal faith that it will re-emerge at some future date – a metaphor of night and daybreak that is utilized both within the novels and in the very titles of such works as *The Lantern Bearers* (1959), *Sword at Sunset* (1963) and *Dawn Wind* (1961). This pattern may also be aligned with a more general belief in history as a cyclical phenomenon, in which large-scale entities such as nations and empires go through predictable phases of growth, decay and collapse, mirroring the life cycles of biological organisms.

For our purpose it is sufficient to reiterate that accounts of the past, whether in fiction or non-fiction, are likely to be written and read under the aegis of one or more historical models. This is important for several reasons, but not least because such models are often implicit rather than explicit, and their ideological force may not be apparent. In a situation such as that we described at the beginning of this chapter, in which children's knowledge of chronology and skill in making informed comparisons between different periods is patchy (at least as assessed by the UK Government inspectors) this is cause for concern. It means that child readers are less well equipped than they might otherwise be to assess representations of the past in an informed and critical manner.

Whether projecting contemporary concerns onto the past, or understanding the present in terms of historical precedent, or discerning some kind of direction or purpose within the movement of history as a whole, the ideological tenor of historical books for children has been one of our recurrent concerns throughout this volume. It has been an important facet of a still wider enquiry into the relationship between historical fact and fictional representation. In the opening pages of this book we pointed to the tension inherent in the phrase 'historical fiction', and over the course of our discussion we have considered some of ways in which this tension manifests itself, in the use of anachronisms and in questions of authenticity, and in the need to find a *modus vivendi* that accommodates the ethical, aesthetic and pedagogic functions of historical texts. British history, in all its variety, has proved a rich territory, and one that continues to stimulate both writers and readers, as the preponderance of recent books amongst those discussed in this volume suggests. In 1976, Robert Leeson wrote of historical fiction as a genre sustained largely by the pedagogic requirements of teachers, and in 1992 John Stephens was almost as downbeat, dourly observing that 'historical fiction continues to be written for children and to some extent read by them' (204). In the last decade this situation has changed dramatically, and children's historical fiction has gained something of the popularity enjoyed by fantasy at the turn of the millennium, with even such popular authors for adults as Philippa Gregory now entering the young adult market. Publishing has its fashions and there is no reason to suppose that this situation will continue indefinitely, but it is a testament to the fact that the past is never definitively outgrown, never made decisively 'irrelevant' to the present. The past may be a foreign country, but it is also our native land.

Notes

1 Introduction: That Was Then?

1. 'Children's literature' refers throughout this book to both children's and young adult texts.
2. For example, in John Stephens's influential discussion in *Language and Ideology in Children's Fiction* (202–40).
3. Mendlesohn gives an account of the experience of her partner, the historian Edward James, at the medieval conference in Kalamazoo. His condemnation by some children's literature scholars for suggesting that children's historical books should teach history and inspire children with the desire to learn more is both amusing and a telling example of the incomprehension that can occur when two disciplinary discourses collide (51–2).
4. Note that this restriction refers to subject matter, not authorship. Several of the texts discussed are by non-British writers.
5. A typical example is Alison Prince's *Anne Boleyn and Me: The Diary of Eleanor Valjean 1525–1536* (2004), which tells of Henry VIII's divorce from Catherine of Aragon from the point of view of Catherine's young lady-in-waiting. This was later repackaged as *Anne Boleyn and Me (My Royal Story): A Tudor Girl's Diary 1524–1536* (2010).
6. At a panel discussion at the World Science Fiction Convention in Glasgow, 2005.

2 The Eagle Has Landed: Representing the Roman Invasion of Britain in Texts for Children

1. Ladybird was quite capable of making conscious intertextual references. Later in *Shopping with Mother*, for example, we see a copy of Peach's own *Alfred the Great* in the window of a shop.
2. Despite the similarity in names, the echo of Dan and Una from Kipling's *Puck of Pook's Hill* (1906) is not deliberate (Browne, personal communication, 2009).

3 Once, Future, Sometime, Never: Arthur in History

1. Sutcliff is explicit about her debt ('Combined Ops' 247), and Treece follows Reed in several striking respects, for example in his siting of the Battle of Badon on the north edge of the Marlborough Downs (Treece, *The Eagles Have Flown* 176).

2. The quotation is from Geoffrey Ashe, *From Caesar to Arthur* (1960), 9.
3. This is at least the most popular identification of Malory, first laid out at length by Edward Hicks in 1928.
4. This is a detail also mentioned by T. H. White in *The Queen of Air and Darkness*, the second part of *The Once and Future King* (1958): 'she was twice his age, so that she had twice the power of his weapons' (308).
5. The differences between the two versions are extensive and more complex than can be adequately addressed here, but both versions are relevant to this discussion, and we shall draw on both. Unless otherwise indicated, references are to the original text.
6. Both by the presence of Robin Hood/Wood, and by the date of 1216 given in the revised version of the book to Uther Pendragon's death (194). However, since Uther's reign is said to have begun in 1066, this dating advertises its own implausibility from the start.
7. The date is 1890 in the revised version.
8. One of the exceptions is Ann Lawrence's *Between the Forest and the Hills* (1977).

4 'She Be Faking It': Authenticity and Anachronism

1. This term, coined by Michael Banton, refers to the practice of viewing 'other historical periods in terms of the concepts, values, and understanding of the present time' (Banton 21).
2. 'Gentlemen's sons should be trained to use a horn, hunt cunningly, neatly train and use a hawk. The study of literature should be left to the sons of peasants', averred a gentleman quoted by the Henrician courtier Richard Pace in his *De Fructu Qui ex Doctrina Precipitur* (Basel 1517).
3. This is the so-called Peacham drawing (c. 1595), which illustrates a scene from *Titus Andronicus* and is currently housed in the library of the Marquess of Bath.

5 Dreams of Things That Never Were: Authenticity and Genre

1. Other current terms for this phenomenon are 'point of departure' (or 'POD'), 'Jonbar point' and 'branch point'.
2. In the final chapter of this book we will consider the alliance between history and fiction further, using Hayden White's concept of 'emplotment'.
3. Clearly, Lane's books also fall within the intertextual category discussed later in this chapter; here, however, we address their quasi-historical aspects.
4. In *Mary, Queen of Scots: A Scottish Queen's Diary, France, 1553* (2010).
5. Others include A. S. Byatt (2009), Anthony Beevor (2009) and A. L. Berridge (2011).

6 Ancestral Voices, Prophesying War

1. Dennis Hamley, personal communication.
2. Not all Home Front books published by writers who were children during the war are quite so autobiographical: Jill Paton Walsh's *The Dolphin Crossing* (1967) and *Fireweed* (1969) and David Rees's Carnegie-winning *The Exeter Blitz* (1978) are examples of novels that contain less of the authors' direct experience, although they are inevitably informed by their wartime childhoods. Rees, for example, lived in Exeter only in later life, but his experience of the bombing in London (and to a lesser extent Bournemouth) gave him plenty of exposure to Blitz conditions (Rees, *Not for Your Hands* 27–52, 160).
3. For more on *lieux de mémoire* as they operate within children's literature, see Valerie Krips, *The Presence of the Past: Memory, Heritage, and Childhood in Postwar Britain* (2000).
4. Victor Watson, personal communication.

7 Patterns of History

1. This is not a phenomenon born with the National Curriculum. More than a decade before the Education Reform Act of 1988 came into force, Robert Leeson was complaining that 'the genre almost depends for its life on the approval of teachers and librarians, as well as the [...] reviewers who act as their reconnaissance corps' (173).
2. See also Ofsted, *The Annual Report* (57).
3. This argument is advanced most explicitly in Hall's ' "House and Garden": The Time-Slip Story in the Aftermath of the Second World War' (2003), but see also her 'Aristocratic Houses and Radical Politics' (1998), ' "Time No Longer" – History, Enchantment and the Classic Time-Slip' (2001) and 'Ancestral Voices – "Since Time Everlasting and Beyond" ' (2003).

Bibliography

Primary Texts

Aiken, Joan. *The Wolves of Willoughby Chase*. London: Jonathan Cape, 1962.

———. *Black Hearts in Battersea*. 1964. London: Red Fox, 2004.

———. *Night Birds on Nantucket*. 1966. London: Red Fox, 2004.

———. *The Cuckoo Tree*. 1971. London: Red Fox, 1992.

———. *The Stolen Lake*. 1981. New York: Dell Publishing Co., 1988.

Austen, Jane. *Northanger Abbey*. 1818. Ed. John Davie, Introd. Terry Castle. Oxford: Oxford University Press, 1990.

Barnhouse, Rebecca. *The Book of the Maidservant*. New York: Random House, 2009.

Bawden, Nina. *Carrie's War*. 1973. Oxford: Heinemann Educational Books, 1975.

Boston, Lucy M. *The Stones of Green Knowe*. London: The Bodley Head, 1976.

Bray, Libba. *A Great and Terrible Beauty*. 2003. London: Simon and Schuster, 2006.

Brocklehurst, Ruth. *The Usborne History of Britain*. London: Usborne, 2008.

———. *Victorians (Usborne History of Britain)*. London: Usborne, 2008.

Browne, N. M. *Warriors of Alavna*. London: Bloomsbury, 2000.

Burnett, Frances Hodgson. *A Little Princess*. 1905. London: Frederick Warne & Co., 1975.

Burton, Hester. *Castors Away!* 1962. Oxford: Oxford University Press, 1979.

Buzbee, Lewis. *The Haunting of Charles Dickens*. New York: Feiwel and Friends, 2010.

Chandler, Pauline. *The Mark of Edain*. Oxford: Oxford University Press, 2008.

Chaucer, Geoffrey. *The Riverside Chaucer*. Ed. F. N. Robinson. Oxford: Oxford University Press, 1988.

Conrad, Joseph. *Heart of Darkness*. London: Penguin, 2007.

Cooper, Susan. *Dawn of Fear*. New York: Harcourt, Brace, Jovanovich, 1970.

———. *King of Shadows*. London: The Bodley Head, 1999.

Crossley-Holland, Kevin. *Arthur: The Seeing Stone*. 2000. London: Orion, 2001.

———. *Gatty's Tale*. 2006. London: Orion, 2007.

Cushman, Karen. *Catherine, Called Birdy*. 1994. London: Macmillan, 1996.

———. *Alchemy and Meggy Swann*. Boston and New York: Houghton Mifflin, 2010.

Davidson, Jenny. *The Explosionist*. New York: HarperTeen, 2008.

———. *Invisible Things*. New York: HarperTeen, 2010.

Deary, Terry. *The Measly Middle Ages (Horrible Histories)*. Illus. Martin Brown. London: Hippo, 1996.

———. *The Slimy Stuarts (Horrible Histories).* Illus. Martin Brown. London: Hippo, 1996.
———. *The Gorgeous Georgians (Horrible Histories).* Illus. Martin Brown. London: Hippo, 1998.
Dromgoole, Patrick. 'Preface'. In Terence Feely, *Arthur of the Britons.* Bristol: HTV Limited, 1974. 7.
Edwards, Eve. *The Other Countess.* London: Razorbill, 2010.
Eldridge, Jim. *Roman Invasion (My Story).* London: Scholastic, 2008.
Eliott, Lydia S. *Ceva of the Caradocs.* London: Frederick Warne, 1953.
Fielding, Henry. *Tom Jones.* 1749. Harmondsworth: Penguin, 1966.
Fisher, Catherine. *Corbenic.* London: Red Fox, 2002.
Foreman, Michael. *War Boy.* London: Pavilion Books, 1989.
Forrest, Martin, with Penelope Harnett. *History: I: Romans, Anglo-Saxons and Vikings in Britain: Ancient Greece: A Past Non-European Society.* Curriculum Bank Key Stage Two/Scottish Levels C-E. Leamington Spa: Scholastic, 1996.
Gardam, Jane. *A Long Way From Verona.* London: Hamilton, 1971.
Gardner, Sally. *I, Coriander.* 2005. London: Orion, 2006.
Garner, Alan. *Red Shift.* 1973. London: Lions, 1975.
———. *Tom Fobble's Day.* London: Collins, 1977.
Grant, K. M. *Belle's Song.* London: Quercus, 2010.
Green, Roger Lancelyn. *King Arthur and His Knights of the Round Table.* London: Penguin Books, 1953.
Hamley, Dennis. *The War and Freddy.* 1991. London: Catnip Publishing, 2007.
Harnett, Cynthia. *The Wool-Pack.* London: Methuen, 1951.
———. *The Load of Unicorn.* London: Methuen, 1959.
Harrison, Cora. *I Was Jane Austen's Best Friend.* 2010. London: Macmillan Children's Books, 2011.
Hebditch, Felicity. *Roman Britain (Britain Through the Ages).* London: Evans, 1996.
Hooper, Mary. *At the Sign of the Sugared Plum.* London: Bloomsbury Publishing PLC, 2003.
Jarman, Julia. *The Time-Travelling Cat and the Roman Eagle.* London: Andersen, 2001.
Jensen, Marie-Louise. *The Lady in the Tower.* Oxford: Oxford University Press, 2009.
Kipling, Rudyard. *Puck of Pook's Hill.* 1906. Ed. and introd. Sarah Wintle. London: Penguin, 1987.
Lane, Andrew. *Young Sherlock Holmes: Death Cloud.* London: Macmillan Children's Books, 2010.
———. *Young Sherlock Holmes: Red Leech.* London: Macmillan Children's Books, 2010.
Lasky, Kathryn. *Mary, Queen of Scots: A Scottish Queen's Diary, France, 1553 (My Royal Story).* London: Scholastic, 2010.
Lawrence, Ann. *Between the Forest and the Hills.* Harmondsworth: Kestrel, 1977.
Lewis, C. S. *The Magician's Nephew.* 1955. Harmondsworth: Puffin, 1979.
Lewis, Hilda. *The Ship That Flew.* 1939. Oxford: Oxford University Press, 1998.

Lively, Penelope. *Going Back*. London: Heinemann, 1975.
———. *A Stitch in Time*. London: Heinemann, 1976.
Lloyd, Saci. *The Carbon Diaries 2015*. London: Hodder Children's Books, 2008.
Magorian, Michelle. *Goodnight, Mr Tom*. Harmondsworth: Kestrel, 1981.
Marryat, Frederic. *The Children of the New Forest*. London: The Juvenile Library, 1847.
Marshall, H. E. *Our Island Story: A History of Britain for Boys and Girls, From the Romans to Queen Victoria*. 1905. Cranbrook: Galore Park/Civitas, 2005.
McCaughrean, Geraldine. *Britannia: 100 Great Stories from British History*. 1999. London: Orion, 2004.
McKay, Hilary. *Wishing for Tomorrow*. London: Hodder Children's Books, 2009.
Morpurgo, Michael. *Arthur, High King of Britain*. 1994. London: Egmont, 2002.
Nesbit, E. *The Railway Children*. London: Wells Gardner, Darton & Co., 1906.
———. *The Story of the Amulet*. 1906. London: Ernest Benn, 1957.
———. *The House of Arden*. 1908. London: Dent, 1967.
Orwell, George. *Nineteen Eighty-Four*. London: Secker and Warburg, 1949.
Paton Walsh, Jill. *The Dolphin Crossing*. London: Macmillan, 1967.
———. *Fireweed*. Harmondsworth: Penguin, 1969.
———. *A Chance Child*. 1978. Harmondsworth: Puffin, 1985.
Peach, L. du Garde. *Julius Caesar and Roman Britain*. Illus. John Kenney. Loughborough: Ladybird, 1959.
Pearce, Philippa. *Tom's Midnight Garden*. 1958. Harmondsworth: Puffin, 1976.
Prince, Alison. *Anne Boleyn and Me: The Diary of Eleanor Valjean 1525–1536*. London: Scholastic, 2004.
———. *Anne Boleyn and Me (My Royal Story): A Tudor Girl's Diary 1524–1536*. London: Scholastic, 2010.
Pullman, Philip. *Northern Lights*. 2005. London: Scholastic, 2006.
———. *The Amber Spyglass*. London: Scholastic, 2000.
Putney, M. J. *Dark Mirror*. New York: St. Martin's Press, 2011.
Rees, David. *The Exeter Blitz*. London: Hamilton, 1978.
Reeve, Philip. *Larklight*. London: Bloomsbury, 2006.
———. *Here Lies Arthur*. London: Scholastic, 2007.
Rosoff, Meg. *How I Live Now*. 2004. London: Penguin, 2005.
Ross, Stewart. *Down with the Romans!* (Flashbacks). London: Evans Brothers, 2006.
Sir Gawain and the Green Knight. Trans. W. A. Neilson. Cambridge, Ontario: In Parenthesis Publications, 1999. Accessed 23 September 2011, http://www.yorku.ca/inpar/sggk_neilson.pdf.
Springer, Nancy. *The Case of the Missing Marquess*. New York: Puffin Books, 2006.
Stolz, Mary. *Pangur Ban*. New York: HarperCollins, 1988.
Sutcliff, Rosemary. *Simon*. 1953. London: Oxford University Press, 1971.
———. *The Eagle of the Ninth*. Illus. C. Walter Hodges. Oxford: Oxford University Press, 1954.
———. *The Lantern Bearers*. Oxford: Oxford University Press, 1959.
———. *Dawn Wind*. Oxford: OUP, 1961.

———. *Sword at Sunset.* 1963. London: Hodder and Stoughton, 1971.
———. 'The Sword in the Circle'. 1981. *King Arthur Stories: Three Books in One.* London: Random House, 1999. 13–354.
———. *King Arthur Stories: Three Books in One.* 1979, 1981, 1981. London: Random House, 1999.
Tacitus. *Tacitus on Britain and Germany.* Trans. H. Mattingley. Harmondsworth: Penguin, 1948.
Temple, Frances. *The Ramsey Scallop.* 1994. New York: HarperTrophy, 1995.
Townsend, John Rowe. *Noah's Castle.* 1975. Harmondsworth: Peacock Books, 1978.
Trease, Geoffrey. *Bows Against the Barons.* London: Martin Lawrence, 1934.
———. *Cue for Treason.* 1940. London: Puffin, 1965.
———. *Bows Against the Barons.* 1934. London: Lawrence & Wishart, 1948.
Treece, Henry. *Legions of the Eagle.* London: The Bodley Head, 1954.
———. *The Eagles Have Flown.* London: The Bodley Head, 1954.
———. *War Dog.* 1962. London: Beaver Books, 1977.
Twain, Mark. *The Prince and the Pauper: A Tale for Young People of All Ages.* London: Chatto & Windus, 1881.
Uttley, Alison. *A Traveller in Time.* London: Faber and Faber, 1939.
Watson, Victor. *Paradise Barn.* London: Catnip Books, 2009.
Webb, Beth. *Fire Dreamer.* London: Macmillan, 2007.
Wells, Rosemary. *Red Moon at Sharpsburg.* New York: Viking, 2007.
Westall, Robert. *The Machine-Gunners.* London: Macmillan, 1975.
Westerfeld, Scott. *Leviathan.* New York: Simon Pulse, 2009.
White, T. H. *The Sword in the Stone.* 1938. London: HarperCollins, 1998.
———. *The Sword in the Stone.* In *The Once and Future King.* 1958. London: Fontana, 1962.
Whitman, Emily. *Wildwing.* New York: Greenwillow, 2010.
Wilding, Valerie. *Boudica and Her Barmy Army.* Illus. Clive Goddard. London: Scholastic Children's Books, 2005.
Wood, Tim. *The Romans.* Illus. Peter Dennis. Loughborough: Ladybird, 1989.
Wrede, Patricia C., and Caroline Stevermer. *Sorcery and Cecelia, or The Enchanted Chocolate Pot.* 1988. Orlando, FL: Magic Carpet Books, 2004.

Secondary Texts

Where authors' comments on their work are published with the work itself, for example as an Author's Note, they are listed under 'Primary Texts'.

Agnew, Kate. 'Interview with Michelle Magorian'. *Carousel.* October 1998. Accessed 29 June 2011, http://www.michellemagorian.com/otherinterviews.htm.
Aiken, Joan. 'A Thread of Mystery'. *Children's Literature in Education* 1.2 (1970): 30–47.
Aiken, Joan. 'Interpreting the Past: Reflections of an Historical Novelist'. *Only Connect: Readings on Children's Literature.* 3rd Edition. Ed. Sheila Egoff et al. Toronto: Oxford University Press, 1996. 62–73.

Alcock, Leslie. *Arthur's Britain: History and Archaeology, AD367–634*. London: Allen Lane, 1971.
'Anglesey Childhood Inspires Saci Lloyd's *Carbon Diaries*'. *BBC Northwest Wales*. 18 March 2010. Accessed 15 July 2011, http://news.bbc.co.uk/local/northwestwales/hi/people_and_places/arts_and_culture/newsid_8574000/8574091.stm.
Ashe, Geoffrey. *From Caesar to Arthur*. London: Collins, 1960.
Ashton, Nigel. *Kennedy, Macmillan and the Cold War: The Irony of Interdependence*. Basingstoke and New York: Palgrave, 2002.
Banton, Michael. 'The Idiom of Race: A Critique of Presentism'. *Research in Race and Ethnic Relations* 2 (1980): 21–42.
Barnhouse, Rebecca. *Recasting the Past: The Middle Ages in Young Adult Literature*. Portsmouth, NH: Heinemann, 2000.
Beevor, Anthony. 'Real Concerns'. *The Guardian*. 25 July 2009. Accessed 29 August 2011, http://www.guardian.co.uk/books/2009/jul/25/antony-beevor-author-faction.
Berridge, A. L. 'Richelieu's Face'. *The History Girls*. 20 July 2011. Accessed 29 August 2011, http://the-history-girls.blogspot.com/2011/07/richelieus-face-by-alberridge.html.
Bradley, Mark. 'Tacitus' *Agricola* and the Conquest of Britain: Representations of Empire in Victorian and Edwardian England'. *Classics and Imperialism in the British Empire (Classical Presences)*. Ed. Mark Bradley. Oxford: Oxford University Press, 2010. 123–57.
Burton, Hester. 'The Writing of Historical Novels'. 1969. *The Cool Web*. Ed. Margaret Meek. London: The Bodley Head, 1977. 159–65.
Butler, Charles. *Four British Fantasists: Place and Culture in the Children's Fantasies of Penelope Lively, Alan Garner, Diana Wynne Jones and Susan Cooper*. Lanham, MD: Scarecrow/ChLA, 2006.
Butterfield, Herbert. *The Whig Interpretation of History*. London: Bell & Sons, 1931.
Byatt, A. S. 'Byatt Attacks Novelists Who Use Real-Life Characters'. *The Guardian*. 13 August 2009. Accessed 29 August 2011, http://www.guardian.co.uk/books/2009/aug/13/byatt-novelists-real-life-characters.
Cahill, Kevin. *Who Owns Britain?* 2001. Edinburgh: Canongate, 2002.
Carpenter, Humphrey and Mari Prichard. *The Oxford Companion to Children's Literature*. Oxford: Oxford University Press, 1984.
Chedgzoy, Kate. 'Horrible Shakespearean Histories: Performing the Renaissance for and with Children'. *Filming and Performing Renaissance History*. Ed. Mark Thornton Burnett and Adrian Streete. Basingstoke: Palgrave Macmillan, 2011. 112–26.
Clute, John, and John Grant, Eds. *The Encyclopedia of Fantasy*. London: Orbit, 1997.
Collins, Fiona M., and Judith Graham, Eds. *Historical Fiction for Children: Capturing the Past*. London: David Fulton, 2001.
———. 'The Twentieth Century – Giving Everybody a History.' Collins and Graham. 10–22.

Collins, William Joseph. 'Paths Not Taken: The Development, Structure and Aesthetics of the Alternative History'. PhD Diss. University of California – Davis. 1990.

Cooper, Susan. 'Swords and Ploughshares'. In *Dreams and Wishes: Essays on Writing for Children*. 1993. New York: Margaret K. McElderry Books, 1996. 137–51.

Craig, Amanda. 'A Fairytale for Our Time'. *The Times*. 30 July 2005. Accessed 29 October 2006, http://www.timesonline.co.uk/article/0,,923-1712079,00.html.

Crossley-Holland, Kevin. Official Web Site. Accessed 8 June 2011, http://www.kevincrossley-holland.com/fiction.html.

———. 'Kevin Crossley-Holland Author of Gatty's Tale Talks with Kati Nicholl'. *Reading Room*. Orion Publishing Group. Accessed 5 October 2011, http://www.orionbooks.co.uk/authors/interviews/kevin-crossley-holland-author-of-gatty-s-tale-talks-with-kati-nicholl.

Dines, Avital. 'Interview with Michelle Magorian'. *kidz-books*. 2005. Accessed 29 June 2011, http://www.michellemagorian.com/interviews.htm.

Edwards, Vicky. 'Interview with Michelle Magorian'. December 2010. Accessed 29 June 2011, http://www.wycombeswan.co.uk/news_details.asp?NewsID=337.

Fisher, D. J. V. *The Anglo-Saxon Age*. London: Longman, 1973.

Fulton, Helen, Ed. *A Companion to Arthurian Literature*. Malden, MA, Oxford and Chichester: Wiley-Blackwell, 2009.

———. 'Introduction: Theories and Debates'. *A Companion to Arthurian Literature*. Ed. Helen Fulton. Malden, MA, Oxford and Chichester: Wiley-Blackwell, 2009. 1–11.

Frye, Northrop. *Anatomy of Criticism*. Princeton: Princeton University Press, 1957.

Grant, K. M. '*Belle's Song* and Help from Chaucer'. 15 February 2011. Scottish Book Trust. Accessed 30 March 2011, http://www.scottishbooktrust.com/blog/teens-young-people/2011/02/km-grant-belles-song-and-help-from-chaucer.

Hall, Linda. 'Aristocratic Houses and Radical Politics: Historical Fiction and the Time-Slip Story in E. Nesbit's *The House of Arden*'. *Children's Literature in Education* 29.1 (1998): 51–8.

———. '"Time No Longer" – History, Enchantment and the Classic Time-Slip'. *Historical Fiction for Children: Capturing the Past*. Ed. Fiona M. Collins and Judith Graham. London: David Fulton, 2001. 43–53.

———. '"House and Garden": The Time-Slip Story in the Aftermath of the Second World War'. *The Presence of the Past in Children's Literature*. Ed. Ann Lawson Lucas. Westport, CT: Praeger, 2003. 153–8.

———. 'Ancestral Voices – "Since Time Everlasting and Beyond": Kipling and the Invention of the Time-Slip Story'. *Children's Literature in Education* 34 (December 2003): 305–21.

Harnett, Penelope. 'Heroes and Heroines. Exploring a Nation's Past. The History Curriculum in State Primary Schools in the Twentieth Century'. *History of Education Society Bulletin* 62 (1998): 83–95.

Hellekson, Karen. 'Toward a Taxonomy of the Alternate History Genre'. *Extrapolation* 41.3 (Fall 2000): 248–56.

———. *The Alternate History: Reconfiguring Historical Time*. Kent, OH: KSU Press, 2001.

Hicks, Edward. *Sir Thomas Malory: His Turbulent Career*. Cambridge, MA: Harvard University Press, 1928.

Hingley, Richard. *Roman Officers and English Gentlemen: The Imperial Origins of Roman Archaeology*. London and New York: Routledge, 2000.

Hutton, Ronald. *Witches, Druids and King Arthur*. London and New York: Hambledon, 2003.

———. *The Druids*. London and New York: Hambledon, 2007.

Jackson, Aaron Isaac. 'Writing Arthur, Writing England: Myth and Modernity in T. H. White's *The Sword in the Stone*'. *The Lion and the Unicorn* 33.1 (January 2009): 44–59.

James, Edward. *Britain in the First Millennium*. London: Arnold, 2001.

———. 'The Limits of Alternate History'. *Vector: The Critical Journal of the British Science Fiction Association* 254 (November/December 2007): 7–10.

Jansen-Gruber, Marya. 'An Interview with Saci Lloyd, the Author of the Carbon Diary Books'. *Through the Looking Glass Children's Book Reviews*. 27 April 2010. Accessed 15 July 2011, http://lookingglassreview.blogspot.com/2010/04/interview-with-saci-lloyd-author-of.html.

Johnson, Rachel. 'Is Beric a Briton? The Representation of Cultural Identity in G. A. Henty's *Beric the Briton* (1893) and Rosemary Sutcliff's *The Outcast* (1955)'. *The Journal of Children's Literature Studies* 7.2 (July 2010): 75–85.

Jones, Diana Wynne. 'Inventing the Middle Ages'. Diana Wynne Jones Official Web Site. Accessed 30 May 2011, http://www.leemac.freeserve.co.uk/medieval.htm.

Kay, Guy Gavriel. 'The Fiction of Privacy: Fantasy and the Past'. *Journal of the Fantastic in the Arts* 20.2 (2009): 241–7.

Krips, Valerie. *The Presence of the Past: Memory, Heritage, and Childhood in Postwar Britain*. New York and London: Garland Publishing, 2000.

Kullmann, Thomas. 'Constructions of History in Victorian and Edwardian Children's Books'. *The Presence of the Past in Children's Literature*. Ed. Ann Lawson Lucas. Westport, CT: Praeger, 2003. 73–87.

Lathey, Gillian. 'A Havey-cavey Business: Language in Historical Fiction with Particular Reference to the Novels of Joan Aiken and Leon Garfield'. *Historical Fiction for Children: Capturing the Past*. Ed. Fiona M. Collins and Judith Graham. London: David Fulton, 2001. 32–42.

Lawson Lucas, Ann, Ed. *The Presence of the Past in Children's Literature*. Westport, CT: Praeger, 2003.

Lebow, Richard Ned. 'What's So Different About a Counterfactual?' *World Politics* 52.4 (July 2000): 550–85.

Leeson, Robert. 'The Spirit of What Age? The Interpretation of History from a Radical Standpoint'. *Children's Literature in Education* 23 (1976): 172–82.

Lewis, C. S. *They Asked for a Paper: Papers and Addresses*. London: Geoffrey Bles, 1962.

Lively, Penelope. 'Children and Memory'. 1973. *Crosscurrents of Criticism: Horn Book Essays 1968–1977*. Ed. Paul Heins. Boston, MA: Horn Book, 1977. 226–33.

Lloyd, Tom. 'Acting in the "Theatre of Anarchy": The "Anti-Thug Campaign" and Elaborations of Colonial Rule in Early Nineteenth-Century India'. *Edinburgh Papers in South Asian Studies* 19 (2006): 2–50.

McGillis, Roderick. *A Little Princess: Gender and Empire*. New York: Twayne, 1996.

Mendlesohn, Farah. *The Intergalactic Playground: A Critical Study of Children's and Teens' Science Fiction*. Jefferson, NC and London: McFarland & Co., 2009.

Montrose, Louis A. 'Professing the Renaissance: The Poetics and Politics of Culture'. *The New Historicism*. Ed. Aram Veeser. New York, London: Routledge, 1989. 15–36.

Nastali, Dan. 'Arthur Without Fantasy: Dark Age Britain in Recent Historical Fiction'. *Arthuriana* 9.1 (1999): 5–22.

Nora, Pierre. 'Between Memory and History: Les Lieux de Mémoire'. *Representations* 26 (Spring 1989): 7–24.

Ofsted. *The Annual Report of Her Majesty's Chief Inspector of Schools 2005/06*. London: The Stationery Office, 2006.

———. *History in the Balance: History in English Schools 2003–07*. London: The Stationery Office, July 2007.

———. *History for All: History in English Schools 2007/10*. London: The Stationery Office, March 2011.

Orme, Nicholas. *English Schools in the Middle Ages*. London: Methuen, 1973.

Paton Walsh, Jill. 'The Art of Realism'. *Celebrating Children's Books: Essays on Children's Literature in Honor of Zena Sutherland*. Ed. Betsy Hearne and Marilyn Kaye. New York: Lothrop, Lee & Shepard Books, 1981. 35–44.

Pearce, Philippa. 'Time Present'. *Travellers in Time: Past, Present and to Come*. Pref. and Introd. Barbara Harrison. Cambridge: CLNE/Green Bay, 1990. 70–4.

Reed, Trelawney Dayrell. *The Battle for Britain in the Fifth Century: An Essay in Dark Age History*. London: Methuen & Co., 1944.

Rees, David. *Not for Your Hands: An Autobiography*. Exeter: Third House, 1992.

North Shields 173. Accessed 28 June 2011, http://www.northshields173.org/2005/02/robert_westall_biography_1.html.

Roberts, Deborah H. 'Reconstructed Pasts: Rome and Britain, Child and Adult in Kipling's *Puck of Pook's Hill* and Rosemary Sutcliff's Historical Fiction'. *Remaking the Classics: Literature, Genre and Media in Britain 1800–2000*. Ed. Christopher Stray. London: Duckworth, 2007. 107–23.

Rustin, Susanna. 'Nina's Wars'. *The Guardian*. 22 November 2003. Accessed 27 June 2011, http://www.guardian.co.uk/books/2003/nov/22/featuresreviews.guardianreview5.

Said, Edward. *Culture and Imperialism*. London: Vintage, 1994.

Schmunk, Robert B. 'Introduction: What is Alternate History?' *Uchronia*. Accessed 5 October 2011, http://uchronia.net/intro.html.

Shippey, Tom. 'Historical Fiction and the Post-Imperial Arthur'. *A Companion to Arthurian Literature*. Ed. Helen Fulton. Malden, MA, Oxford and Chichester: Wiley-Blackwell, 2009. 449–62.

Sibbery, Elizabeth. *Criticism of Crusading, 1095–1274*. Oxford: Oxford University Press, 1985.

Sidney, Sir Philip. *An Apology for Poetry*. c. 1580. Ed. Geoffrey Shepherd. London: Thomas Nelson, 1965.

Springer, Nancy. 'Interview with Author Nancy Springer'. *Books for Sale*. [no date] Accessed 5 September 2011, http://www.books-for-sale.org/313/interview-with-author-nancy-springer/.

Stephens, John. *Language and Ideology in Children's Fiction*. London and New York: Longman, 1992.

Sutcliff, Rosemary. 'Combined Ops'. *Only Connect: Readings on Children's Literature*. Ed. Sheila Egoff et al. Toronto and New York: Oxford University Press, 1969. 244–8.

Thorpe, Lewis. 'Introduction'. Geoffrey of Monmouth, *History of the Kings of Britain*. Harmondsworth: Penguin, 1966. 9–47.

Trease, Geoffrey. 'The Historical Novelist at Work'. *Children's Literature in Education* 7 (1972): 5–16.

Tsarion, Michael. 'The Rape of Tara, Hill of Kings'. *The Irish Origins of Civilization*. Accessed 16 August 2009, http://www.irishoriginsofcivilization.com/appendices/rapeoftara.html.

Venuti, Lawrence. *The Translator's Invisibility: A History of Translation*. London: Routledge, 1995.

Waller, Maureen. *Ungrateful Daughters: The Stuart Princesses Who Stole Their Father's Crown*. London: Hodder and Stoughton, 2002.

Webb, Beth. 'Interview with Beth Webb'. *Just Imagine Story Centre*. Accessed 17 October 2011, http://www.justimaginestorycentre.co.uk/node/6126.

———. *The Beth Webb Site*. Accessed 9 August 2009, http://www.bethwebb.co.uk/tegensworld.html.

Westall, Robert. *Children of the Blitz: Memories of Wartime Childhood*. Harmondsworth: Penguin, 1985.

———. 'About *The Machine-Gunners*'. 1990. Official Web Site. Accessed 27 June 2011, http://robertwestall.com/the_machine_gunners_by_robert_westall.html.

Westerfeld, Scott. 'Teatime with Scott Westerfeld'. April 2011. Accessed 6 June 2011, http://www.youtube.com/watch?v=ecrjXezcMZg.

White, Gabrielle. *Jane Austen in the Context of Abolition*. Basingstoke: Palgrave Macmillan, 2006.

White, Hayden. 'The Historical Text as Literary Artifact'. *The Writing of History: Literary Form and Historical Understanding*. Ed. Robert H. Canary and Henry Kozicki. Madison, WI: Wisconsin University Press, 1978. 41–62.

Index